CW00828147

Dear Paul,

Happy Birthday

love,

Maya

Gallery Books
*Editor*  Peter Fallon

INTIMATE CITY

Peter Sirr

# INTIMATE CITY

Gallery Books

*Intimate City*
was first published
simultaneously in paperback
and in a clothbound edition
in June 2021.
Reprinted August 2021.

The Gallery Press
Loughcrew
Oldcastle
County Meath
Ireland

www.gallerypress.com

ISBN 978 1 91133 816 1 *paperback*
        978 1 91133 817 8 *clothbound*

A CIP catalogue record for this book
is available from the British Library.

*Intimate City* receives financial assistance
from the Arts Council of Ireland.

# Contents

*for Enda and Freya*

*We drifted through the intimate city*
*like dust, like light*
*settling briefly, silent but alert*
*looking for an opening*
                              — 'The Hunt'

## 'Someone is leading our old lives'

Again and again we walk through the city, inventing what should be there. We walk through the hollowed-out core, the broad Georgian streets with their soft red or beige brick, their fanlights and steps and brass plates, their So-and-So Lived Here and So-and-So Lived There, famous windows, famous bricks, famous vistas, the secret park that you can only get into if you live on the square. We can see someone in there now sitting on a bench like a daytime ghost, the pepper canister church that must have a salt shaker equivalent maybe on the other side of the mirror city, and what we notice, as we always notice even in non-plague times, is that no one lives here, no one is leaning against an upper window with a cup of coffee in hand, no one is resting a bag of shopping on the porch while fumbling for a key, no one is kissing in the hall or unlocking their bike from the railing outside and promising to come back soon, no one's quarter inch of cigarette goes flaring down to Baggot Street, so we're here in this double quiet, the emptied out pandemic quiet where if we do happen on someone we jump off the pavement into the middle of the street, and the decades-old quiet of houses long abandoned to doctors, solicitors, graphic designers, antiquarians, anaesthetists, credit management services, assessors and adjusters, consulates, institutes, management consultants, fund managers, recruitment services, and so we invent them, the people who should be here, the people who used to be here, whose furniture should be glimpsable in upper windows, whose music should be leaking into the streets, whose rows should be annoying the neighbours, the poets, artists, costume designers, programmers, couples, triples, quadruples, pharmacists, estate agents, nurses, teachers, actors, students, dancers, journalists, electricians, software developers, personal trainers, impersonal trainers, sexologists, neurologists, aromatherapists lured back from their suburbs and dormitory towns by reasonable rents, park life, pubs, groceries, museums, the way the light will catch the brick just before sunset.

It's not a very elaborate vision, it's what you get when you walk around Edinburgh or Berlin or Copenhagen or Amsterdam or any number of ordinary liveable cities. The Pepper Canister Church, St Stephen's Church if we need a formal introduction, Anglican, 1824, Greek-columned, chapel of ease, services first Sunday of the month, rector the Reverend David Gillespie, concert venue, sits at the heart of a crescent, Mount Street Crescent, and we have fallen in love with the bend of the crescent as you veer off Mount Street proper and into it. Trees greet us, a wild front garden, a secret sculpture, a kind of robot or android, grave in his greenery, watching me photograph him. I lean into a railing to try to get the bend. Across the road Birdy perches on the ledge of Crescent Hall, about to fly off.

Why does this tiny bend matter? The dog sniffs at the kerb, unimpressed. My wife eyes the barbarian concrete Starbucks behind the church where I badly want to queue up and say, a flat white and a sledgehammer, please. I try to photograph both of them at a railing on the bend as if, what exactly? As if we lived here? As if this were our neighbourhood? It is, in a way, it's part of our portable mental neighbourhood, our psychic neighbourhood, one of the places we walk around to remind ourselves why we live in the city and not the country, but also, maybe, because it's a weird kind of dreamland, its surfaces alluring, its cast vanished. Birdy surveys us, still perched on her ledge. I think of Rowan Gillespie's naked woman scaling the wall of the Treasury Building, now removed, as if her naked gesture troubled the economy. At least his Birdy is still ready to fly, her aspiration secure. A bronze child swings from a lamppost below her. You have to be a statue around here to swing from a lamppost. A little further up a bronze John B Keane towers over a bronze Brian Friel. I admire Brian Friel's jumper and sternly folded arms. Like Keane, he seems to be contemplating an absent stage. There's not enough action here for either. Writer statues are a troublesome bunch, holding still is not a writerly thing. We wander into Herbert Street, thinking of Behan, 'a released bull', toppling into John Montague's basement . . .

> *A light is burning late*
> *in this Georgian Dublin street:*
> *someone is leading our old lives!*[2]

Maybe a descendant of that poem's cat, 'tiny emissary/of our happiness', since all the basements are unoccupied now. Krapp's mother died here, number 21, the Merrion Nursing Home, 'after her long viduity', as did his creator's mother. It sits forlorn and abandoned-looking at the end of the terrace behind a faded purple door in its Greek portico, the kind of place you would not be surprised to end up in after a long viduity. A mind city, the bits and pieces of imagination strewn around, our footsteps circling, staking out territory, extending their reach, wanting to draw things in. Things, people, books, windows, streets. A kind of greed, all this wanting, which maybe is what this book is, a chain of linked desires: to explore the city past and present, to walk it, to drink in details, the light on the brick, the barges in the canal, the rushes on the bank, rooms and walls, the footscraper outside a front door, listening for the steps of those who've been here before, tradesmen and artists, market sellers, beggars and beadles, mapmakers and builders, to greet time, stop it on the pavement before it scurries off. Look, I keep wanting to say, again, the black stone of the Lutheran church, *Gottesdienst Sonntags, 11 uhr*, the sun on the Eye and Ear, the tram clattering. Stop, that's enough, but of course it never is.

# The Hurdle Ford, or The Monster's Breast

One by one they dissolve. Calatrava's Samuel Beckett is tugged back to Rotterdam; off go the O'Casey, the Talbot Memorial, the Loopline, Butt Bridge, O'Connell Bridge, The Ha'penny Bridge, the Millennium Bridge, Grattan Bridge, O'Donovan Rossa Bridge, Fr Mathew Bridge, the first of them all, great bridge, bridge of the Osmen, Dublin bridge; then Mellows Bridge, the slippery James Joyce Bridge, not to be crossed on a wet day, also by Calatrava, through whose steel wings you can see the house of 'The Dead', 15 Usher's Island; the blue bridge that came from St Helen's Foundry in Lancashire, Frank Sherwin Bridge, Heuston Bridge and so on down past Chapelizod to Lucan Bridge. The quay walls have melted away, the reclaimed land to the east has emptied itself back, and the river, the Ruirtech, *ro-ritheach*, the strong-running, flexes its muscles and rushes eastward to the nearer sea. And now that the bridges are gone, there is the serious problem of getting across.

For a long time I can't get past hurdle. *Áth Cliath*, the ford of hurdles. I understand that the hurdles involve woven rods of willow or hazel, but they seem too flimsy, too haphazard, too much exactly the kind of unlikely artefact you expect the past to concoct to test your credulity. But isn't there also something beautiful about the sheer provisionality of this passage? The hurdles were laid flat on the riverbed, weighed down with stones, and provided a route across for people, beasts, maybe even chariots, when the tide was low. It must have required constant repair and rebuilding, must have been constantly on the brink of disappearance. A virtual bridge, an almost invisible pathway.

It didn't always work:

> *770. The overthrow of the Uí Téig by the Ciannacht at Áth Cliath. There was a great slaughter of the Laigin. A number of the Ciannacht were drowned in the full tide as they returned.*
> — Annals of the Four Masters

Or, if you prefer:

> *765. The battle of Áth Cliath, by the Cianachta Breagh, against Ui Tegh; and there was great slaughter made of the Leinstermen, and numbers of the Cianachta were drowned in the full tide on their returning.*
> — The Annals of Inisfallen

Two annals, only five years in the difference — possibly a chance it happened, or at least that something happened. What, though, of the unrecorded who misjudged the tides or were caught by a sudden flood?

Many roads converge on this point. Mythical roads, routes from the Iron Age: *Slí Chualann*, from Tara to Wicklow, *Slí Mhidhluachra* from Ulster, and on the southern side of the ford *Slí Mhór* from the west, *Slí Dhála* from Munster. No one has identified the exact location of the ford. Some think it was where the first bridge was erected, but how did people get across while that was being constructed? Others think it would have been a little west of the bridge. As he pores over his Ordnance Survey map Hermann Geissel sees four ancient roads converge on the point where the crossing might have been: Stoneybatter, Upper Church Street, Bolton Street and Parnell Street. He is particularly excited when he walks the area and realizes that the four roads seem, once the present street system is set aside, to be converging on Bow Street, which becomes Lincoln Lane as it reaches the river, not more than an alley running along the side of St

Paul's Church on Arran Quay. As I read his account I'm peering at the Google map of Dublin on the computer.[1]

I decide to have a look. I walk up Blackpitts, New Row South, Francis Street, across Thomas Street and down St Augustine Street to the river. I line myself up with St Paul's of Smithfield and peer across. As the contemporary traffic roars behind me I imagine the centuries of traffic shuffling across the hurdles: men, women, children, cattle, horses, armies. Where I am standing now, leaning against the quay wall, would have been part of the river; to my left would be Usher's Island, properly islanded again. I take several photographs of the lane that might have led to the ford and of Fr Mathew Bridge. Then I walk up to the James Joyce Bridge and observe the river from there. Eventually I make my way back home. Later, I realize that almost every street I walk on daily formed part of the ancient routes. Francis Street and New Street were part of *Slí Chualann*. Cork Street, Ardee Street and The Coombe continued the route from Munster, *Slí Dhála*. And when I descended St Augustine Street and looked up Lincoln Lane towards Bow Street I was following the line of *Slí Mhidhluachra*.

In his *Dublin, An Urban History* Niall McCullough superimposes these routes on a map of the city. They were, he says 'of incalculable importance in the city structure and remain important streets to the present day — gritty urban places hard to imagine as tracks across open landscape'. He feels strongly that they are 'the real skeleton of the city structure and they meet, not on the hill or at the Liffey but at the crossing of the Poddle at Cross Poddle, roughly the junction of present-day Patrick Street, Kevin Street, the Coombe and Clanbrassil Street'.

It's interesting the extent to which these Iron Age routes still resonate with a contemporary architect even as he recognizes that no trace of them is reflected in the current planning. What, though, could be more significant not just to the understanding but to the imaginative apprehension of the city than a sense of their primary, mythical arteries? The present-day names, the widened streets with their endless stream of traffic conceal the ancient routes; cities disclose themselves obliquely, the past runs quietly down the old routes like the network of rivers under these streets on their way to the iron grilles that release them into the Liffey. But some signal, maybe, survives, some faint pulse of vanished journeys . . .

Hermann Geissel's real interest, the subject of a television documentary and a book, is less in the ford than in one of the roads it led to: *Slí Mhór*, the *magna via* which would have run up from the river to Cornmarket and then out of the city westward along Thomas Street. The road is also known as the *Eiscir Riada*, after an esker or ridge that people thought of as a continuous feature made up of sand, gravel and boulders that originally bisected the country into its two rival halves, the *Leith Chuinn* and the *Leith Mhogha*, as well as providing a highway to the west. Actually, the *Eiscir Riada* is a series of ridges with many gaps between them, and the road may not always have followed it — its continuity was more imagined than real, and the route therefore a mental construct as much as a physical passageway. The television programme and book are attempts to reconstruct its route.

One of the major sources for information on the route is a paper, 'The Ancient Roadways of Ireland' by Colm Ó Lochlainn, published in 1940.[2] Geissel's conclusions often diverge from Ó Lochlainn's, but I go to the library to investigate the original paper. There is something irresistible about the history of a road, particularly if the route is ancient, obscured by the passage of time and centuries of reconfiguration and infilling, and perhaps even more irresistible if the evidence is inconclusive, or disputed, or gained by poring over old manuscripts or *dinnsenchas* put together by poets or annalists with dark agendas of their own. One of the most powerful images of a road is the Iron Age trackway excavated in Corlea, County Longford, by Professor Barry Raftery of University College Dublin.[3] It was built in 148 BC and consists of oak planks laid on birch runners. It took between 200 and 300 mature oak trees to construct the trackway, which runs across the bog for about a kilometre, at a time when the bog was a much more forbidding wetland than it is now. It is wide enough to have allowed wheeled traffic but there are no signs of wheel ruts; like so much else from the Iron Age its purpose remains obscure. We don't know who crossed it or why, or why the road seems to have been abandoned at a certain point, as evidenced by the piles of timber found near the centre of the bog. We do know that the construction of the road was, in Barry Raftery's words, 'a gigantic undertaking comparable to the effort involved in the erection of the linear earthworks or in the building of the great royal centres'.[4] The fact that it is not far from a centre of royalty and ritual like Cruachain in County Roscommon or Uisneach in County Westmeath which was dedicated to the festival of Beltaine, indicates that it might have been part of a pilgrim route. He reminds us that road building on this scale was seen as a heroic task in the early literature, and begins his account of it by quoting a passage from *The Wooing of Étaín* in which one of the tasks given to Midir by Eochaid, king of Tara, after he loses a game of chess is to build a trackway across an impassable bog.

The Corlea trackway begins and ends in the imagination, crossed by travellers shrouded in mist, surrounded by dark, dank pools of water. In the same way the hurdle ford stretches out of history into myth, reminding us how long this patch of land has been occupied. The land has changed, the river has changed, a city has grown and spilled out over the map in all its complexity, its eternally shifting politics and struggles for ownership and control. The ford, though, is everyone's, and no one's . . .

As I read Colm Ó Lochlainn's article in the glass and concrete fortress of the Ussher Library in Trinity College I find myself less interested in the conjectured route of the ancient roadways and their likely purpose than in the way he applies himself to his task. Early Irish literature, he reminds us, is full of movement: armies and cattle crossing large tracts of country, constantly raiding and returning, as well as accounts of saints and their retinues travelling all around the country. All this movement is accomplished with a speed and efficiency that imply even if they don't specify a working transport infrastructure. By the time the Vikings arrive they are able to leave their boats and go on a two-day march inland and come back laden with plunder. Likewise, the Normans 'have little difficulty in moving bodies of heavily clad mailed warriors north, south, east and west without the preliminary military work of making roadways'. The roads are not mentioned in the literature; they are however mentioned in the law texts which make very specific recommendations on road building. Assuming, then, that they did exist, it should, Ó Lochlainn reckons, be possible to reconstruct their routes from the various itineraries undertaken in the literature.

The first thing he did was to list and to mark on the Ordnance Survey map all places which contained 'any of the following words: *Áth*, a ford: *Béal Átha*, mouth of a ford, *Droichead*, a bridge, *Bearna*, a breach, gap, chasm: *Bealach*, a gap, passage, road, *Bóthar*, a cattle track: *Ród*, a roadway: *Tóchar*, a flagged path, a causeway: *Ceis*, a wattled path: *Casán*, a footpath: *Slighe*, a high-road (possibly a way cut through woodlands)'. I stare out the window over the green of College Park, taking in the poetry of the names, the range of possibilities they offer, the efficient bureaucratization of the human need to move around. He also looked for names indicating a river crossing (*snámh*), a weir (*coradh*), a sandbank (*fersait*), a rocky outcrop (*scairbh*). He then examined journeys in the early literature: *The Life of St Patrick, Táin Bó Cuailnge* etc and worked out that 'in the minds of the storytellers and chroniclers, from the sixth to the tenth centuries, the idea of a great road system existed quite clearly — just as, in our day, the run of the main railways in Ireland is familiar to all'. The system is articulated in the tradition 'that five great roadways, radiating from Tara, made a magical appearance at the time of the birth of King Conn Céadcathach (circa 100 AD)'.

Whatever about their magical appearance, and the still unsolved mystery of Tara itself, ultimately he argues for the truth of the long established tradition. In the case of *Slí Mhór*, for instance, he establishes a route as follows: Dublin, Lucan, Celbridge, Taghadoe, Timahoe, Monasteroris, Road, Croghan, Kiltober, Durrow Abbey, Ballycumber, Togher, Ballaghurt, Clonmacnoise, Ballinasloe, Aughrim, Kilconnel, Bellafa, Kiltullagh, Clarinbridge. For me part of the attractiveness of a route like this is that it can't be verified. Despite Joyce's famous claim we know we couldn't actually reconstruct Dublin by consulting *Ulysses* — the architects and engineers would be left scratching their heads at the lack of concrete physical data. But imagine some scholar of the future poring over a map of Dublin constructed entirely from Joyce's writings, or from a combination of his work, the plays of Sean O'Casey, the poetry of Patrick Kavanagh, the novels of Roddy Doyle. The city of the mind or imagination that would be plotted there might lack in technical data, might miss out whole other districts of the mind as well as centuries of brick and dust, but it would be a place worth investigating, worth wandering around and getting lost in . . .

A dotted line crosses the river, pursued by a series of continuous lines on either side. The tide is out and the interwoven rods of willow hold firm. Conn of the Hundred Battles is in the neighbourhood, or maybe Conchobar Mac Nessa and his cranky agent-provocateur poet Aithirne Áilghesach who specializes in exercising his poet's right to demand any tribute he chooses: an eye from Eochaid, the one-eyed king; cows, women, whatever else he can get out of the Leinstermen. The main thing is to start a row. It is at his bidding that the hurdle ford is constructed, to get his cattle and the wives and daughters of the Leinster nobles, whom he has also demanded, across to Ulster territory:

Ath Cliath, canas ro ainmniged?
Ni ansa .i. cliatha caolaig doriginset Laigin hi flaith
   Misgegra
fo cosaib caorach Aitherne Áilgesaigh . . .

*(Where does the name Áth Cliath come from? /*
*Leinstermen made hurdles during the reign of*
*Misgegra / under the feet of the sheep of Aithirne*
*the Importunate . . . )*

Sheep too, clearly — everything, as always, depends on the
version. And in case that doesn't satisfy, there's this, from
the same source, *Prose Tales in the Rennes Dindshenchas*.
Or else, says the writer, keeping his options open:

*When the men of Erin broke the limbs of the Matae,*
*the monster that was slain on the Liacc Benn in the*
*Brug maic ind Óc, they threw it limb by limb into*
*the Boyne, and its shinbone (colptha) got to Inber*
*Colptha (the estuary of the Boyne), whence Inber*
*Colptha is said, and the hurdle of its frame (i.e. its*
*breast) went along the sea coasting Ireland till it*
*reached yon ford (áth); whence Áth Cliath is said.*

# A Pair of Curtains

There is a particular kind of desolation that can only be achieved by curtains: ancient net curtains rotting into the windows whose rooms they protect, curtains that proclaim their dejection to everyone curious enough to look, curtains that have given up, whose folds hold the grime of decades. Here's one whose thin plastic cord has expanded through old age or exhaustion and is now sagging a quarter way down the tall window. The curtain itself is ragged, unkempt, forlorn. What kind of life gets lived behind a curtain like this? You imagine misery, but joy likes these spaces too — spaces that are occupied temporarily, provisionally, spaces no one is responsible for but some faceless, distant landlord who has long forgotten the curtains he bought in a hurry in the discount shop on the quays thirty years ago, who may well have forgotten the flat they adorn, or, to judge by the broken fanlight and the paint peeling from the door, the house itself. It is a monthly rumble of activity in a bank account, an invoice for a broken toilet seat, a bill from a plumber called to fix a leaking bath. Unless he's the kind of landlord who likes to collect his rent in person. A friend of mine lived in a house in Rathmines and every Saturday in the early hours of the morning the guard who owned it would appear in his uniform, hand out for the weekly cash. It is unlikely, if this one does arrive to collect his rent, that he notices his declining curtains, any more than he notices the slow death of the mildewed couch or the pile of metal in the hall that used to be a hoover. He comes, he goes. The furniture stays, the curtains sigh in the draught.

# Disremembering Dublin

Cities remember, cities forget. Hundreds of thousands of people pass through a street and leave the phantom print of their feet, their breath, their voices. Lives are lived behind bricks and windows and when they are over the city shrugs them off as if they had never happened. Nor are the famous, the memorialized if not remembered, immune from oblivion. I'm standing on Lennox Street, in Portobello, reading a brief inscription on a stone plaque on the wall of number 28. Sculptor John Hughes lived in this house 1890-1901. I must have passed it hundreds of times before finding out anything about him. I now know a few things, enough to imagine the outlines of a life, and his passage in and out of this street for a decade at the end of the nineteenth century, the decade when he was at the height of his powers.

He was born in Dublin in 1865 and died in Nice in 1941. When he was eighteen he entered the Metropolitan School of Art in Thomas Street and was a part-time student there for ten years. I wonder if he encountered W B Yeats who was born the same year as he was and spent two years at the college from 1884 to 1886. Hughes did well at the art school and won scholarships to the South Kensington School of Art, London, and then Paris. He travelled to Italy for further studies and eventually came back to teach in the Metropolitan School. In 1902 he became Professor of Sculpture in the Royal Hibernian Academy School. In 1903 he left Dublin and lived in Italy and France, where he died in 1941.

So much for the procession of facts. What of his work? His 'Man of Sorrow' and life-size 'Madonna and Child', both completed in 1901, can be seen in Loughrea Cathedral,

24

and his statue of Charles Kickham, author of *Knocknagow* — poet, novelist and above all PATRIOT, reads the inscription — sits in state on a huge plinth in his stone topcoat, contemplating Kickham Square in Tipperary town.

But his most famous work is famously absent. In 1904 King Edward VII unveiled his bronze sculpture of Queen Victoria on a granite plinth outside Leinster House, then the headquarters of the Royal Dublin Society. When the new state acquired the buildings for Oireachtas Éireann there were rumblings of discontent that the colonial queen should still be sitting outside its parliament buildings and calls for it to be removed were made repeatedly from 1922 onward. Her fate was of concern beyond Ireland too, as the following passage from *Hansard* shows:

> *Professor Savory: I asked the Under-Secretary of State for Dominion Affairs whether his attention has been drawn to the declaration by the Prime Minister of Éire that his Government have under consideration the request of the Dublin Corporation for the removal of the statue of Queen Victoria from its position in front of the Parliament House in Dublin; and whether, to save this statue from the indignities inflicted on those of King William III and King George II, His Majesty's Government in the United Kingdom will make an offer to the Government of Éire to purchase this statue for removal to the United Kingdom?*

> *The Under-Secretary of State for Dominion Affairs (Mr. Emrys-Evans): The point raised by my hon. Friend is a hypothetical one. He will have seen that in a recent statement in the Dáil Mr de Valera indicated that no decision had been taken in this matter which was not regarded as one of urgency.*

> *Professor Savory: May I ask whether the hon. Gentle-*

> *man will take some steps to save this statue from the*
> *fate meted out to that of King William III, which*
> *was blown up in 1929 in College Green, and the*
> *statue of King George II in St Stephen's Green,*
> *which was threatened with a similar fate, was blown*
> *from its pedestal, but was saved for the City of*
> *Birmingham through the activities of Professor*
> *Bodkin?*

> *Mr. Emrys-Evans: I do not think the statue is in any*
> *immediate danger.*

> *Professor Savory: Beware.[1]*

Queen Victoria was, of course, in severe danger. The story
of her eventual removal is told in Yvonne Whelan's
*Reinventing Modern Dublin: Streetscape, Iconography and
the Politics of Identity* (UCD Press 2003), which reproduces
a photograph from *The Irish Times* in July 1948 showing
the roped and shackled Queen being winched by a crane
from her plinth and lowered onto a truck under the careful
eyes of Dublin Corporation workmen as a large crowd of
ministers, deputies and the general public looks on. The
image has become an icon of postcolonialism. It is the cover
image of a collection of essays published by Oxford University
Press, *Ireland and the British Empire*. The statue, turned on
her back in order to get through the gates of Leinster House,
was brought, fittingly enough, to the Royal Hospital in
Kilmainham. Her reign wasn't quite finished, however;
there were requests from London, Ontario, and Victoria,
British Columbia, but neither could raise the funds necessary
to transport the statue. And then, in 1983, the authorities
in Sydney began a worldwide search for a statue to grace
the Queen Victoria Building. By then the statue had been
further exiled to Daingean, County Offaly, where Neil
Glasser, the QVB's Director of Promotions, found it

*behind a brick wall belonging to a derelict reforma-
tory school seated on damp ground, exposed to the
inclement weather of Ireland. For forty years she
had served as a favourite perch and nesting place for
the local birds. Bush and brambles had sprung up all
around and although undamaged, her time outside
had left her discoloured with the bronze well hidden
under a coat of black and greens.*[2]

The decision was finally made in 1986 to give the statue to
the people of Sydney and it now stands in the Bicentennial
Plaza.

It is Hughes's bad luck that he should be known to us
largely as the creator of a vanished imperial icon. Thomas
MacGreevy, the poet and Director of the National Gallery
in the fifties, goes further. For MacGreevy, Hughes was a
great sculptor who produced 'archetypes individualistic,
fastidiously graceful, consciously aesthetic, above all, philo-
sophic, rather in the Leonardesque way'. He is writing in an
essay on Loughrea Cathedral, where he is struck forcefully
by Hughes's 'Madonna and Child' and his figure of Christ
resurrected, the 'Man of Sorrow' who has returned to earth
'with all the agony of Calvary still imprinted on His Features'.
'It is a tragedy,' he says, when the statue was still very much
present in the city, 'that this great Irish sculptor should be
best known to his own countrymen by his heavily dignified,
rather forbidding statue of the Famine Queen outside
Leinster House.'

*She was small-minded, stupid, pig-headed, arrogant,
bigoted — see her letter to Lord John Russell about
Father Mathew — without magnanimity, and in her
whole attitude to people outside her own narrow
world, obsessed with self-conceit. What could Hughes
do? In life she was a little thing, only four-foot-ten
in height. Presumably as a concession to the great-
ness racket, Hughes made her an outsize figure*

> *physically. For the rest, he gave her such vitality as truth could give. The result is a statue that has the vitality of truth. It is probably the most vitally truth- ful statement about Queen Victoria in all the art devoted to her apotheosis. Sculpturally it is probably better than any other statue of her. Certainly it is better than any I have seen in England or Scotland. But for a statue set up as a public ornament and for public delectation, goodness and beauty are neces- sary as well as truth. And to find these in Kildare Street one has to turn from the main personage of the group to the subsidiary figures, particularly to the exquisite figure of Ireland crowning the Irish soldier dying in the South African War.[3]*

That subsidiary figure is now in the garden of Dublin Castle Conference Centre.

For all its indignities Victoria's fate was gentler than that endured by other symbols of British government. The statue of King William III was damaged in an explosion and removed by the Corporation from Stephen's Green in 1928; the equestrian statue of George I was moved from Essex Bridge to the back of the Mansion House and later sold to the City of Birmingham; the statue of Viscount Gough in the Phoenix Park was blown up in 1957 after three attempts; the statue of Viscount Carlisle was blown up in 1958, and of course Nelson's Pillar was blown up in 1966. The fate of these memorials reminds us of the provisionality of com- memoration in disputed spaces. In any regime change the first things to go are the civic symbols, the monuments and statuary that asserted the power and dignity of the old regime. Hughes' Victoria belonged to a particular monu- mentalist moment. One scholar that Yvonne Whelan quotes gauges the rate of statue erection during Victoria's reign as one a month and also reminds us how 'The streets of even modest-sized German towns bristled with patriotic sculp- ture: in a single decade some five hundred memorial towers were raised to Bismarck alone.'⁴

The statues of Carlisle and Gough were the work of John Henry Foley, a Dubliner, and the pre-eminent public sculptor of his day, a specialist in imperial icons. His statue of Victoria's husband, still one of his best works, survives undamaged and unmoved on the other side of Leinster House. Thomas MacGreevy wrote a piece in 1955 for the Dublin magazine *Pictorial* in which he reflected on the city's imperial monuments.⁵ Nelson's Pillar, the work of Armagh man and architect of the GPO, Francis Johnston, he considers 'the finest Doric pillar in Great Britain or Ireland'. Nelson himself, sculpted by Corkman Thomas Kirk, 'a very fine sculptor', seems to be a good piece of work but MacGreevy acknowledges that the pillar might be better off with Napoleon. He argues, vainly as it turned out, for the preservation of the Foley Carlisle and Gough statues, though recommending that these, like others likely to give offence in the Republic, for their own safety, should 'be removed to a place where they could be regarded as museum pieces, segregated somewhere apart for the study by scholars in relation to the art history of our country'. His piece ends with a flight of fancy as he imagines a better replacement for Nelson:

*Myself, I have a hankering for a symbolic winged female figure of Belfast. It could be a gracious addition to the masculine line of figures in O'Connell Street. Think of them! O'Connell with his right leg out, Smith O'Brien with his right leg out, Sir John Gray with his right leg out, Nelson with his right leg out, Father Mathew, wearing his habit, with no legs, and Parnell with his left leg out! A 12 or 15 foot figure, comparable with those of the cities of France on the Place de la Concorde in Paris, under Partition or even when Partition ends, it would be a reminder of our great sister Irish city of the north and could be an inspiring presence as we walk up O'Connell Street. And the buses with 'Belfast Pillar' on them . . .*

If the public symbols of cities are subject to rapid changes of favour, the buildings at least are more secure. And even street names prove to be lodged deeper into the city's psyche than you might think. I'm standing, after all, in Lennox Street, named for a British Viceroy, like nearby Richmond, Harrington, Heytesbury and Camden Streets; and the neighbourhood itself, Portobello, like its London namesake, commemorates the capture by Admiral Vernon in 1739 of Porto Bello on Panama's Caribbean Coast, during the conflict between the United Kingdom and Spain, better known as the War of Jenkins' Ear. The British only occupied the Porto Bello for three weeks before withdrawing, having destroyed its fortifications, port and warehouse, but the neighbourhood is still thriving, oblivious of its Caribbean heritage and the severed ear of Captain Robert Jenkins.

Cities remember, cities forget. John Hughes is a brief inscription on a stone plaque in a small Portobello street. I pause to photograph some of the neighbouring houses. The paint is peeling off some of the doorways, the timber above a fanlight is damaged, and some of the ornate console brackets at the top of the doorcases, one of the highlights of these streets, are chipped. The most neglected houses are those with the most bells, with ten or more flats packed into a house. A door swings open and a tenant comes out, giving me an odd look. Opposite, a smart new restaurant in one of the oldest houses on the street, which just a few months ago was an auctioneer. The Lennox Irish Breakfast, with bacon, sausage, black pudding, sauté potatoes, tomato and choice of egg. The Lennox Ultimate Caesar Salad . . . Suddenly hungry, I call in to 'The Bretzel' on the corner for some bread.

## At the Front Gate

He's well dressed, particularly for a Saturday, striped shirt and suit. He's ringing the neighbours' bell as I come home from the market.

'Have you lived here long?' he calls over.

I try to remember. 'Seven or eight years, I think.'

He gives up on the neighbours and comes over. He seems a little disappointed that I haven't been here longer.

'Did you know the people next door?' he asks.

I knew the old lady who lived next door, who used to play her Frank Sinatra records in the early hours of the morning and who remembered the orchards that were here before they built the houses, and one of her sons who used to visit, and who sold the house after she died. He knew the family, it seems. He grew up around the corner. He points at the corner, at the office of the estate agent specializing in Polish property. That was the baker, he tells me, McHenry's.

And it was a baker again, for a brief couple of years, I am able to tell him, run by an Iranian family. It was called Taybah, and I was partial to its pastries, although I could never work out whether the female hand that passed them in from the hatch behind the counter took them from an oven or a delivery box. From the day it opened it had a bleakness about it, as if the enterprise had been cursed before it began but must nonetheless continue to set out its meagre supply of pastries on the glass shelves. But that's all too recent to be meaningful. The man is in a mood to talk and he tells me about his childhood in the neighbourhood, how he wandered all over the city with his friends, up to the Phoenix Park and back. He remembers the smell from the slaughterhouse, a heavy, sweet tang barely noticeable to the residents except as the sure smell of home but commented on by everyone who left the South Circular Road to enter the area. They boiled horse carcasses to make glue, he tells me, though I already know this from my own haphazard researches. He remembers the flies that swarmed in every direction within a mile radius of the slaughterhouse, and the maggots that had to be cleaned out of the gutters. He remembers how cold the houses were in winter. Now he lives in a distant suburb and drives his big car everywhere.

'There were orchards here before the houses,' I offer. 'Fairbrothers' Fields I think they were called.'

'That's right,' he nods. And then he switches back into the present, and the future, to tell me about a new political party he is founding, and I'm half curious, half anxious to get the shopping inside and dinner under way, so I neglect to ask him for a card or a leaflet, and let him return to his car, away from the sudden press of the past into the brisk campaigns of the future.

# In the Double City: James Whitelaw's Dublin

Thomas Street manages to be both within the city and outside it at the same time, as if the walls were still in place and
this stretch of the highway outside still a distinct suburb. A
stone's throw from Christchurch, a brisk walk to the Front
Gate of Trinity College, yet the air is different, the light is
different, and the smell is different. On this cold February
day I cross the wide trafficky expanse of High Street and
Cornmarket towards Thomas Street. The traffic acts as a
kind of wall, funnelling cars out to the south and into the
centre and north of the city, increasing the sense of a passage
from one district to another. As you pass St Audoen's, the
limit of the old city, and stare down the sharp incline of
Bridge Street where the sun hits the pale brick of Cook
Street flats, you realize that you are walking across a high
ridge above the river, and this again reinforces the sense of
exiting one kind of space and entering another.

There are other signs. In spite of the tiny distance, fashion
has never made the crossing. The city has never bothered
much with Thomas Street; it seems to exist in permanent
neglect, many of its fine old buildings on the brink of collapse,
torn down, altered, eternally endangered, at the mercy of
the dreams of developers and the chaos of the markets.
The street survives, tough, resolute, working-class, with a
bohemian sprinkle of cafés near the art college like a daub
of icing on a crumbling cake. Here is the suit hire shop,
the communion shop with the tailor overhead; here is
Chadwicks builders' supplies with its arched gateway like
the entrance to another domain; here are the discount shops,
the pawnbrokers, the stalls with stacked toilet papers and

chocolate bars; here is Mannings bakery and what used to be Frawley's department store, now an outsize clothes shop and soon to be a student accommodation block. For years it was the central shopping anchor of the street, drawing shoppers in from outlying areas, and spawning market stalls outside it to serve the crowds on their way in and out. It was, effectively, a department store for the poor. If you were the kind of person who shopped in Switzers or Brown Thomas you didn't go to Frawley's, you probably never even heard of the place. After a century of trading it ended up in the hands of a now broke developer who intended to demolish it and erect a retail and office complex on the site and has since been bought from the receiver by another developer. In the end part of the physical structure of Frawley's was saved by history; it turned out that its hardly imposing exterior hides a mansion in the form of twin 'Dutch Billys' built in 1710 and once owned by Joseph Fade, a banker and one of Dublin's first developers, who lived here with his twenty-one children. The site is also within the grounds of the medieval Augustinian friary that gave the street its name, and who knows what treasures lie underneath its foundations.

The whole street is like that, a brooding, dark-eyed presence living on the ghosts of lost or forgotten riches. A great deal of it is derelict, particularly the western stretch from St Catherine's Church to the Fountain. Weeds grow out of the brickwork, windows are broken, shops and pubs boarded up and shuttered, as if desolation must always be the default mode here. New businesses have sprung up and put down roots, the Bosnian supermarket, a Brazilian market, an Asian market, outposts of hipsterdom — coffee shops, a sour-dough pizzeria, but it's still as if the city has never quite forgotten or forgiven the district's heritage of disaffection. This was always the mob's city, the seething, lawless under-city that could be counted on for riots or murder. In the midst of the dereliction, the great squat bulk of St Catherine's Church, with its Doric columns and pediment — 'the finest

façade of any church in Dublin' according to Maurice Craig
— looms vividly. Until recently it was one of the most
miserable sights in the street, its beautiful mountain granite
darkened by centuries of grime, the interior falling asunder
after long neglect. I remember I used to pause here years ago
in the darkness of 6 a.m. on bleak December mornings on
my way to work in James's Street Post Office as a Christmas
postman. The building then seemed the epitome of gloom;
it seemed entirely appropriate that Robert Emmet should
have been hanged and beheaded outside it — the forbidding
building might have been constructed for no other reason
than to have someone butchered in front of its façade.
Things have improved since then. The exterior has been
cleaned up so that it now looks much as it must have done
when it was built in the 1760s to the design of John Smith,
who was also responsible for St Thomas's Church, on
Marlborough Street, and the spire of St Werburgh's, both of
which have vanished.

A spire was planned for St Catherine's too, but, like so
many others in this city of missing spires, never left the
drawing board for lack of funds. I'm here today not just for
the building but for James Whitelaw, one of the first Rectors
of St Catherine's. Inside there's a monument to him.
Outside, maybe, his spirit prowls the district and inspects
the populace. If we double back to September 1803 we
might find him standing outside his church watching the
oddly makeshift arrangements for Emmet's execution, the
planks set on top of barrels borrowed from a local brewery
for the platform, the table and cleaver borrowed from a
butcher's, maybe the shop that supplies his own table. No
doubt his well-organized and meticulous mind is offended
by the slipshod arrangements. You expect the state to be
grander in its judicial killings, to accord them the pomp of
its judges and law courts and highly wrought language of
condemnation. I think of the elaborate rhetoric of Emmet's
speech from the dock, or the extraordinary letter to the
Chief Secretary, which he begged permission to return to his

cell to write as he was being led to his death. The casual set design is either part of the punishment — the contempt meted out to the body will also be accorded to the machinery of its destruction — or sheer messy improvisation. An order is passed down, time is short. Is a contingent of soldiery despatched afterwards to return the bloody table and cleaver, or does the butcher have to sue the Corporation for compensation? Do the barrels go back to Manders' brewery to be filled with beer? In Iran they borrow cranes from building sites to hang the condemned, after which the cranes are driven back to the building sites for the rest of the day's work. Manders goes out of business not long after the execution — it may be that the customers don't want beer from its tainted barrels. Or maybe their beer is just no good.

If he is horrified by the events in front of his church, or by the violence on Thomas Street the previous July, the Rev James Whitelaw is unlikely to be too surprised. The rebellion that degenerated into a murderous riot must have involved at least some people he knows from his wanderings in his own parish and further afield. In many ways he knows more about his city than anyone else alive . . .

1798: the year of the United Irishmen rebellion that sees between 15,000 and 30,000 killed. Most of the events take place outside Dublin, due largely to the authorities discovering and raiding the planned assembly points, but the city is alive with the currents of conspiracy and counter-insurgency. In the Castle Major Sirr briefs his spies. In May he surprises Lord Edward Fitzgerald in the feather-dealer's house in Thomas Street, and shoots him in the shoulder. Fitzgerald is taken to the Castle in an open sedan chair, and thence to Newgate where he dies of his wounds. In the unusual heat of that summer James Whitelaw is busy with his own plans. He meets with his assistants and they pore over John Rocque's map of the city. It's time to start the great work that has been preoccupying him for some years: to count the citizens of Dublin and establish at last the population of this city. Is this work part of the Government's intelligence gathering? Is it directed by Major Sirr as a means of keeping tabs on the disaffected? Whitelaw has in fact obtained the government's permission and approval, but the project is his own initiative and he will pay for it himself. The troubles, he realizes, will actually make his job easier. The Lord Mayor of Dublin has issued an order requiring a list of all residents to be affixed to the door of every house in the city, making enumeration a straightforward exercise at least in the better regulated and better off areas of the city. It doesn't quite work in his own parish and surrounding districts, where the lists, when legible, are rarely accurate. This means that he will have to investigate each house for himself. And his assistants will have to go back and double-check. It has to be an accurate survey, otherwise there is no point. And so they set out. Surprisingly, maybe, they meet little resistance. One of his assistants, less than diplomatic, questions a butcher in Ormond market about the number of occupants in his building. There appears to be some discrepancy here. The list states clearly . . . The butcher has had enough; he lifts a bucket of blood and offal and throws the contents over the assistant, who slinks off, humiliated. Other than that, the work goes smoothly.

Order is everything. It is necessary to know how the numbers are distributed among the various classes: upper class, middle class, servants, lower class. How many servants there are in this city. One in ten serves master or mistress. But when you leave the fine houses and come to examine the parish of St Catherine's . . . Unless you have seen them, it is difficult to believe the conditions these people are living in. Whitelaw trudges through the dark alleys and stinking lanes, thinking of himself as an historian of wretchedness. He gets up early and often finds himself in a room less than fifteen-foot square where between ten and sixteen people lie stretched on a wad of filthy straw, crawling with vermin, not a blanket between them. Nor is it any surprise to encounter between thirty and fifty in a single house. In a house in Braithwaite Street he counts a hundred and eight occupants. The exact numbers are important. Perhaps, he thinks, when the facts have been irrefutably established, the way will lie open for properly administered charity and educational opportunity. After all, it is in no one's interest to breed disaffection. Surely it is evident that misery is an impediment to governance?

Joseph's Lane, near Castle Market. A sudden rainstorm beating down. It is not always easy to gain entry to these houses. As he steps across the threshold he is suddenly halted by a bloody mess, alive with maggots, which has burst in through the back door from the slaughterhouse adjoining the house. The hall is buried under the stinking flood. There is no way he can get in. But the job must be done somehow, so he retreats back into the lane and finds an old plank and some stones. Having constructed his bridge, he makes for the stairs, attracting interest from the residents who simply wade through the blood. As he climbs the stairs he sees water pouring through the house. The roof is in disrepair, as it so often is in these houses, and he knows it will remain in that condition as long as the house is standing, just as he knows that the rent will continue to be collected punctually. He stops at each room and takes his count. He can barely endure the stench now. No one remarks on it. Can it be that they don't smell it? In the garret he finds a shoemaker and his family, seven in all. The room has no door. They explain to him that because the shoemaker couldn't pay the week's rent, the enraged landlord has taken the door away in hopes that they will quit the building. This house holds thirty-seven people. Whitelaw does a quick calculation and concludes that out of this ruin the landlord gets more than thirty pounds a year, with rent coldly extracted every Saturday night.

It is a double city, one visible and regulated, the other hidden and ignored, and utterly wild. He finds himself getting angry, not just at the conditions he encounters but the maddening passivity of the occupants. As long as they can fill their bellies they don't seem to care where or how they live. If there is filth and mess no one shifts to move it. 'Why should I? Who will pay me to remove it?' In July he visits a house in Schoolhouse Lane almost comical in its desolation. The side of the four-storey building has collapsed and fallen into the adjoining yard, killing an entire dairy of cows. The tenants are still here, continuing to live just as before, and the landlord comes as usual every Saturday for his rent. Money-grubbing, grasping wretches, living comfortably in the best parts of the city, who would still come for their rent were the whole district to collapse. 'What, do you think the air is free?' There should be legislation to make them answerable for the conditions of their buildings.

As he patrols his parish he frets about the number of brothels, soap factories, slaughterhouses, glasshouses, lime-kilns, distilleries and dram-shops. Thomas Street, he notes, contains 190 houses, and fifty-two of those are licensed to sell spirits and are open at every hour of the day and night, providing a spectacle of unceasing profaneness and intemperance. Misery, irreligion and drunkenness — no wonder, the rebellion found its focus here. The district is so crowded even the dead find themselves evicted from their graves and flung anywhere to pollute the neighbourhood.

~

James Whitelaw stands with his feet firmly planted in his seething parish. He has spent two years meticulously tabulating the results of his survey; it will be another five before his *Essay on the Population of Dublin* is published. He continues with his parochial work, lobbying hard for relief, promoting subscriptions to allay distress. These are hard times in St Catherine's. In the wake of the Act of Union many businesses have failed, many families been reduced to starvation. Tirelessly, he works for the establishment of relief committees. There is more trouble afoot; in a depot nearby, muskets, pikes, grenades are stored. Beams of wood are hollowed out to conceal them. The conspirators go over the plans, discuss the signals that will be used. The spies take note and report back to Sirr. Whitelaw also finds the time to write his highly prized 'Parental Solicitude' and *A Map of the Grand and Royal Canals of Ireland.* And what is the result of his great survey? Will it make a difference? The authorities take his figures and examine them. He has corrected the vanity of the metropolis, which imagined itself to be inhabited by above 300,000 souls. He and his assistants have found 182,370, of which a fifth might be considered of the upper and middle class. Major Sirr goes through the lists. The authorities realize the importance of decent statistics. They take down their maps and with sharpened pencils divide the city into wards, to be inspected by Conservators. That should make things easier. They are less concerned with the living conditions of the mob. One question they would surely like to have answered was the one that Whitelaw didn't feel able to ask. He had been so keen to establish how many belonged to each religious sect but found that 'the temper of the times seemed to discourage enquiry', and he had to give up the idea. He satisfied himself with establishing the number of Protestants in each of the parishes surveyed; a simple deduction from the gross population figures would provide the number of Catholics. In his own parish of St Catherine's, out of a total population of 20,000 about a tenth were Protestant, and the rest were Catholics. Within forty years another census would reveal that the Protestant population of the city was 27%, down from 50% in 1730. Even if his statistician's mind would have appreciated the figures, Whitelaw, unlike many others, shows no particular preoccupation with the religious question. There are more pressing concerns in this city of gross inequalities. Life goes on. Whitelaw's dangerous daily round to the homes and bedsides of his parishioners continues. A biographical dictionary published in 1822 tells us: 'On every occurrence of epidemic distress, he was always the first to promote a subscription, and apply it judiciously to the relief of the afflicted.' It gives an example of one occasion where due to 'a stagnation of business 2643 families were reduced to starvation' but through his perseverance relief committees were established in the various districts (from the *Biographia Hibernica*).[1] He was to be found at all hours 'moving from one miserable abode to another; at the side of the sick, however contagious the disease'. In the end it is his charity that undoes him. He goes to offer comfort to a parishioner in the Fever Hospital and catches the infection which causes his death in 1813, at the age of sixty-five.

His church is still there, its century and a half of slow decline now arrested. It was closed in 1966 and deconsecrated the following year, but after its refurbishment in the 1990s it was reconsecrated and is now 'an evangelical and charismatic expression of worship within the Church of Ireland', in a city more diverse than Whitelaw might have imagined, and which we can imagine his curious, meticulous ghost quietly surveying.

# A Morning Walk

Because it will end soon I'm possessed by a sudden urge to memorialize it, this ritual the morning offers us, or rather the series of rituals through which we enter the day. After breakfast we leave the house, my five-year-old daughter, the dog and myself. The leaving is itself a complex ritual. The dog waits at the top of the stairs, anxious and excited. Will it happen, or will they forget me? Will I have to content myself with looking out the living room window and hurling myself against the glass if any other creature appears? His tail thumps against the stair carpet as he watches us putting our coats on. I go back into the living-room to get the lead. I give it a mild shake, a tiny wrist-flick. It's enough; the dog comes bounding down the stairs in a fever of excitement. He jumps up on his hind legs, and butts the door, almost as if the issue were still in doubt and we might yet fail him. I'm tempted to clip the lead quickly onto his collar and get him out before he explodes, but that is my daughter's task, and I know better than to disturb any part of her ritual. It takes her a while to control the dog enough to get the lead on, but eventually it's accomplished, and we can leave. She is the gate opener and the gate closer.

Finally, we're on the pavement, and the journey can begin. We set off, the three of us, three different but connected journeys. I hold my daughter's hand as she skips down the street; in my other hand I hold the lead firmly as the dog wheels and lunges, imposing himself, warning off any creature foolish enough to break the circle of power he throws around himself. We walk up to the great noisy thoroughfare of Clanbrassil Street, packed with slow-moving cars, motorcycles, bikes. We stand on the edge of the pavement, waiting for a gap to get us across to the central island. Even here the dog is foolish enough to race after a cat or another dog. I shorten the lead and hold tight. Eventually we cross the swarming river of traffic and escape into St Kevin's Parade by the side of Bu-Ali. This is the entrance to another world, an island of redbricked quiet patrolled by cats. Freya greets the two ginger cats generally to be found near the side entrance of the takeaway or outside the door of the cottage alongside it. The owner leaves out food for the strays. The ginger cats are fearless and merely stare at the dog, but the smaller, darker cats dive under cars and his dignity is appeased.

We round the corner and now we have the long strip of Lombard Street West with its cherry blossom trees and orderly Victorian houses. Like most of the small streets around here it was built in the 1870s in small lots by different developers, which accounts for the variations in the houses. Most are single-storey but there is one block of two-storey houses. Many of the houses have bay windows, but some present a straight line to the street. The doorcases are similar but again there's much variation, as there is in the different styles of fanlights above the doors. There's coherence, but it's a slightly higgledy-piggledy coherence bound together by small differences.

Right now it's cherry blossom season and the pavement is littered with the pink confetti. Although we are in the heart of the city there is hardly any traffic here and we rarely encounter anyone. My daughter skips along happily and we make up stories about the streets we walk through or stop to inspect signs on letter boxes or cats on windowsills. Lombard Street is quite long and my natural inclination when faced with any long stretch of road is to veer off it down a side-street; to walk, for me, is to zigzag rather than keep a straight course. As we approach the second corner I have an inclination to veer into Desmond Street and take the next right into McMahon Street, the next street down from

43

Lombard Street. It's a tiny, toy-like street and because of the slope of the road when you turn into it you almost feel as though your head will touch the roofs of these cottages with their pretty bay windows and scaled down brightly coloured doors. They stretch back and are perfectly spacious inside but the front they present to the street is of a decorous modesty. This used to be our daily route until one day I didn't take the turn and continued down Lombard Street, and for some reason my daughter was so taken with the altered route that it locked fast in her mind and became an absolute part of the journey. I feel her hand tugging me sharply back from my attempted variation and give up the attempt. I can always enjoy it later, I think.

There are certain pre-ordained stops along the route: in one garden an old yellow wellington boot has been converted into a plant pot and each morning Freya pauses to inspect both boot and the creeper that seems happily housed in it. Then there is the poodle in Arnott Street which waits for us on a table in the basement level kitchen and barks furiously up at us as we pass. Get off my path! How dare you cross my territory! Get away now or I'll . . . His taut poodle body quivers with rage. Even if it's a precise replication of his own antics at our front window, our dog is unimpressed, and ignores him.

We cross the road and a little further on they are still working on a block of new houses on the corner. One of the houses has a mirror set in the concrete and Freya pauses there to examine herself. Once she's satisfied, we can advance. The mirror house marks the end of the little district that began with the cats on St Kevin's Parade. Its southern border is the South Circular Road and its northern limit is Long Lane. The long stretch of Heytesbury Street is the eastern boundary. Beyond that the brick colour lightens and the house type moves up a scale in grandeur. We cross over busy Heytesbury Street and go around the corner into Pleasants Street. We're now in the neighbourhood of Camden Street, and the little streets we have just left have no bearing here, and no one who lives here would be drawn to them; they're much more likely to feel the magnetic pull eastward towards the axis of Camden, Wexford, Aungier and George's Streets with their coffee shops, restaurants, groceries, butchers, hardware and electrical goods stores, and on into town.

We are nearly at the end of the morning ritual but neither of us is in any hurry to bring it to its conclusion. The Montessori is in a basement and I tie the dog to the railing before we descend. My daughter sits on a step or on the edge of the raised garden and waits for me to ring the bell. The world will begin when the door opens and she walks in, and this moment of waiting is a small effort by both of us to prolong the ritual of the journey through the streets. The journey is too short, the ritual is over in only fifteen minutes, and I think we both realize that the ceremonial walk from house to school is a magical space, a sort of transition between worlds that is itself a wholly absorbing world.

There will be other trips out during the day, including a repetition of this route when I collect her, but somehow that's different, those excursions are stitched into the day; the morning walk occupies a separate space, almost a private city: our own interaction with ourselves, but also an interaction with space, time, with bricks and light and urban greenery. Strange how effortlessly these details, and our passage through them, print themselves on our receptors; our bodies as well as our minds become used to them, and used to the trace of the ritual journey. Walk somewhere a few times and the body's software will absorb the route and then reproduce it automatically. Sometimes if I leave the house without thinking about where I'm going I'll find my legs moving resolutely for the habitual route; or I'll find myself halfway up Lombard Street before I realize I'm supposed to be walking in the opposite direction. I have to make a conscious effort to divert my body from its programmed navigation. This particular software configuration will lodge in the permanent map-room of the brain, so that even if I were to come back here twenty years from now I wouldn't have to think about where I was going. But the ritual will have vanished. It will be a route rather than a ceremony, it won't be now, a morning in May, the three us walking together into our day.

I know that my current morning route has only a couple of more months in it, before my daughter starts school, and that's partly why I have this urge to memorialize it. I'll walk this way again, but it will be different, it won't be a fixed trajectory hardwired to the brain; it won't be now.

*2010*

# The Poet and the Mapmaker

Why is a map of a city so evocative? It is, after all, in many ways a reductive representation, reducing the din, excitement and variety of the urban experience to a dry sketch, an outline plot, an aid to navigation or administration. It offers, maybe, an illusion of control: you gaze down at a city captured in its entirety, enjoying the bird's eye view, as if you might swoop down into a park or street and bear off an exotic snack or trinket. For all its apparent dryness and strict functionality a map holds a pure appeal to the imagination. To look at a map of a city you don't know is to inhabit it virtually, dreaming your way from Avenida 25 de Mayo to Avenida Scalabrini Ortiz, from Prinsegracht to Sarphatistraat or from the Riva degli Schiavoni to Piazza San Marco.

Technology has intensified this experience so that we can test a city before we visit it, using Google's street view to survey the restaurants near the hotel and scope out our evening stroll, swinging round through three hundred and sixty degrees like a prison governor at the centre of his panopticon to peer at windows, traffic lights and parked cars. It's as if you could try on a segment of your life before submitting to the experience of it. In this sense technology robs cartography of some of its ancient magic, which for me also is a childhood magic. Maps are part of the unforgettable iconography of childhood, maps of imaginary lands, treasure islands, fabulous cities, maps of ancient Greece or Rome, maps of the underworld. Maps can be daunting or frightening. In a pub today a friend visiting from Japan pulled out a map of the Tokyo underground in Japanese, and we looked with a fascinated horror at the dense network of criss-crossing lines and the script of the station names.

However intriguing it is to look at a map of a place we might conceivably go to or where we are actually standing, to look at an old map of a city is more powerful, more evocative. You look down at the image of a place from which everybody who lived there has disappeared, every dog or prowling cat has crumbled to dust, every meal has been long forgotten, every conversation obliterated, and yet you are confronted everywhere with images of endurance: routes that have survived, streets and street names, churches and public buildings, the remains of old fortifications, the river meeting its estuary.

One of the iconic images of early Dublin is John Speed's 1610 map. It's the oldest existing map of the city, and this, certainly, is part of its appeal. It seems, when you look at it, to belong to an even earlier period. Surely the city must have been bigger than this, you think. As it turns out Speed's map was based on a map completed in the 1570s by another English cartographer, Christopher Caxton, but there were probably few enough changes in the interim. The tiny city described in Speed's map is still an essentially medieval town. You see the walled old town — the area between St Audoen's and the Castle, from the river to Patrick Street, with a few outcrops to the north, west and east. You can see the gate houses: Dame Gate, St Nicholas Gate, New Gate, Ormond's Gate. Thomas Street stretches westward outside and to the south of it lie the lands and buildings of the dissolved monastery of St Thomas the Martyr in Thomas Court. A single bridge crosses the Liffey where the present Fr Mathew Bridge is, leading to the extensive settlement on the north of the river, although only three buildings are actually named on the map: St Michan's Church, St Mary's Abbey and The Inns or law courts. Standing in its distant suburb at the eastern edge of the map is 'The Colledge', the recently founded Trinity College — recently founded, that is, on the site of the confiscated Priory of All Hallows.

The city looks frail and vulnerable, as if it might collapse at any moment, or be swallowed up by a modest invasion party. You can well imagine the Ranelagh massacre in Easter Week 1209 when five hundred recent immigrants from Bristol were killed by 'the Irish enemie', and the annual municipal ritual that developed afterwards, with the citizens trooping out defiantly to the spot to commemorate Black Monday. Or, as your eye rakes over the few thoroughfares where everyone must have known everyone else, you can understand how the mayor was able to give his personal blessings to everyone who married in the city.

You could, if you had time, count the houses. If you attended a service in each of the fourteen Protestant churches named on the legend — Speed doesn't show any Catholic places of worship — it probably wouldn't detain you more than a day or two. The population of Dublin in 1610 wasn't more than about ten thousand, which was about half of the numbers in the city nearly three hundred years earlier. Historians estimate that there were twenty thousand people packed in to the city before the Black Death in 1348. The plague, and the successive plagues that followed it, halved the population and it took several centuries to recover. As recently as 1575 a plague had killed a third of the population:

> *Grass grew in the streets and in the church door-ways, those who could fled the city, and the mayor and sheriffs held their courts in Glassmanogue. The garden of All Saints was set apart for the sick, a great gate was erected and a guard set to prevent escapes. As a deterrent against concealment of the malady it was proclaimed that any inhabitant failing to give notice of the outbreak would, on detection, be liable to imprisonment for 80 days, have his premises closed for the same period, and then be banished from the city for evermore . . .[1]*

Speed's map shows Dublin poised between the middle ages and early modernity. By 1700 there would be sixty thousand in a much-expanded city and by the end of the following century the population would have reached almost a quarter of a million, making it the largest city in the British Empire after London.

But that's all in the future as we contemplate the toytown map of 1610. Part of its power is that the city it shows us is still so recognizable, that the old city persists inside the skin of the new. It's not a particularly accurate map — some of the streets are too wide, simply to get the names in, some of the names are wrong, and it seriously underestimates the actual number of buildings in the city. But the street names have almost all survived; the streets and the roads in and out of the city are still there. The cathedrals are there, the Castle is there, some segments of the wall are still visible. The medieval core of Dublin is very much present in the current layout of the city; it is simply that the city has grown and expanded in all directions around it. The names, though, have a particular magic, and probably the more so since they are such a dominant feature of the map as we know it. This is because the legend is printed on the map, covering a good deal of its right-hand side, so that your eyes are drawn as much to the names as to the buildings and the ships sailing right into the heart of the city. S Mihans church; S Maryes Abbey; The Bridge; Wood Key; Marchants Key; The Castel; White friers; Schoolhouse Lane; Christchurch; S Warbers Street; The Come; S Francis Street; St Patrick's church . . . And of course, DUBLINE itself, suspended with a decorative flourish over Oxmantown.

This effect, it turns out, was not intended by Speed. The map I'm squinting at in the City Archive, though not identified as such, is a poor photocopy of a nineteenth-century reprint of a much later edition, the version produced in 1780 by Robert Pool and John Marsh who published it alongside a plan of the city in 1780. This, in turn, was copied from a version published in the *Dublin Magazine* in 1762.[2] Many hands have busied themselves with this view of the city. Even if he may not himself have tested it the map bears the characteristic box in the bottom left corner showing 'A scale of pases'. A scale of paces seems a particularly attractive measurement for a city map. A pace was five feet, which is a serious stretch, and the scale of his Dublin map is 3.5cm to 200 paces.

Of the sixty-nine numbered features on the map seventeen are churches, the rest are public or municipal buildings, defences and individual streets. This is the nature of maps, to pluck out the worthy urban symbols which collectively form a notion of the city. 'Maps, once made, / leave the impression of a place gone dead', as the Scottish poet Alastair Reid has it[3]. You want to know where and how everyone lived, you want to see the timber and wattle of ordinary houses, the racks of wine outside the vintner's, the loaves of bread stamped as the law required with the baker's own mark, the food sellers of Cook Street, but the citizens have removed themselves and their doings from the cartographer's eye. The city hides in its own image. I move my eyes from the legend to the numbers sprinkled on the map, eager for the comfort of recognizable streets. There's Skinners Row, where I lived for several years, though today it's called Christchurch Place. Christ Church itself is barely standing, and down the road the Tholsel, the city hall, just about holds itself up. The south wall and roof of Christ Church had collapsed in 1562, and the nave vaulting of St Patrick's had gone in 1554. The city is a set, a performance, lying quiet in its moment, its throng and bustle whitened out. The city, in fact, was still dusting itself down after the Great Explosion of 1597, when a huge cargo of gunpowder shipped in from the Tower of London to quell the rebellious Irish under Hugh O'Neill ignited as it was being winched onto the quays. Colm Lennon has given a vivid account of it:

*The clock over the Bridge Gate had just chimed the hour of one o'clock as the sling of the crane swung four barrels towards the quay.*
*Suddenly, a blinding flash and a thunderous roar*

*occurred and the scene was one of devastation. A smoking crater beside the crane denoted the place where the 140 barrels of gunpowder had been stacked. The crane and cranehouse had been obliterated. Everywhere there were strewn shattered bodies and parts thereof. Many of the stout cage-work houses of the merchant patricians which had proudly fronted the river were flattened or almost totally ruinous. Back from the Liffey in the maze of streets and lanes of the town venerable buildings and churches as well as private houses were displaying signs of the blast. An eerie stillness lay over the zone where the explosion had centred, broken then by the shouts and alarms of those who came to rescue and inspect.[4]*

The explosion left 126 dead, of whom 76 were citizens and 50 'strangers'. The dead included the craner, Stephen Sedgrave, his wife and three of their children who lived at the Cranehouse. Between twenty and forty houses were destroyed by the blast. In the investigation which followed it transpired that industrial unrest was one of the causes of the explosion — there had been a strike of carters and porters resentful of their treatment and poor wages. A sorry tale emerged of intimidation and exploitation of labourers by John Allen, a royal official, who for his part had gone off 'to drink a pot of ale' when the explosion happened. Allen was tried and imprisoned for his role. There's a very contemporary feel to the account — it's like opening up the paper and reading about Polish or Latvian workers being badly treated on the Dublin building sites of today. These labourers were necessary to the economy of the city but kept at arm's length and, except in exceptional circumstances, kept off the record.

The explosion placed a heavy burden on an already cash-strapped city and the Corporation had to mortgage civic lands to finance rebuilding and to import Dutch engineers to rebuild the Cranehouse. The city had hardly yet recovered from the effects of the Nine Years' War during which thousands of British soldiers were billeted with the citizens who were obliged to feed them and put up with all the attendant inconvenience and disease. Speed's map shows gaps in the houses of Wood Quay and Winetavern Street, which Colm Lennon surmises might well be explosion damage. If maps could talk this one would surely unleash a torrent of oaths.

There's something familiar too about the glumness of the city. Looking at the map and reading the account of the explosion and its effects is very like revisiting the Dublin of the 1980s, with its derelict quays and grand streets interrupted by wastelands or desolate car parks. Cities repeat the same kinds of histories again and again — if we were to transplant an alderman from Speed's Dublin into the current council chamber he might not find himself entirely bewildered.

Those gaps in the 1610 map might be an argument for Speed's actual presence in the city. No one can say whether the most famous mapmaker of his day actually came to Dublin or not. It doesn't seem likely. His involvement in many, if not most, of his maps, was as cartographic editor, enhancer. The Dublin map was part of his greatest work, the *Theatre of the Empire of Great Britain*, published in 1612. The *Theatre* was the atlas that accompanied his *History of Great Britain*, but it's as a mapmaker rather than an historian that he is remembered. His maps were quite consciously based on the work of others — he claimed himself in the introduction to the *Theatre* (a facsimile of which is in the Map Library in Trinity College) that he only personally mapped two towns: 'it may be obiected that I have put my sickle into other mens corne, and have laid my building upon other mens foundations'.[5]

Mapmakers don't suffer from anxiety of influence, but happily walk, or edit, the spaces where others have gone before. Speed was an organizer and synthesizer whose work served very useful administrative and political purposes. One of the maps included in the atlas is 'The Kingdome Of Great Britain And Ireland' showing the unity of the two islands under one Crown as if inevitably ordained. The left of the map carries drawings of Irish gentlemen and gentle-women, but there's also a wild Irish man with his mantle and spear as if to suggest the idyll might be interrupted.

It was precisely the political uses of cartography that ensured the patronage that made the work possible. Speed's map wasn't part of a Rough Guide to Dublin for seventeenth century tourists but part of an assertion of political control. Every empire needs its maps, and its mapmakers. In a country as yet incompletely mapped it was all too easy for the natives to conceal themselves, as Edmund Spenser noted: 'a flying enemye hiding him self in woodes and bogges from whence he will not draw forth but into some streighte passage or perilous forde wheare he knowes the Armie must nedes passe'.[6] Speed wasn't a wealthy man, and his path to map-making was actually quite unlikely. This, for me, is one of the interesting things about him. He began as a tailor, in Cheshire, and continued in that profession until, at the age of thirty, he came to London in 1552. Maybe the intensity and spectacle of the city sparked his interest in history, or maybe it was the turbulence of recent English history. This was, after all, one of the most dramatic periods of English history. The Wars of the Roses were a recent memory, and the effects of the Reformation and Henry VIII's dissolution of the monasteries were still felt.

Speed, though, overlooked the troublesome recent past in favour of ancient history. His first work of mapmaking was a four sheet map of Biblical Canaan, which was published in 1585, and it was shortly after this that he came to the attention of the nobleman Fulke Greville — later Treasurer of the Navy and Chancellor of the Exchequer, and created Baron Brooke by James I. Greville got Speed a sinecure in the Customs Service which let him get on with his real passion and he also put him up for membership of the Society of Antiquaries, whose members included the greatest scholars of the day, the likes of Willam Cambden, Robert Cotton and William Smith, all of whom made a contribution to Speed's work. [7]

It seems entirely appropriate that Speed should have been liberated into his true work by a man who also harboured a private passion. Fulke Greville is one of the most interesting English poets of his time, but pretty much everything he wrote was published posthumously. He's best known today for his poem-cycle *Caelica*, a complex meditation on love that is a triumph of a hard-edged plain style and one of the greatest poetic works of the sixteenth century. Here's one poem from it, where poetry and cartography might be said to intersect:

> *Whoever sails near to Bermuda coast,*
> *Goes hard aboard the monarchy of fear,*
> *Where all desires (but life's desire) are lost,*
> *For wealth and fame put off their glories there.*
>
> *Yet this isle poison-like, by mischief known,*
> *Weans not desire from her sweet nurse, the sea;*
> *But unseen shows us where our hopes be sown,*
> *With woeful signs declaring joyful way.*
> *For who will seek the wealth of Western sun,*
> *Oft by Bermuda's miseries must run.*
>
> *Who seeks the god of love, in beauty's sky,*
> *Must pass the empire of confused passion,*
> *Where our desires to all but horrors die,*
> *Before that joy and peace can take their fashion.*
>
> *Yet this fair heaven, that yields this soul-despair,*
> *Weans not the heart from his sweet god, Affection;*
> *But rather shows us what sweet joys are there,*
> *Where constancy is servant to perfection.*
> *Who Caelica's chaste heart then seeks to move,*
> *Must joy to suffer all the woes of love.*
>
> — *Caelica*, LIX

Greville's public career was an unending arc of success: knighthood, peerage, the grant by James 1 of Warwick Castle and Knowle Court. Yet he came to a bizarre end, stabbed in his seventies by an aggrieved servant and dying in agony four weeks later. After stabbing Greville, the servant, a man called Ralph Heywood, killed himself with the same knife. Greville was buried in St Mary's Church in Warwick — the grave is still there — with the epitaph he composed himself: 'Folk Grevill Servant to Queene Elizabeth Conceller to King James Frend to Sir Philip Sidney. Trophaeum Peccati.' He had known the poet and courtier Sidney, 'the flower of chivalry', since his schooldays in Shrewsbury and the two were close friends. He encouraged Greville as a poet, and also the young Edmund Spenser, whose knowledge of Ireland would soon be more intimate than Speed's. I briefly indulge myself in plotting a novel in which Greville and John Speed visit Spenser in his estate in County Cork, maybe introducing his neighbour Walter Raleigh. Speed maps the estate while Spenser puts the final touches to his genocidal *A View of the Present State of Ireland* . . .

Greville was badly shaken by Sidney's death at the Battle of Zutphen against the Spanish, and he wrote both an elegy and an account of his life. His own epitaph doesn't mention himself as a poet, which gives some idea of his cast of mind. It's as if he's an accomplice in his own oblivion. Or maybe he knew that poetry, like murder, will eventually out, and didn't require a monumental push. Not the least attractive aspect of the poetry is that he starts off unremarkably enough, sounding pretty much like his Elizabethan contemporaries, but goes on plugging away at it in what leisure his courtly activities afforded him, getting better all the time, and finally becoming a real and unforgettable poet in his plain style laced with a grave wit.

As for John Speed, he lived one year longer than Fulke Greville and died in 1629. The two were almost exactly contemporaneous and lived almost the same generous span of life. Speed is buried with his wife in St Giles-without-

Cripplegate in the City of London. His bust is in the church, lucky to have survived the bombing in 1940 when the church was showered with so many incendiary bombs that even the cement caught fire. The connection with tailoring was never entirely lost, for the cast for the niche in which the bust is placed was provided by the Merchant Taylors' Company, of which John Speed remained a member. The Speeds had eighteen children, and I learn from the St Giles-without-Cripplegate website that a few years ago two of his descendants from America, William and James, visited the church. I wonder if any of those descendants are carto-graphers, or if they've been to Dublin.

# Directions . . .

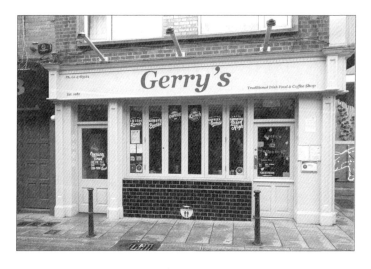

'How do I get there from Stephen's Green?' James asks. He's coming from Cork to stay the night and can't remember from his last trip how to get to our house. Nothing to it, I email him, just walk south from the Green into Harcourt Street and when you get as far as Jonah Barrington's house turn right into Montague St, then keep straight through Camden Row, Long Lane, Malpas Street, Blackpitts, follow the road around and keep going. It couldn't be simpler. 'Sounds like a poem,' he replies, and of course he's right. Even as I was giving him the directions I felt as if I were chanting a spell, or at least establishing something more than a set of instructions; it felt more like a rite of possession. Anyone who gives directions to his or her home is also issuing an intricate map of personal associations. In the case of these particular instructions, which make up one of the pos-

sible routes home, the names are more suggestive and resonant than the streets themselves, which are really a series of
laneways, little connecting strips across more salubrious
and significant routes. But it doesn't matter — the nature of
the streets isn't important. Nor is the length of stay at the
particular address. Sometimes what the directions advertise
is precisely the provisionality of the occupation. Today I'm
here, next month I'll be somewhere else. Directions are an
intimate flourish, an invitation to a home, a life.

In the same way, to give directions on a street to a stranger
is an invitation to a city. Being asked for directions is a test
not just of your knowledge of the city but of your intimacy
with it. If you fail the test you feel as if you've somehow
failed the city. You sway uncertainly in it, not more than a
visitor yourself, no matter how long you've been there. But
if you pass it, and despatch the stranger efficiently, you walk
away with a little jump of pride and the streets seem to greet
your steps like an old familiar, an adept, at home and in
control. And yet I think of all the times I have been unable
to give directions to a location not more than a few streets
away, as if the internal map had shrivelled and vanished the
moment it was needed, or the linguistic resources needed to
translate the instinctive route into a coherent and easily
graspable form refused to make themselves available.

And likewise I think of all the times I have been unable to
issue meaningful directions to my own home, sometimes
out of pure enthusiasm, my internal map flashing frantically,
offering so many possible and competing routes that I can't
choose between them, and what emerges is less a route than
a labyrinthine plot to prevent arrival. Part of my absurd
pride in the route I offer James is because I know it's easily
accomplished; failing complete disasters there's a strong
chance it will deliver him to the front door, or at least to an
adjacent street. But then I'm struck again by the sparseness
of the visual metaphor that is a map: lines on a page, names.
What he really needs, I imagine, is the character of the streets
he will pass through. He'll need the Italian restaurant, the

59

milk bar, the post office, Gerry's Coffee Shop, the barber, the two gambling clubs — the Colossus and the Jackpot — and, once he crosses Wexford Street, he'll need the side wall of the gourmet burger place painted with bullocks, Whelan's pub, St Kevin's Park, formerly a graveyard, burial place of the martyred Archbishop Dermot O'Hurley and various members of Thomas Moore's family. The ghost bus visits nightly and the tour leader, who has his own key, brings the customers inside to inflict the mild terror of cursings and hauntings before bringing them up to St Audoen's to look for the green lady on the forty steps. Then the Meath hospital, the tyre garage, and Blackpitts.

But all of this is superficial information. To really experience the streets he should study their history, he should look at old maps to witness them serve a dozen generations of feet; his body, his bones need to absorb their sounds, their smell, their essence. I have, recently, become obsessed with the study of old maps of the city and I know that this route, this little westward line through the city, is hundreds of years old. How can I convey this to James? Perhaps I should direct him to the City Archive for a couple of hours first, to prepare himself for the journey. Perhaps I should work up a course of study for him in the weeks before he leaves his house in the country. And yet, and yet, he might argue, isn't the whole point of a map to remove a city from its contingent present, its layers of history, and abstract it to a layer of pure formula? Isn't one of the pleasures of visiting a foreign city precisely a negotiation of the grids and lines of a map which says Hamburg, Vienna, Rome and offers the illusion of total ownership, total control, that this is all you need to master it? Maps are powerful fictions — without them we would be lost in the chaos of the real. So I reinforce the names of the streets with a Google map — the plain map view rather than the street view with its rooftops and parked cars, including, I now see, my own in its habitual spot just down from my front door, and finally, exhaustedly, click *Send*.

There are other kinds of maps, after all. And there is also

the pleasure, even, you could say, the necessity, of being lost. I think of Walter Benjamin, who couldn't read a street map, and who derived an aesthetic from being lost, from straying. To him a city — in this case Paris — was a maze of paths and tunnels, the Métro stations like shafts offering a glimpse of the underworld, but it was also a labyrinth at whose centre lay an erotic prize, a Minotaur's chamber with a three-headed monster, 'the occupants of the small brothel on rue de la Harpe in which, summoning my last reserves of strength (and not entirely without an Ariadne's thread), I set my foot'.[1]

Benjamin's comments remind us how much of the imagery of urban exploration, of the tradition of the *flâneur*, is a displacement of solitary male sexuality. It's like the famous Baudelaire poem, 'À une passante', when the poet glimpses a woman in mourning passing on the street, lifting the hem of her dress as the watcher, rapt, tense, maddened, drinks from her eye, *La douceur qui fascine et le plaisir qui tue.*

Fugitive beauté —
Dont le regard m'a fait soudainement renaître,
Ne te verrai-je plus que dans l'éternité?

Ailleurs, bien loin d'ici! trop tard! *jamais* peut-être!
Car j'ignore où tu fuis, tu ne sais où je vais,
Ô toi que j'eusse aimée, ô toi qui le savais!

*(Fugitive beauty / Whose glance suddenly brought me to life again, / Will I never see you again except in eternity // Elsewhere, far from here, too late, perhaps* never *I have no idea where you fled, you don't know where I go, / You whom I could have loved, you who knew it!)*

For Benjamin this was the archetypal urban poem with its vision of the city as a constant theatre of possibility. The

Peter Sirr

crowds pass by like an endlessly fascinating river, offering tantalizing glimpses of possible lives:

> *The delight of the urban poet is love — not at first sight, but at last sight. It is a farewell forever which coincides in the poem with the moment of enchantment. But the nature of the poet's emotions has been affected as well. What makes his body contract in a tremor — crispé comme un extravagant, Baudelaire says — is not the rapture of a man whose every fibre is suffused with eros; it is, rather, like the kind of sexual shock that can beset a lonely man.*[2]

Poetic trips around a city don't have to be impelled by eros: I think of Charles Reznikoff pounding the streets of Depression-era New York. He walked anything up to twenty miles a day every day of his life and it's no accident that one of his collections is called *Going To and Fro and Walking Up and Down*. He was a lawyer by profession and maybe because of that poetry was always testimony for him: he liked to restrict himself to the evidence provided by his eyes. The New York he saw on his walks fills his poems, but the observation also provided the method: a focus on brief moments in lives and, as much as possible, releasing the potential of what is seen. This is what he understood by 'objectivist', a writer 'who does not write directly about his feelings but about what he sees and hears; who is restricted almost to the testimony of a witness in a court of law . . .'

One aspect of this is a kind of deadpan kindly noticing and recording, as in a poem on Cooper Union Library:

> *Men and women with open books before them —*
> *and never turn a page: come*
> *merely for warmth*
> *not light.*

The poems are also remarkable for the way in which the city

is a continuous living and radiant presence for him; nature is always framed by the human machinery of the city, 'clouds, piled in rows like merchandise'. Streetlamps, subway stations shine in the poems with the pure force of attention, 'those little islands of existence which Rezi saw with so much love', as George Oppen put it:

> *Coming up from the subway stairs, I thought*
>    *the moon*
> *only another street-light —*
> *a little crooked.*
>         — *'Jerusalem the Golden'*, 20

> *Walk about the subway station*
> *in a grove of steel pillars;*
> *how their knobs, the rivet-heads —*
> *unlike those of oaks —*
> *are regularly placed;*
> *how barren the ground is*
> *except here and there on the platform*
> *a flat black fungus*
> *that was chewing-gum.*
>         — *'Jerusalem the Golden'*, 18

If he sees the clouds and the lights he also records how 'the milliners, tacking bright flowers on straw shapes, / say, glancing out of the window, / It is going to snow . . .' Reznikoff isn't a soft-hearted urban pastoralist; there's always someone working, always a keen sense of the life within the city; factory chimneys are his Cedars of Lebanon, and livelihoods are often precarious. The early self-published books are full of vignettes of families on the brink of disaster: this is the New York of immigrant pushcart peddlers, garment makers, boarders and broken English. One offers a version of a family story that had large resonance for Reznikoff — the destruction of his grandfather's poetry. In the poem, after the unnamed businessman dies, his children find 'the manuscript so carefully written and rewritten', scribble on it and tear it up. 'At night the mother came home and swept it out.' That vision of an inner life extinguished may well have intensified the poet's desire to record the life of his city and his people, almost as if that registering and recording might somehow restore the voice of the lost.

Or I think of Lola Ridge, the Irish-born, New Zealand raised poet writing the New York poems that were published in her radical 1918 collection *The Ghetto*:

*The heat in Hester Street.*
*Heaped like a dray*
*With the garbage of the world.*

*Bodies dangle from the fire escapes*
*Or sprawl over the stoops ...*
*Upturned faces glimmer pallidly —*
*Herring-yellow faces, spotted as with a mould,*
*And moist faces of girls*
*Like dank white lilies ...*

It makes a difference, of course, if the city is not your own; it's much easier to see the strange, and it's much more amenable to myth-making, but Ridge sees her adopted city with a searing intensity that owed much to her commitment to socialism and her experience of the poverty of the working class.

◡

Here is another kind of map, an exercise taken from Benjamin, who amused himself with it while waiting for a friend in a Paris restaurant. A personal cartography, an erotics of place. I take a pen and begin a line in the garden of a house in Waterford, towards the end of the garden, the forbidden orchard at the bottom of which is the wide expanse of the river. From there I draw a line which ends in the

garden of a Victorian house in a Dublin suburb. The line
enters and wanders through the various rooms of the house,
then veers off into the field behind the house, and into the
streets of the surrounding neighbourhood, the grounds of
Stratford College, St John of Gods, Marianella. It veers
towards Rathmines and the years of school there, and into
the streets of the city itself. It settles in Trinity College and
strikes out from there all over the city, landing in parties and
beds and parks and expeditions and pubs and conversations,
as the city opens up and reveals its inner life. Every street
walked through seems to offer rich possibilities. Every
lighted window seems to beckon, is an invitation to a possible
life. And many rooms are entered unexpectedly. The pencil
follows a line out from a pub to a suddenly conjured aftermath
in a flat in Leeson Street, Appian Way, Beechwood Avenue,
Leinster Road. The lines go on, to hospitals, graveyards,
registry offices, churches, to other cities, other countries, to
particular unforgettable interiors, to the point at which one
life seemed to end and another to begin, to airport terminals
and apartment buildings, avenues and alleyways. And so the
pencil goes on, veering back and forth, crossing and recross-
ing, doubling back and venturing out again, constructing its
map of one quick version of a life, a kind of cartographical
idiolect that brings together the inhabited territories, the
explored interiors, the places of emotional attachment that
will stay on the map even if the rooms themselves vanish, as
well as the passages of complete loss, when you walk out a
door and realize that you have no idea where you are.

It's the early hours of the morning when the bus finally
stops somewhere in the centre of the city. I climb down into
the empty space of the square and look around. I don't see
anything familiar. I hesitate and look around, waiting for
something to clarify. Not far away I hear a derisive laugh
and then, *Kijk, hij is verdwenen, hij heeft keen idee waar hij*

*is, stomme toerist.* This idiot doesn't know where he is. That makes up my mind. I strike out briskly, away from the hecklers, as if the place had suddenly come alive in my brain. It hadn't of course, but it hangs back from recognition, a dark sleeping mass of unfamiliar buildings and canals. There is that low anxiety of being lost in a strange place, but also a sense of a necessary rite of passage. This is the place I have come to live in, after all. Maybe part of the price of coming here is to wander through it until it gets under my skin, until the map sinks into my brain and my feet and I can negotiate its streets by day or night. When you walk through a foreign city every stone seems to press itself on your consciousness, every building announces itself with a peculiar angular insistence, every street name flaunts its strangeness, every door and every lock cries out for attention. You live, until the place begins to settle down, in a fever of alertness. Meanwhile I walk on and find myself walking along the side of the Zoo. There's a cardboard poster with a large tiger in the act of pouncing on some invisible prey, and it's an image that takes hold, as if I'm trying to creep up on the city and somehow sink my claws in it. I keep walking and eventually things begin to clarify. This is the street where I had to bring the cat to the vet last week. Once I cross this canal I'll be near the Tropical Museum and the Oosterpark. By lucky accident I've managed to hit on the route home to the east city, and so one street leads successfully to the next and I'm staring down the tree-lined expanse of the Linnaeusstraat, around the corner from the Indische Buurt, the neighbourhood each of whose streets commemorates the Dutch imperial adventure in Indonesia: Balistraat, Madurastraat, Molukkenstraat, my own Javastraat. I make my way up by the deserted Dappermarkt, by day a great market throng, and finally put the key in the door of number 20 and climb up to the apartment. I feel foolishly elated, as if I have accomplished some great mission. Still, I have accomplished something. Here I am, after all, at home. It's not my first night in the city but it feels like the beginning of something, a kind of entrance that other days can build on; it feels like a kind of arrival.

# Noises Off: Dublin's Contested Monuments

As I walk down O'Connell Street on a September evening I cross over to inspect the parapet of the bridge in which a small bronze plaque is inset. It reads as follows:

THIS PLAQUE COMMEMORATES
FR. PAT NOISE
ADVISOR TO PEADAR CLANCEY.
HE DIED UNDER SUSPICIOUS
CIRCUMSTANCES WHEN HIS
CARRIAGE PLUNGED INTO THE
LIFFEY ON AUGUST IOTH 1919.
ERECTED BY THE HSTI

To the right of the inscription is a relief of the unfortunate priest's head. The poor man, I think, plunging into the murky waters of the river. What exactly were the circumstances? Peadar Clancy was a republican activist so it's possible this was an act of the British secret service. Maybe they thought Clancy was in the carriage. So what did they do exactly? How do you cause a carriage to plummet off O'Connell Bridge into the Liffey? It can't have been easy. And what happened the horses, or the driver? Did they survive? As it happens we know the answer; we know that, in a sense, everyone survived, because no one died, no one fell into the river, there were no circumstances suspicious or otherwise, there was not even a Pat Noise, and as for the HSTI, whatever it is, the organization never existed. Not that anyone noticed, at least for a couple of years after the plaque was set in the bridge. That happened in 2004 when the two hoaxers, dressed as council workers, laid it in the depression left after the removal of the control box for the ill-fated 'Millennium Countdown' clock that was installed in 1996. The clock, weighing nearly a thousand kilograms, was placed just below the surface of the Liffey and its illuminated numerals were supposed to count the seconds remaining until the dawn of the millennium. You could have a postcard made showing the exact number of minutes and seconds left. The engineers, however, hadn't counted on the uncooperativeness of the river. The digital numerals were soon caked with a greenish slime and were barely visible through the dark waters, which was probably not a bad thing as the water seemed to inter-fere with the clock, which was often wrong. In the end, nine months after its installation, the clock was fished out and the citizens counted their own way to the millennium. But the depression remained on the bridge, and eight years later it was quietly filled. Pat Noise from *pater noster*, our father.

For two years he lay at the heart of the city unnoticed, until a journalist spotted the memorial. Its discovery caused a dilemma for the City Council. It was clearly in breach of planning regulations, and it didn't even commemorate a real person. Some councillors argued for the substitution of the plaque with a memorial for an actual, recognizable Dubliner. Some were particularly aggrieved that the plaque had lain undetected under their noses. When it seemed likely that the plaque would be removed Dubliners began laying flowers and ironic tributes on the bridge.

Eventually, at a meeting in December 2006, a motion for the retention of the plaque was put to a meeting of the South Eastern Area Committee in City Hall. There was a certain amount of huffing and puffing; a councillor muttered about the dangers of condoning vandalism until it was pointed out that the Council was itself responsible for gouging a hole out of the bridge and leaving it unfilled; the hoaxers had merely measured the area and inserted the appropriately sized memorial. Another worried about the dangers of setting precedents. What if the city were to be covered with fake memorials? How could we tell the real from the imagined history of the city? What effect might the confusion have on tourism? Imagine the poor Germans and Italians and Americans returning home with their minds addled between hoax and history.

In the end the motion was carried on the grounds that it was a monument to eccentricity and added to the colour of our lives, and so Fr Pat Noise has escaped oblivion and remains inscribed in the civic memory, all the more firmly inscribed, maybe, because he doesn't exist. The more conscious attempts to represent the city in public art have been much more problematic.

There's another aspect to the Pat Noise saga. Its language of commemoration, its invoking of republican activism function as a sly reminder of a tradition of commemoration associated with the founding of the state, and a reminder, too, of the contested nature of commemoration in this city where almost every gesture in stone or bronze is bound to be offensive to someone.

How many statues peer down on the people of the city? How many great figures are locked in the air above the city, perched over the citizens in their stone and bronze gravitas, arms raised, outstretched or folded, in full flight, cloaks and frock coats, swords, scales and trumpets? They stand proudly in the full regalia of great personages and contemplate their achievements, or look back to the glorious day of their unveiling. Or they're nervous and awkward, stuck forever in their moment. A character in Joyce's *Exiles* declares that 'All statues are of two kinds . . . The statue which says: How shall I get down? and the other kind . . . the statue which says: In my time the dunghill was so high.' They may seem as if they'll be there forever, but their tenancy isn't always secure. Many were blown up because they were deemed to have outstayed their welcome, or were more prosaically removed, winched off and hidden away or shipped off to more appreciative climates. And others came to take their places. Right now, I'm in College Green, taking in Edward Delaney's Thomas Davis. It stands on the spot where William of Orange once sat astride his magnificent horse, his back to Trinity College. Grinling Gibbons' equestrian monument, erected in 1701, was made of iron, and its strong inner framework was coated with lead. William was crowned with laurel and dressed in suitable classical costume.

The unveiling was a great occasion: a public holiday was declared and all the shops were closed. The church bells rang and the Lord Mayor and Corporation marched in procession from the Tholsel opposite Christchurch to the country suburb of College Green. The procession marched three times around the statue as the city musicians beat their kettledrums and blew their trumpets. The Recorder of Dublin delivered a panegyric to the King after which the Dublin Militia fired off a volley. And the crowd wasn't forgotten either: several hogsheads of claret were set on stilts and opened up.

King and horse began to settle into the city. They absorbed

the weather, looked down on the lives of merchants and beggars and observed the ritual procession from the Black Dog Prison in Cornmarket to the gallows in Baggot Street. None of this prevented the statue from being regularly vandalized. First up was a pair of students from the college it turned its back on. On the night of the 25th of June, 1710, not long before the anniversary of the Battle of the Boyne, the students, Graffon and Vinicome, climbed up and covered the King's face with mud and removed his sword and baton. The Corporation immediately put up a substantial reward and the pair were caught. They got six months imprisonment, a hefty fine, were expelled from the university and were also ordered to stand before the statue for half an hour with a placard that read: 'I stand here for defacing the statue of our glorious Deliverer, the late King William', although apparently that wasn't carried out. A new baton was entrusted to the King with due ceremony but disappeared again four years later.

Then as now there were always street artists lurking in the shadows waiting to intervene, and at midnight on the 3rd of July, 1805, a man purporting to be a painter approached the watchman and told him he had been sent by the Corporation to decorate the statue. The watchman gave him a leg up and went back to his duties as the painter worked long into the night. Eventually he came down, told the watchman he needed to get more paint, and left, never to return. The city woke to see the King still with the paint bucket round his neck and covered with a mix of grease and tar. More serious attempts were made on the statue as the century continued. In 1836 there were three separate attempts to blow it up, and finally on the 7th of April a bomb went off, smashing all the glass in the neighbourhood and toppling the King from his horse. His legs and arms were broken and the horse was smashed to smithereens. This time two rewards were offered, one by the Viceroy and one by the Corporation, but no one was caught. The King was duly mended and restored, and a second unveiling took place the following year. Dillon Cosgrave, the historian from whom I've taken these details, tells us that on the night of the explosion 'a wag called at the house of Sir Philip Crampton, the eminent surgeon, who was believed to be much attached to the society of persons of rank, and told him that a gentleman of high distinction lay near College Green, seriously wounded, and needing his care'. Cramtpon arrived in Church Lane to find the broken iron patient.[1] In total, the statue was bombed six times before the last attempt, in 1929, finally consigned it to the forge for recycling, and the site was razed.

It was replaced, in 1966, by Edward Delaney's Thomas Davis. Cast in the Fonderia d'Arte in Milan, Delaney's Davis is a great hulking figure, standing still with long, almost monstrous arms dangling by his side, with four roughly textured bronze heralds (achieved by wrapping the wax models in hemp cord) below him whose trumpets function as waterspouts for the fountain that is also part of the monument. Six bronze panels illustrate Davis's poems: 'The Burial', 'The Famine', 'We Must not Fail', 'Tone's Grave', 'The Eviction', 'Penal Days'. It was unveiled by Éamon de Valera at Easter 1966 on the fiftieth anniversary of the Rising. Some took exception to the statue because they felt it didn't deliver an accurate enough representation of the man. They felt that it was the duty of the artist to replicate the subject's physical form. The statue is ageless, its mass firmly planted, but Davis was dead at thirty-one, his brief but dazzling career as Young Irelander, propagandist and nationalist poet cut short by scarlet fever. The sculptor concentrated on his own vision of the man and his achievement, maybe reckoning that if a man is to be on a plinth he may as well dominate all before him and ignoring the fact that in life Davis was small in physical stature. 'Perhaps in 1966 we are not allowed to say that never since *homo sapiens* emerged, except in the last stages of dropsy, did a man ever stand upon such legs as Mr. Delaney has given him,' the editorial in *The Irish Times* fulminated after the unveiling. But if the

commission was a product of a particular moment in the
State's history, the looming presence of Delaney's vision
owed as much to his grounding in post-war German and
Italian practice, as well as the physical impression his time in
post-war Germany had left on him. He worked with Toni
Stadler and Giacomo Manzù (whom he thought 'the greatest
sculptor in Christendom'). Both of these artists produced
work directly influenced by the devastation wrought by the
Second World War. Thomas Davis has some of the blocky
monumentalism of Stadler's figures; there's nothing polished
about it, or about the rough heralds with their (malfunction-
ing) water trumpets. Their twentieth-century moment is also
a kind of ahistorical timelessness, as if they might have been
unearthed from a buried Troy or Nineveh. To critics who
took issue with the roughness and scale of his monument —
one called it 'elephantine-footed' — Delaney retorted: 'Truth
lies in proportions, not in size.'

There was something spiky and rough about Delaney
himself; he was the hard man of Irish sculpture, the man
who had, according to legend, turned up at art college without bothering with entrance tests, and who had come back
from Germany with a letter of introduction to Jack Yeats
from Oskar Kokoschka, which he then tore up on discovering that Yeats had died before he could visit him. He had left
school at fourteen, joined a circus in Claremorris, worked
for an undertaker putting mountings on coffins and was
fired for putting the decorative clasps on upside down. He
had hung around bohemian Dublin with Brendan Behan.
An Arts Council scholarship allowed him to enrol at
Akademie der Bildenden Künste in Munich, and when the
money ran out he kept himself going by welding tram tracks
at night.

It's interesting that this commission to celebrate the independence of the state should produce a figure at least partly
derived from the ravaged world from which it had, at least
officially, kept itself aloof, yet if Ireland and Europe meet
in the sculptor's vision, it's a fruitful encounter. Delaney's

second major commission in the city was the Wolfe Tone monument in Stephen's Green and I make my way up Grafton Street and down along the Green to look at it. Like everyone else who goes in and out of the park I have been looking at it for years without really seeing it. I see the park, the couriers eating their sandwiches in the plaza in front of Tone, but Tone himself slips past the eye; he has blended into the city in that contradictory way of statuary, their mass strangely invisible. Seeing him requires a deliberate act. I pause by the couriers and stare at the bronze figure and the granite pillars that cause Dubliners to call it Tonehenge. In fact, it's a double monument. Tone is at the front, backed by pillars. On the other side, in the park, is the famine monument. Tone faces a broad plaza and enjoys the light of the city. The famine figures, three emaciated, misshapen Giacometti-like figures, crouch in the dank dark of that corner of the park, disregarded.

Like Davis, Tone is a massive figure, over ten feet tall, square-shouldered, square-jawed, an oversized hand tugging at the collar of his coat. The figure was cast in Delaney's back yard in Dún Laoghaire using the lost-wax method he had learned in Germany and Italy. His son, Eamon, has written that one of his earliest memories is of 'Wolfe Tone being lifted by crane from our back garden and over the little houses'.[2]

> *There is a picture of him inside the workshop, with his head to the ceiling. He looks like he's moving, just as in the Green, and heading towards the door, with his shoulder forward: this room is too small for me now; I'm getting out of here.*[3]

As with Davis, the figure is more archetype than particular individual and the conjunction with the famine figures on the other side of the granite columns reminds us that this is as much a commemoration of failure as an icon of nationhood. Not that this prevented it from being attacked. In 1971

the UVF planted a bomb which blew the statue into four
pieces. Undaunted, the sculptor welded Tone back together,
and made a few improvements. '"There's a few things I didn't
get right the first time," my father said with a wink, ever the
wag. He also said that the statue's arm would now move
outwards, with the other tucked in, just as if Tone is marching — marching back to life.'⁴

He used the incident to clarify his feeling about his sculpture: 'Tone's is not a victory monument. He wanted all of
Ireland independent and united. The failure of Tone's expeditions led to a decline in national morale and presaged
the Famine or Great Hunger. If Tone had succeeded I doubt
if the Famine would have been allowed to happen. . .'

Tone and Davis, icons of a young state, idealistic heroes who
failed. Likewise, Emmet, or the 1916 Proclamation signatories.
As soon as they're monumentalized, or turned into train
stations or blocks of flats, their youth vanishes, they become
ancient, or rather, entirely ageless, their mortality robbed by
memorializing art . . .

⌒

As I move back to College Green my mind's eye is filled
with a photograph I first saw in Niall McCullough's *Dublin,
An Urban History*. The worn looking image shows a huge
crowd gathered in College Green around a temporary monument, the Ginchy Cross. The occasion was Remembrance
Day, the 11th of November, and the crowd was marking
the participation of the 16th (Irish Division) in the First
World War. The cross was originally erected on the Somme
to commemorate 4,354 men of the 16th who died in two
battles. The generally accepted statistics are that two hundred
thousand Irish soldiers fought in the war and almost fifty
thousand died. The Dublin Fusiliers alone lost almost five
thousand men in France and Gallipoli. The history of the
Irish state, the focus on the commemoration of Easter 1916,
and the politicization of the commemoration of the Great

War, pushed that event to the fringes of public recognition until very recently, but the photograph is a reminder of how important it was to Irish people in the decades after the war. The *Irish Times* report of the 1928 commemoration, which was held in Stephen's Green, states that one hundred and twenty thousand were present. There were also those who objected and tried to disrupt the event with a smoke bomb. And then I recall that the statue of William III was blown up on the 11th of November, 1928, while a simultaneous attack was made on George II in Stephen's Green.

The timing of the attacks suggests that the attackers were not only striking at remaining monuments of imperialism but at the memory of a war some were determined to erase from the national consciousness. Irish participation in the war was itself deeply political, and bound up with contested identities of the State, so it's not really surprising that its commemoration should prove divisive. The ceremony itself ended up being banished from the city proper to the limbo of the Phoenix Park. This and the other remembrance ceremonies tended to end with a rendition of 'God Save the King'

and to be seen effectively as a celebration of Empire by other means. The problem was that the State, with its own cherished commemoration rituals, couldn't find a way of incorporating the Great War into the official memory and the result was that a huge part of the people's historical experience was swept out to a kind of Phoenix Park of the mind.

Maybe this is what makes the photograph so haunting. We see the bulk of Trinity College and the Bank of Ireland, we see Grattan in full oratorical flight, and the frail looking wooden cross in the centre, the moveable Cenotaph. But most of all what we see are the crowds crammed in to what McCullough calls the Assembly Room of Dublin, College Green, for a profound civic occasion. The conjunction of the provisional, temporary cross and the permanent, unshakeable statue is striking. The cross, about four metres high, was made from elm timbers from a ruined French farmhouse and had previously been erected between the battlefield villages of Ginchy and Guillemont. It's now housed in Edward Lutyens' extraordinary memorial in the Irish National War Memorial Gardens in Islandbridge. The memorial perfectly encapsulates the ambiguity of the state's response to the First World War. On the one hand is the fact that the gardens were designed and built with government support to commemorate all 49,000 of the Irish dead in the Great War. The government also donated the site, on the southern side of the Liffey looking across at the Phoenix Park, and even ensured that it was built by a workforce drawn equally from former British Army and Irish Army men. This was a generosity that crossed party boundaries. Yet de Valera, having initially agreed to attend the formal unveiling in 1939, pulled out, and the state never got around to opening the memorial, or to seeing that the gardens were properly maintained, and they fell into serious neglect. Eventually it seemed that the city had forgotten about the beautiful memorial on its edge; it wasn't until the mid 1980s that they touched the consciousness again and work began on their restoration. The first official opening of the memorial took place on the 90th anniversary of the Somme in 2006 and was attended by President Mary McAleese and representatives of all political parties. You feel sure, looking at the old photograph, that the crowds around that wooden cross a few years after the end of the war would be happy to see its final resting place, and to know that the war, in all its complexity and terrible human cost, has been incorporated into the national memory.

⌒

If you're a statue with any ambition the place you want to be is O'Connell Street, the biggest theatre of all and the most contested site. The street opens and closes with high drama: at one end the domineering solemnity of John Henry Foley's O'Connell, at the other one of Augustus Saint-Gaudens' masterpieces, the Parnell Monument, an obelisk of Galway granite at whose base, startlingly close to us, is the statue of Parnell in full oratorical flight. Saint-Gaudens is an interesting figure. He was born in Dublin to a French father and an Irish mother who immigrated to New York when he was six months old. At nineteen he travelled to Paris where he studied at the École des Beaux-Arts. His first big commission, and the one which established his reputation, was a monument to Civil War Admiral David Farragut, in New York's Madison Square. Other commissions included the Standing Lincoln in Lincoln Park, Chicago, and the Robert Gould Shaw Memorial on Boston Common. Shaw was the colonel in command of the African-American 54th Regiment of the Union Army and was killed in a failed attempt to capture Fort Wagner in South Carolina. Robert Lowell gives a brilliant description of the relief in 'For the Union Dead':

*Two months after marching through Boston,*
*half the regiment was dead;*

*at the dedication,*
*William James could almost hear the bronze*
*Negroes breathe.*

'Their monument,' the poem continues, 'sticks like a fish-bone / in the city's throat . . .' There were undoubtedly many for whom Parnell's monument performed the same function. Shaw said once that one Englishman couldn't open his mouth without offending another; in the same way, at least half of a city is likely to be offended by a new monument. How many love the great silver needle of the Spire towering over O'Connell Street where Nelson's Pillar used to be? Many cities seem to need a phallic gesture in the centre.

For a hundred and fifty-seven years the phallus was Horatio Nelson on top of a column one hundred and thirty-four feet and three inches high. A hundred and sixty-eight stone steps led up to the parapet from which, on a clear day, you could see, as well as the spread of the city and its bay, as far north as the Mountains of Mourne. The city had rushed to celebrate the fallen hero years before he appeared in Great Yarmouth and Trafalgar Square, and the unveiling was another of those days when official Dublin put its best foot forward with the obligatory procession of horse and foot yeomanry led by the Lord Lieutenant, the Duke of Richmond, with the Provost and Fellows of Trinity College, and a host of sailors, officers, sheriffs and aldermen. To some, even then, it was an eyesore. The Wide Street Commissioners didn't want it in what was then Sackville Street, because it effectively divided the street in two and ruined the vista of the city's major thoroughfare.

Throughout its history there were many proposals to remove or relocate it as it was an obstacle to traffic. Maybe the most memorable suggestion was that made by the waspish Anti-Parnellite MP Tim Healy that not only the Pillar but also all the statues should be removed from the street: 'If it is desired to commemorate the dead, the statues ought to be placed somewhere where they will not be in the way of the living.'[5] The end, or at least the beginning of the end, came at 1.32 am on Tuesday morning, 8 October 1966, when a massive explosion, the work of a group of former IRA volunteers, blew the Pillar in half, leaving seventy feet of truncated column and pedestal. The Irish Army had to be called in to finish the job, a pretty thankless one and one they made something of a meal of, causing more damage to the surrounding area than the original explosion had done. This was the ignominious end of one the most famous of all Dubliners, thirteen foot of Portland stone — if a hundred and fifty odd years of leaning on a capstan high above the city is enough to qualify you as a Dubliner. Nelson's head underwent further indignities, being leased by a group of Dublin art students to a London antique dealer to raise funds for the students' union, taking part in an ad for ladies' stockings shot on Killiney beach and even appearing onstage with The Dubliners in the Olympia. It now lies untroubled and at peace in Dublin City Library and Archive, Pearse Street.

~

Blowing up statues is not for the fainthearted. Nine years before Nelson was toppled from his column the IRA had assaulted another of John Henry Foley's works, the fifteen-ton equestrian statue of Field Marshall Viscount Gough (1779-1869) in the Phoenix Park. Gough was depicted in his uniform of Colonel of the Guards reviewing his regiment, field-marshal's baton in his right hand. The IRA had brought over a plastic explosives expert from France to help them

accomplish the job, and Gough and his horse were hurled efficiently from their base. In his recreation of the event in *Foley's Asia*, a dramatization of the sculptor and his subjects, Ronan Sheehan has the bombers retire to Chapelizod for a post-explosion meal of tagliatelle and pesto. The statue ended up in storage at the Royal Hospital in Kilmainham; an old photograph shows Gough's severed head in a cupboard. The base remained intact and stayed in the Park. No one can have been entirely surprised at the assault. The hero of the Peninsular War and 'Hammer of the Sikhs', even if he was from Limerick, was never likely to be a popular virtual citizen of the city. It's something of a surprise that the statue was commissioned in the first place. When he died in 1869 his friends had tried to persuade the Corporation to erect a monument in a prominent city location. Carlisle Bridge (O'Connell Bridge), Foster Place or Westmoreland Street were suggested, all of which were vetoed by the Corporation. Having him on Carlisle Bridge would have meant having two Foley sculptures of ideological antagonists staring each other down across the Liffey. Foley was less concerned with the politics than with the opportunity to have a go at another big equestrian commission after the success of his Lord Hardinge outside Government House in Calcutta and Sir James Outram, also in Calcutta, often considered his master-piece. 'I need scarcely repeat how gratifying the task would be to me,' he wrote, 'and how willing I am to forgo all consideration of profit in my desire to engage myself upon it. I feel that the time has arrived for our native country to add to the memorials of her illustrious dead an Equestrian Statue, and that Lord Gough at once presents a worthy subject for such a memorial.'[6]

His enthusiasm for the commission contrasts strikingly with the lack of interest he showed in the work for which most Dubliners know him best, the O'Connell Monument. When Dublin Corporation ran a competition for the project Foley didn't enter it. When the competition failed to produce a winner the Corporation appealed to the Dubliner who was the Empire's leading sculptor, who had produced the statue of Prince Albert in the Albert Memorial in Hyde Park, and whose Dublin work included Goldsmith and Burke outside Trinity College, and Henry Grattan in College Green, and eventually he accepted the commission, much to the displeasure of many who thought him too deeply implicated in Empire to appreciate the achievement of the Liberator. But the model was enthusiastically accepted when it was exhibited in City Hall in 1867. In the event Foley died before either the Gough or O'Connell statue was completed and both were finished by his pupil Thomas Brock. The O'Connell Monument wasn't unveiled until 1882. Meanwhile the Corporation found a site for the Gough statue at a discreet distance from the city, in the Phoenix Park, but the inauguration was a nervous affair, packed with soldiery in case the citizens got out of hand. It was so much an icon of Empire that it was in fact subjected to repeated attacks. On Christmas Eve 1944 Gough was beheaded and his sword removed. Twelve years later the right hind leg of the horse was blown off, and the following year the final blow was struck. After nearly thirty years in storage it was eventually sold off to Robert Guinness, but only on condition that it leave the country. Guinness gave it to a descendent of Gough, Sir Humphrey Wakefield, and it's now in Chillingham Castle in Northumberland, England, having been painstakingly restored by Newcastle black-smiths.

And that would have been the end of it, another minor saga of unloved imperial statuary, but Gough, or at least his horse, reappeared in Dublin, replicated by artist John Byrne for his sculpture *Misneach* (the Irish for courage), unveiled in Ballymun in September 2010. The dimensions are the same, and the pose is the same, head down to the side, right leg pawing the air, but this time the rider is a young girl in bronze track suit and Velcro-fastened runners, and she's riding bare-back. The image was problematic for some in the local community; the tradition of children riding horses bareback in Ballymun and other working class suburbs isn't appreciated by everyone and many in Ballymun are weary of the image, perpetuated for the world to see in *The Commitments*, where a horse is seen being led to a tower block lift because 'the stairs would kill him'. Byrne's sculpture was commissioned by Breaking Ground under the Per Cent for Art scheme that was part of the redevelopment of the area (under the terms of the scheme, one per cent of development costs must be spent on art). Byrne wanted to subvert the tradition of equestrian statuary in Ireland and Europe, and when he found out that the Gough statue had ended up in England he went to Chillingham and got permission to copy the horse. The figure for the rider is a local girl, Toni Marie Shields, chosen from open auditions. She was scanned with 3D software to make the mould, which was then combined with the mould from the model of Gough's horse to make the bronze sculpture. Byrne then distressed the bronze by applying a green patina at the end of the process, to make it look as if it had been standing out in the weather for a century or two. It's now in a school in Ballymun and may be transferred to the Main Street if the Metro rail project is completed. Wherever it ends up, it seems entirely fitting that Foley's Arab deconstructed and re-imagined stallion should be prancing in the city again.

All these illustrious dead. Part of me sympathizes with Tim Healy's impatience with them. What are they doing here, in the middle of the city with their frozen gestures? They inhabit their alternative city, their pigeon space, above the living, Kelly's Larkin, Father Mathew, Jesus of the Taxi Drivers, Hibernia, Fidelity and Mercury looking down from Francis Johnston's GPO, Oliver Sheppard's dying Cúchulainn in the ground-floor window. Sheppard's bust of James Clarence Mangan is in Stephen's Green, and I never go into the park without going over to inspect it, drawn by its sharp clear lines and the expression somewhere between gentleness and ferocity, with just the single word MANGAN on the base. That's been there since 1909 but in recent years there's been a rush to commemorate the city's writers on the streets. Here, in North Earl Street, is Joyce, swaggering in bronze outside the Kylemore Café. There's always something strangely literal about statues of writers. Writers, after all, live in their heads; they don't ride horses or inspect troops, they don't lift up their arms and orate, unless in the privacy of their bedrooms. Marjorie Fitzgibbon's bronze is based on a photograph of the author, but for all the jauntiness of the pose, the cane and the broad brimmed hat, it still looks odd and stilted. It was commissioned by the local businesses, presumably to add a bit of lustre to the street, but North Earl Street doesn't really need Joyce or anyone else to stand like a sentinel at its gateway. It's not as bad as the lurid kitsch of Oscar Wilde in Merrion Square. Kavanagh sitting on a bench by the Grand Canal, or Brendan Behan at a safe distance on the other side of the city, on the banks of the Royal Canal, work better because they at least depict the writers in a plausible attitude and occupation, staring into water and hatching plans.

The city doesn't stop at replicating writers, but also attaches their names to new bridges across the Liffey: The Sean O'Casey Bridge, The Samuel Beckett Bridge, The James Joyce Bridge. I'm not sure if this really works either. A street maybe, or a square. A modest plaque in the brickwork. Rue de la Poésie . . . A bridge, though, seems grandiose, a kind of monumentalization the writers themselves, you feel, might well resist if they had any say. There have been other attempts to represent writers in the cityscape. The city's first attempt to bring a writer into the circle of official celebration was the James Joyce Museum in the Martello Tower in Sandycove, the building where the opening of *Ulysses* is set. Apart from its spectacular location in Sandycove, I think this museum works not least because the building has such a strong imaginative resonance. Joyce only spent a few troubled days there but the fact that the opening scene of *Ulysses* is set there, with Buck Mulligan and Stephen Dedalus gazing down at the waters of the bay, the snotgreen and scrotumtightening sea, makes it a more real place than many carefully preserved writers' houses with their kitschy appeal to the literal. The museum has a very specific and selective brief: to focus on the life and works of Joyce, only displaying original material from Joyce's own time. There are information panels and photographs; in the gunpowder magazine various items are assembled: the death mask, a piece of Nelson's Pillar, a Clongowes pandybat, a photo of Throwaway, the twenty-to-one outsider which won the 1904 Gold Cup, an empty Plumtree's Potted Meat pot like the one Bloom finds when he eventually gets home, its contents eaten by Molly Bloom and Blazes Boylan. Samuel Beckett presented the museum with Joyce's famous family waistcoat; Maria Jolas donated his last cane, Sylvia Beach brought photographs, a prospectus for *Ulysses*, notes in Joyce's hand.[7] The opening, on Bloomsday 1962, was a gala drink-fuelled Dublin occasion with a huge crowd in attendance, including Maria Jolas, Frances Steloff, Joyce's sisters, Louis MacNeice, Mary Lavin, Brendan Behan, Anthony Cronin. One of the first curators was the poet Michael Hartnett from whom Paul Durcan bought his first copy of *Ulysses*. Many volunteers helped to staff the tower, including the actor Eamon Morrissey, who used tell the more credulous visitors that Joyce was imprisoned in the tower by the British for his seditious activities. This museum was followed many years later by the privately run James Joyce Centre in North Great Georges Street and the ill-fated James Joyce House of the Dead in Usher's Island, and the recently opened MoLI (geddit?) Museum of Literature Ireland in Stephen's Green.

And, of course, there's the annual Bloomsday celebration, a jolly middle-class fancy-dress party with a few lectures and performances thrown in. The statue is a further attempt to integrate a writer who spent most of his adult life in exile from his native city into the bustle of its commercial life, but his gaze is upwards, away from the commotion of North Earl Street, and he doesn't look like a willing participant in the tourist industry. I try to imagine him at the meeting I attended, hosted by the tourism industry, whose main object was to discover ways of monetizing 'the literature product'.

One institution which tries to do just that is the Dublin Writers' Museum. Again, the notion of a 'writers' museum' is problematic. It tries to construct a product out of the idea of writers by assembling books, busts, objects: letters, portraits, typewriters, Oliver St John's Gogarty's driving goggles, Brendan Behan's Painters and Decorators Union membership card. 'Did you know, for example, that Oscar Wilde was a promising pugilist during his days at Trinity College, and that Samuel Beckett, had he not turned out to be one of the most influential writers of the twentieth century, would also have made a name for himself in the TCD cricket first eleven?' It attempts to compress centuries of literary achievement into an easily digestible narrative that can be read off the walls and listened to on the handset that comes with the admission ticket. There is a library, but it consists of locked bookcases, so that what is really on display is the idea of a library, a virtual representation of reading.

The Gallery of Writers is a sumptuous Georgian drawing
room with an ornate ceiling by Stapleton and portraits of
dead writers. Living writers are outside the frame of the
narrative. The museum wants fixity and certainty, the stasis
of the past unruffled by new pretenders; once the panels and
objects and audio guide are in place there will be no need
for the tourist industry to revisit the exhibit or revise the
narrative. It's the Dead Zoo model: the main work is in the
collecting and the installation, but once that's done you only
have to polish the cases occasionally. MoLI is more sophisti-
cated. A partnership between UCD and the National Library
of Ireland, housed in the freshly imagined space of the Aula
Maxima of Joyce's old university in Newman House, it makes
much of the Joyce connection, proudly displaying 'Copy
No. 1' of *Ulysses*. It also features changing exhibitions on
contemporary literature and it has already established itself
as a challenging addition to the city's literary culture.

How should a city represent its writers other than by
organizing festivals, events and exhibitions or displaying
their ephemera in museums? One way is to find a way of
stitching their texts into the fabric of the city. In 1988, as
part of the Millennium celebrations, Robin Buick placed
fourteen plaques in city pavements, tracing Leopold Bloom's
movements through the city in the eighth chapter of *Ulysses*,
Lestrygonians. The texts were chosen by Robert Nicholson,
the curator of the Joyce Museum. Each plaque, about the
size of an A4 sheet of paper featuring a bowler-hatted
Bloom and brief quotation, is set at a point on Bloom's
lunchtime route from O'Connell Street to the National
Museum via Davy Byrne's pub.

There's something attractive about this mapping of the
imaginary onto the literal, this plantation of an imagined
journey onto the streets of the city. Maybe it's also attractive
because it makes no obvious demands on the citizens, it
doesn't come into their line of sight, it's almost secret. Just
to see them you have to shuffle along the street, head down
to the pavement, looking for the plaques between the feet of

hurrying citizens.

A much louder, though of its nature temporary, attempt to map Joyce onto his city was undertaken in 1999 by Frances Hegarty and Andrew Stones when they placed nine fragments of Molly Bloom's soliloquy rendered in cerise-pink neon at a series of locations around the city. The neon was lit both night and day, but it was only at night that the project came alive as Molly's thoughts came out from Eccles Street to blazon themselves from prominent locations in the city. ' . . . I hate an unlucky man . . . ' was placed above a bookmaker's; ' . . . it'd be much better for the world to be governed by the women in it . . . ' looked down from its prominent site on City Hall, while on the side of Trinity College appeared ' . . . I wouldn't give a snap of my two fingers for all their learning . . . ' The quotes chosen are all humorous, sceptical of men and their self-importances. One might be taken as a sly critique of the way cities commemorate themselves and their dignitaries: ' . . . a stranger to Dublin what place was it and so on about the monuments and he tired me out with statues . . . '

What was maybe most attractive about it was its projection of the private into the public space, the sense that the city could reflect back the private life of its citizenry through the words of one of its most memorably imagined citizens. It was a reminder, precisely, that a city is the sum of the interior life of its citizens and that one of the functions of art, even public art, is to attempt to represent that. The neon ramblings didn't want to improve us or set before us a massive icon of nationhood or historical memento. 'We hate poetry that has a palpable design on us,' Keats said, and this can also be true of public art. As I walk up O'Connell Street I pause to admire another creation of light, Julian Opie's LED panel on the central median, 'Walking Down O'Connell Street'. Each side of the panel shows an animated figure walking down the street, electronic shoppers taking their place in the pedestrian life of the city, mirroring the street's activity, blending in with it. Opie apparently came up with the idea for the LED panels when he noticed that LED taxi meters in South Korea display a small galloping horse when switched on. His figures in bright orange light, here on the street and in front of the Municipal Gallery, The Hugh Lane, in Parnell Square, which commissioned them, are elemental, childlike, yet they move with a fluid sensuousness. They go about their business just like the rest of the city, except that their motion is without destination, circular and repetitive, nothing but motion. How jealous they must make the rest of the street's figures, frozen forever in a single gesture.

# The Lost Train

*FIVE days a week, Michael Kiernan, 50, a computer network administrator, makes the 90-minute commute home from the Bronx County Courthouse, where he works, to suburban Long Beach on Long Island. Like a lot of New Yorkers, he has it down to a science. He leaves work at 4:45, walk-jogs across 161st Street, then hurries into the subway, where he gets into the first car on the D train. He stands by the door, riding two stops to 145th Street, then races up the stairs for the A train, a downtown express. Again he stands, in the first car, by the third door, which at 34th Street opens at the stairs to the Long Island Rail Road. If all goes well, he catches the 5:20 home.*
— Michael Winerip, 'As Luck Would Have It . . . '
*New York Times*, 8/11/2009

This is the opening of an article about a man who collapses on a subway in New York, having suffered an arrythmia, a near-fatal loss of heartbeat, which I happen to read in the *New York Times* on the plane after a trip to the city. There happened to be a doctor in the same carriage, and the train happened to stop in one of the five stations out of a total of 146 in Manhattan that have defibrillators. The story has a happy outcome, and the man is returned to the workforce and his fine-tuned commute after ten days. The outcome turns on a series of remarkable coincidences — the train happening to stop at the 59th Street station which had the defibrillator, the cardiologist happening to have left work early and positioned herself in the first car to be as close as she could to her own exit.

But it's also a story, in its way, of the pure poetry of public transport, in this case of a transport system so regulated and reliable that you can plot a series of complex transfers, moving yourself around like a counter in a game so that you are always optimally positioned to advance to the next level. I'm reminded of a friend who always drank after work in Kennedy's pub beside Tara Street Dart station, pint in one hand and Dart schedule in the other, in the days before smart-phones, so that he could calculate with maximum efficiency the time between the last draught of Guinness and the next departing southbound train. Transport systems demand a precise relationship with time which is one of the character-istics of urban living. The routes of the system take up residence in the mind and body of the city dweller. As in Flann O'Brien's theory of molecular transference between man and bicycle in *The Third Policeman*, a shift takes place between train or bus and human so that they all become part of the same continuum of motion. Imagine, though, as the systems become ever more complex, how the possibilities multiply; how, as a system makes more connections to other parts of itself, its connectivity increases exponentially until eventually it becomes infinite . . .

Last year I visited Buenos Aires and on the second

evening of the trip I found myself standing on a platform on Line D of the *subte*, the city's subway system, on my way with friends to see a concert by Bela Fleck and the Flecktones in the Gran Rex. The system is radial, much like Dublin's bus system, in that the various lines mostly radiate from the centre and if you need to get from a station on one line to a station on another you have to travel back to the city centre first. This didn't prevent the *subte* from being used as the location for the film *Moebius*, a dark, brooding mystery about the disappearance of a subway train and its passengers.

The film is the work of a group of advanced students from the Universidad del Cine in Buenos Aires under the direction of one of their professors, Gustavo Mosquera. It's an adaptation of a classic 1950s science fiction story 'A Subway Named Moebius' by astronomer and writer A J Deutsch, set in the Boston Underground. A new tunnel means that all seven lines of the Boston subway system are connected. Now, a train on any line can travel to any station in the system, but this apparent perfection is exactly what triggers disaster, and on the 4th of March train number 86 carrying three hundred and fifty Bostonians disappears. The story's hero is a mathematician who tries to unravel the mystery by applying his understanding of topology. 'The System is a network of amazing topological complexity,' he explains to the distracted general manager, who is none the wiser for the news. The new tunnel 'has made the connectivity of the whole system of an order so high that I don't know how to calculate it.' The system has turned into a Moebius strip, along which the train hurtles eternally, occasionally heard but never seen. The Borgesian plot has an obvious attraction for an Argentinian director and in fact at one point in the film the camera pans slowly over the station name BORGES as the hero finds himself trapped in the missing train. Menacing shots of tunnels achieved by the director hanging over the front of the train with his antique reconditioned 35mm camera and riding back and forth for hours are interspersed with bewildering mathematical theories delivered at a furious pace. The starkly real and the nightmarish crash into each other.

There's another edge to the film, a darker resonance: the missing train is a clear allegory of the 30,000 'disappeared' during the days of the junta. The sinister group of men who gather to decide how to deal with the situation have no interest in the train or its passengers but are anxious to sweep the problem aside. They refuse to listen to the driven young mathematician played with a searing intensity by Guillermo Angelelli. 'It never happened,' one hisses menacingly at the general manager as the train eventually turns up empty. The poetry of the film is all the more convincing for its fidelity to its own dark language, its own theatre of images. And the other trains that begin to disappear as the credits start to roll will equally be erased by the state. It's a haunting, powerful film, made itself in a side tunnel of the implacable, unchangeable commercial film system whose producers repeatedly tell Mosquera that 'Hollywood is not in the business of making movies for intellectuals'.

The train pulls in and bears us off safely. Hanging from my strap I think how the subway systems of the world connect up with each other in a Moebius strip of elective affinity. Close your eyes in New York and open them in London, Paris, Buenos Aires, looking at the date on the page of your edition of *The New York Times, The Guardian, Le Monde* or *Clarín*. And don't forget your copy of *Fantasia Mathematica*, with the story by Armin Joseph Deutsch, who also lent his name to a crater on the far side of the moon, along whose western edge passes a ray from another impact crater, Giordano Bruno, a long way now from the flames of the Campo dei Fiori.

# Like Vast Sarcophagi

*On shining lines the trams like vast sarcophagi move*
*Into the sky...*
>                — Louis MacNeice, 'Birmingham'

There's a story that the late Garret Fitzgerald rose with the sun sometime in the mid 1990s and went into town to measure the turn from Dawson Street into Nassau Street. I'm not sure if he had an engineer with him, but his measurements satisfied him that any tram making the turn would be sure to crash into the side of Trinity College. It's probably apocryphal — he denied it himself — but his was only one of many voices raised against running a tram line through the city centre. I think of the story, and those irate voices, every time I sit on the Green Line tram gliding down past Hodges Figgis and around into Nassau Street. And then I think of all the trams that used to be here . . .

First there's the noise, the clatter, the hiss and crackle of the trolley on the wires, the arm sucking in power, the blue sparks of electricity, the pavement rumbling under the weight, then the bright slender monster bearing down. Leopold Bloom, already grazed by the lanterns of passing cyclists, is almost knocked down by one on Cormac's Corner. 'Hey, shitbreeches, are you doing the hat trick?' roars the driver, and Bloom, once he recovers from the shock, contemplates reporting him. A brush with impatient modernity in the form of an electric tram of the Dublin

United Tram Company, three separate tram systems united by William Martin Murphy. By 1901, three years before Leopold Bloom's close shave, the whole system has been electrified. There are about sixty-six miles of tracks and two hundred and eighty trams, including a special unnumbered Director's Car from which Murphy and his fellow directors can inspect the system. This is a suitably regal construction, the only three-windowed tram in the fleet, all its internal pillars carved as classical columns, the panels carved with Celtic designs, illuminated by elegant lamp clusters, carpets, armchairs and a wine cabinet — the Custom House of the tram system, as Michael Corcoran has described it.[1] It's a great combination of the modern and the paternalistic, a steel hymn to the Victorian lust for inspection, but also a sign of the prestige of the system. Dublin was regarded as a pioneer in tram development and visiting dignitaries from other cities were taken out in this car to see the system in operation.

A schedule from 1910 shows seventeen routes, mostly radiating out from Nelson's Pillar, the epicentre of the system. Each route has its own symbol, displayed above the destination board: a red triangle for the Terenure route, a green shamrock for Dalkey, a two impacted blue diamond for Donnybrook, a brown lozenge for Rialto and Glasnevin, a green crescent for Sandymount and Ringsend and a white square for the cross-town routes. These symbols, introduced in 1903, aren't just about aesthetics; they're a recognition of the fact that a very large percentage of the system's users are illiterate. For forty years the trams are at the heart of Dublin life and an established feature of its iconography. There are many photographs of the trams and their passengers and operators, though sadly a great deal more were lost when the headquarters of the DUTC was destroyed during the civil war. Among the photographs of the earlier trams one particular driver is featured several times, apparently because he bore a strong resemblance to Edward VII.

Like all pleasing systems it is more than simply functional.

Looking at images of the different generations of trams —
the Open-top, the Balcony, the Standard and Luxury — what's
immediately striking is their physical beauty. Tall, slender,
immaculately finished, they are models of modern progress,
sleekly efficient machines that still manage to retain a sense
of bourgeois grace and formality. In the old horse tram days
the drivers were asked to actively solicit trade from genteel
pedestrians. 'Carriage, madam? Carriage, sir?' Something of
the ethos survived electrification. Here are three from 1912,
during what seems to be a major public event, all in a line,
each crammed with passengers. Bowler hatted men hold on
to the rail at the rear and crane out to see what's happening
in front; passengers stand on the crowded upper decks,
straining to see or hear. Here's another, in the distance,
making its way up Rathmines Road as a horse and trap passes
in front of it, the driver or motor man standing on his open
platform. Motor man was the official designation of the
driver in the electric era and it was an important social
distinction. The motor man was a skilled operative, whereas
the driver in the horse era was little above a general labourer
in status. So many of them were countrymen that Dubliners
believed there was a deliberate policy of the DUTC to
recruit from outside the city. And here is the Phoenix
Park tram, No. 80, top hats, bowlers, caps and fashionable
millinery. The trams, at the insistence of Murphy, were
all made in the city, in the tramcar works in Spa Road,
Inchicore, and this continued into the electric days: the Dalkey
'windbreakers' and the eight wheelers from Terenure. The
fleet had many different kinds of car, as Denis Johnston,
writing in 1951, remembers:

> *Terenure had its No. 191, affectionately known as*
> *'The Coffin' from its hexagonal ends. This was the*
> *first tram in the world to have vestibule front and*
> *rear platforms for the protection of driver and con-*
> *ductor from the weather. Does anybody remember*
> *No. 268 on the Rathmines run, one of the two early*

*double-deckers that were fully roofed on the upper deck but with a shorter glassed-in space on the top floor than down below? Or that remarkable six-wheeler on the Donnybrook line, No. 286, with a pair of centre wheels that used to emerge sideways whenever she went round a curve? Or No. 80, built with a specially high clearance to get through floods on the road to Clontarf? She was called 'The Submarine', and I have recently seen a photograph of her, with the green shield for Dollymount borne on two spikes above the destination indicators . . . [2]*

Shaws Sausages. Jeyes Fluid. Theatre Royal. Bovril. Craven A. Deer Park Hotel. Reckitt's Blue. Enamelled ads placed on what were called 'decency boards', the boards placed at the side of the upper decks when it was discovered that the ankles of female passengers could be observed by the citizenry.

The web of wires cast over the street, either side of a parade of iron poles, are an indelible part of the cityscape. The DUTC had to fight Dublin Corporation to allow the overhead wires but eventually in 1898 they were given permission to run an electric tram to Nelson's Pillar, and thereafter the electrification took off, powered by generating stations in Ballsbridge, Clontarf and Ringsend. From our perspective, our love affair with oil on the decline, it's fascinating to look back at this heyday of electricity in the city and to admire the engineering achievement and the resourcefulness of the system. It wasn't for everybody, though. As the system grew lines were added, but a glance at the route map shows that this was still essentially transport for the middle classes. Whole areas of the city were ignored: the Liberties, the North Wall, areas where the poor predominated. This was business, not universal provision, and the DUTC was one of the wealthiest tram companies in the world.

The trams spark and rattle around the city. The system is popular, and overcrowding such a concern that the matter is raised in the House of Commons, as is the fact that children over three have to pay the full fare. For almost the entire life of the trams there is a penny fare; the distance it covers decreases but the fare is retained.

Dolphin's Barn. Rialto. Sandymount. Haddington Road. Terenure. And then the great silence of the trams, the 1913 Lockout, when, at a pre-arranged time, the drivers walked off their trams in the middle of Horse Show Week in response to William Murphy's dismissal of several hundred workers suspected of union membership. The employers' response was devastating: led by Murphy, over four hundred of them obliged their workers to sign a pledge that they would not join James Larkin's Irish Transport and General Workers' Union or engage in strike action, precipitating the worst industrial dispute in the country's history. The employers locked out their workers and brought in blackleg labour from England. For months the dispute dragged on, the workers and their families barely surviving on handouts from the TUC in England. This was the Dublin of teeming slums, the worst housing in Europe with thousands of families crammed into single rooms, the highest infant mortality rate in these islands. An evocative photograph shows a large crowd awaiting the arrival of the first food ship from Britain in September 1913. Starvation eventually drove the workers back, but relations between labour and business had shifted fundamentally, and though the unions suffered as a result of this defeat and the First World War, they were built up again and the ITGWU became the dominant force in Irish trade unionism. The most memorable telling of the story is James Plunkett's 1969 novel *Strumpet City*. Not long after the workers went back Murphy, a Redmondite nationalist, converted tram No. 242 into a recruiting car, travelling around the network encouraging men to join the British Army.

The trams are lodged in the city's psyche, icons of a defining moment in its labour history. I sometimes wonder if the events of the Lockout somehow detached the citizens from their trams, associating them, however vestigially, with a brash and brutal capitalism. A contemporary cartoon shows the Dublin-Howth tram with the slogan *William Murder Murphy's Trams* on the side of the upper deck and *Don't forget August 13* on the lower. This is probably fanciful. The tram company itself fully assisted in its own dismantlement. The DUTC opened its first bus route in 1925 and began the process of replacing the trams, ultimately becoming a bus company. It had the great misfortune to be run in its last years by the tram-hating founder of a bus company. The last DUTC tram, the No. 8 to Dalkey, closed in 1949, an event which necessitated the presence of '60 guards, including 2 superintendents, 1 inspector, 8 sergeants and 3 motorcyclists' as souvenir hunters descended on the tram.[3] The Hill of Howth tram survived until 1959. It is commemorated in a short film, *Once Upon a Tram*, made by James Maguire and John Sarsfield in 1958. Narrated by Cyril Cusack, it's an account of a single summer's day in the life of the trams that connected Sutton and Howth railway stations via the Summit and, watching it, you wonder how anyone in their right mind could have wanted to close the line. It was a machine made for happiness; everyone on it is smiling as it climbs through the greenery towards the Summit or makes its way back down again. Anyone riding that tram was much more intimately involved with the landscape around them than they were when they negotiated the two bus routes which replaced it. The buses were sometimes suspended if the roads were icy, unlike the trams which operated in all weathers.

Trams continued to be a primary method of urban transport in many European cities: Amsterdam, Oslo, Milan, Lisbon, Budapest, to name a few. The largest tram system in the world is in Melbourne, which has 499 trams running on 249 kilometres of track. In Dublin, as in English, American and Canadian cities, once the bus appeared trams were doomed. Buses were seen as cheaper, especially in the context of expanding cities. It was easier and cheaper to reach the new suburbs with buses.

A successful tram system is more than just a means of transport; it's the expression of a particular vision of a city, a concentrated space with a small footprint, a space that is essentially urban rather than suburban. The decline of the tram system in Dublin paralleled the drift to the suburbs that characterized urban planning from the 1920s onward. When light railway systems begin to return to the city, with first the Dart and then the Luas, they are essentially suburban commuter systems ferrying passengers in and out of the city.

Something else was lost with the demise of the old system. A tradition of building trams, and of urban design, a sense of public transport as something aesthetically pleasing as well as efficient. To look back at the history of the DUTC is to realize that Dublin achieved something remarkable with a tram system among the finest in the world, an achievement now largely forgotten. The first trams in the world to be roofed in on top were built in Inchicore (1904); the power station in Ringsend was visited by engineers from all over the world; in it a system of automatic points was invented which allowed the motor man to select his route by letting the trolley move over an attachment to the overhead wire.[4] The main thing, though, is that the city conceived and built a transport system itself that suited its own character perfectly, and added significantly to its visual repertoire, and it's hard not to feel that a part of the soul of Dublin was lost with the trams. Maybe the new ones will rekindle a little of their spirit. In the end the old trams died a pretty undignified death, ransacked and vandalized, and then left to rust and rot. One, No. 253, became a sewing classroom and was then converted into four-bedroomed sleeping quarters in a convent in Dun Laoghaire. The nuns would sleep in the tram when retreats in the convent were overbooked. It has since been restored and made a triumphant return to the streets in a St Patrick's Day parade. The famous Director's Car spent years in a Dalkey garden and was eventually moved to the Transport Museum where it is still awaiting restoration. Most of the tram bodies were sold off. The citizens got their hands on as much as they could before the tracks were ripped up. Here's Denis Johnston's account of his journey on the last tram from the Pillar:

> *It was a very fantastic ride — back as far as Nassau Street in the wrong line, since we could not cross over to the left until we got there. And all the way out a mass of crazy poltergeists were taking the tram to bits. First the lights went out, then the curtains came down. Then the fittings were wrenched off, and the Fare Sheet, Byelaws and Board of Trade regulations disappeared. At Haddington Road the very seat underneath me seemed to disappear, and from there to Ballsbridge, where I got out, a bonfire was blazing in the middle of the road.*
>
> *Like a ghost tram the darkened and half-wrecked vehicle crossed the bridge and clanked its way out past the Showgrounds. From the upper windows arms waved in the night air, and from the blackened interior came the howling of many banshees. That was the last of the Dublin trams.*

It's rush hour and the tram is crowded. I hold onto my strap and plot my route to the door. I'm consoled by the fact that mine is one of the almost 42 million journeys on the Luas this year. The press of flesh is testament to the city's hunger for public transport. The trams are about to get longer as extra carriages are added to cope with the demand. As I twist my way off and walk towards Haddington Road I salute the ghosts of the vanished trams.

# In the Dream Rooms: Artists' Spaces and Writers' Rooms

It's more than looking at pictures; it's looking at people looking at pictures, inhaling the building, the light of the rooms, like Peter Redgrove

> *Dipping into the Tate*
> *As with the bucket of oneself into a well*
> *Of colour and odour, to smell the pictures,*
> *To sniff up the odours of the colours, which are*
> *The fragrances of people excited by the pictures. . .*
> — 'Into the Rothko Installation'

Sometimes it's possible to go through a gallery without really looking at anything, but taking everything in as an atmosphere, a radiance, as if the place were an external embodiment of an inner dream. All good buildings are like that, and museums and galleries are the great dream-spaces of the city. Today, though, I've come to peer once more into a room within a room, a room which was taken apart in another city, then shipped here and reconstructed item by item with absolute precision. The room is more than a room; it is the artist's imagination, a space whose apparent clutter and disorder were not simply a by-product of a place where art was made, but a source of images, a provider of comfort and stimulation. The room and the art became inseparable, each unthinkable without the other.

Most rooms in most lives are continuously swept clean and re-made, returned to an ideal state that disguises or conceals habitation, but this room was left to grow and accumulate until every spare inch of floor was covered. I look through the windows at hundreds of paintbrushes in jars, cups, paint cans, taking in the brightly lit mayhem of the room, the cardboard boxes, the easel, the paint-spattered mirror like the centre of a triptych with wings of black paint, the paint-spattered walls, an old record-player, cloths, corduroy trousers, an old dressing gown, a chair, photographs, old newspapers and magazines. He used to cut up the corduroy trousers and dressing gowns to apply the paint with a rougher texture. I look at the studio door, covered in blues and blacks and reds, an improvised palette. On the walls outside blown-up texts tell the visitor what Francis Bacon felt about this room: 'For some reason the moment I saw this place I knew that I could work here. I am very influenced by places — by the atmosphere of a room.' The statement is from an interview with Melvyn Bragg in the actual studio in 7 Reece Mews, South Kensington, which plays on a loop in the adjoining room. Bacon surveys his room affectionately, 'This mess around us is rather like my mind; it may be a good image of what goes on inside me, my life is like that.' Most important of all, 'I feel at home here in this chaos because chaos suggests images to me.'

In the real house, in London, the fruitful chaos of the studio contrasted with the spartan cleanliness of the kitchen-cum-bathroom and the bedroom. Bacon's companion and heir, John Edwards, has described his own first impressions of the studio. 'As we sat at the dining table in the bedsitting room I noticed the door to his studio was ajar. Through the gap I saw an unbelievable mess.' The chaos then was apparently much worse than later, or than what is in front of visitors to the Hugh Lane Gallery today. Edwards filled about ten bin bags with newspaper cuttings, magazines, old books and tins of hardened paint, all of which was covered with the orange and pink dust of the raw pigment. At that stage the studio had become too chaotic to work properly in and Bacon could barely move in it. Edwards found wads of money tied up in bundles, set aside for a rainy day and then forgotten, much of it so old the notes were no longer legal tender. Bacon was pleased with the clear-out and asked him to continue the work by destroying twenty or so large canvases in the studio, which he did by slashing them with a Stanley knife. These have survived in the reconstructed studio.

Bacon had many opportunities to occupy different spaces but he never considered moving. Nor did he ever contemplate modifying or improving 7 Reece Mews: in all the time he lived there, Edwards tells us, he made no attempt to change anything. He had found a space that worked for him, and its particular suggestive, orderly chaos couldn't be replicated elsewhere. It was his dream room; once he pushed the door open and stepped inside he was in instant communion with everything he had created there and with the possible future works whose seeds lay somewhere in the mess. Many artists are attached to their workrooms and studios and, once established there, find it impossible to contemplate working anywhere else. The rooms become part of their mental furniture; the lure of place mixes with the lure of habit to form a richly associative physical space. The fact that Bacon's studio was imported to Dublin says something about the power of our interest in the places where things are made, where the currents of imagination flow. It reminds us of the power of objects and atmospheres and transports us to our own dream-spaces.

This must be part of the fascination of the series, Writers' Rooms, that ran in *The Guardian* several years back, which every week offered a photograph of a writer's writing room or study, with accompanying commentary on the photographer's image. The featured rooms, from which the writers themselves were absent, were mostly models of order — large, airy spacious rooms with well-made shelving, decent height, chrome table lamps, sofas for relaxing, discreet computers, jars of pens and pencils, assorted fetishes arranged on desks inherited from monasteries and big enough to sleep on. They seemed to come out of a central casting of writerly success, writers' studios as imagined by Hollywood. There were some concessions to austerity — the desk facing a blank wall as a disincentive to daydreaming, the desk that is actually a door resting on four steel filing cabinets. Some cultivated an aesthetic ugliness as further proof of seriousness:

> '*I admit that the décor — if that's not too strong a word — is the subject of some hilarity to female interviewers.*'
>
> — Sebastian Faulks

If we give the writers the benefit of the doubt and assume they didn't embark on a furious bout of tidying up before the photographer appeared, the orderliness is still surprising. Only a couple of rooms begin even to approach the fringes of Bacon-like accumulation — 'Once it was a light-filled, pale green space, but it has accreted 17 years' worth of manuscripts and books' (Maggie Gee). The nearest to a genuine mess shows a mattress on a floor where the writing is done, no sign of a desk, a talismanic crocodile on a wall, a scatter of clothes and books. The occupant fondly remembers his previous workplace, 'a Suffolk shooting lodge by woodland' where he would sit fifteen feet up in a deer-shooting perch strapped to a tree. 'That was the best study of all time: 5 a.m., wrapped in blankets, with my gasman's clipboard, a thermos of coffee, and deer trotting below me through the mist' (Alexander Masters). One other bed features in the series, arrived at after much trial and error and research. 'I was reading a biography of my great hero-writer Robert Louis Stevenson and discovered a photograph of him towards the end of his life, lying on his bed in Samoa, propped up on a pile of pillows, a writing book resting on his drawn-up knees. So that's how you write *Treasure Island*, I thought. I went up to my bedroom, piled up all the pillows I could find and began to write . . . ' (Michael Morpurgo).

For some the presentation of the workroom allows them to disclose their often frighteningly productive work habits

— 'I normally begin my first paragraph just before I break for lunch and then work solidly through the afternoon. I start cooking supper at about half past five or six and then go back to the Mac for a final blitz before drinks. Every three or four days, I'll finish a chapter, which James reads over drinks, while I try not to watch his expression . . .' (David Starkey).

Not every writer, of course, feels the need for a dedicated space. Some prefer to work in the neutral atmosphere of a sitting room or bedroom, or at a kitchen table, tricking the mind by the very absence of the kind of ritual stimuli that work in dedicated studios, huts, attics or treehouses. A writer is not bound by the demands of materials and can move around the house with impunity or even escape the private shelter completely, yet only one of the writers in the series ventured outside for the working day. That writer, a novelist, gave as his workroom the Rose Reading Room of the 42nd Street branch of the New York Public Library. The photograph shows the beautiful, serious space with its vaulted windows, its rows of desks lit by an enormous chandelier. No human beings with their litter of books, laptops and personal belongings clutter the ghostly perfection of the room, which is like a writer's fantasy of scholarship, or the library we might carry in our minds as an ideal repose, a place in which to unlock the mysteries of the world or simply to sit and dream. Almost as a corrective to the published image the writer adds that he has since changed neighbourhoods and now works in a branch of the library in Brooklyn where the habits of the users might seem to be an orchestrated undermining of the idea of contemplative solitude. It's a dose of reality the writer welcomes, however:

> *In Brooklyn, people regularly carry on cellphone conversations at their desks, regularly sing along to the music they are listening to through their earphones (why wear earphones at all?), regularly have conversations (which are regularly about illicit*

*things), regularly fall asleep — apropos of I can't imagine what, a guy at the next table slapped the bookshelf behind him and screamed, 'Fucking pussy!' (true) — regularly prepare and eat meals, stare, hum, hoot, and get in scarily heated arguments with the roaming policemen about what's acceptable behaviour. It's my best argument for why Brooklyn is the superior borough: it's real.*

— Jonathan Safran Foer

Reality isn't always what you want in a library, though. I think of the various libraries I've frequented specifically to work there, sometimes having to flourish some arcane interest to provide a right of entry, or to order a book I had no intention of reading just to be able to sit in peace in a great public space and watch the light pour through the windows onto the shelves. There is something irresistible about working in a shared space and communing with the spirit of scholarship even if it's really only a route into your own mind. To have nothing in front of you except a desk, a few books and a notebook or laptop is a great incentive to work. But I think too of the great serious impoverished scholars and writers for whom the library was the only possible space in hostile circumstances. I think of Walter Benjamin working in the Bibliothèque nationale in Paris researching the interior spaces of the nineteenth-century city for his swelling *Arcades Project*. He was so much a regular there that when he returned after a prolonged absence the other scholars stood up to applaud him as he made his way back to his usual desk.

Most of the writers in the series prefer their own company, and the beloved objects with which they share their spaces:

*The oar in the corner is a work of a few years ago by my son Conrad Shawcross — it was inspired by the prophecy that Odysseus will know the place of his death when he meets a man who mistakes the oar he is carrying for a winnowing fan. The sculpture's an impossible object, an enigma, and I find it very good company. Next to it you can just see the 1930s-style kidney-shaped table I work at, which was made by Stephen Owen when he was just out of Parnham furniture-making school.*

— Marina Warner

I think of the sheer physicality of Bacon's studio, its sea of brushes and paint. The writers' rooms, by contrast, are cerebral spaces, and betray little of the fury, torments or exultations of the creative process. What isn't strictly utilitarian is decorative and, when it comes to the implements that produce the words, the writers tend to be reticent. Although most of the desks displayed in the series reveal laptops or desktop computers, it's striking how few of the writers mention them. Indeed, for many the presence of technology is an embarrassment, or a not entirely trustworthy successor to the time-honoured tools of the trade: 'I agree with John Updike that writing on a computer produces a particular tone and texture. All my novels are written longhand; I revise them by hand and then type them on the iBook' (Justin Cartwright). I think of one of Randall Jarrell's polished dismissals of a book which 'gave the impression of having been written on a typewriter by a typewriter'. The ballpoint, in its day, must have attracted the same kind of opprobrium, and no doubt the line of disapproval stretches all the way back to the newfangled and prose mangling ways of the chisel. One writer, however, explicitly mentions his laptop, an ordinary machine which contains 'an extraordinary writing program' (Richard Sennett), WordPerfect 6.0 for DOS, a programme so old the IT department of the London School of Economics has deemed it 'illegitimate'. The writer's mention of this venerable DOS programme is, for me, the equivalent of the floor covered in paintbrushes and paint pots in the artist's studio. What WordPerfect offered, and continues to offer to those willing to make the effort to get it to run on modern machines, is a kind of Zen simplicity combined with power and sophistication. Its bare blue screen is a kind of pure room, a clear mental space that invites concentration. For that alone it has earned its place in the history of computing. For a writer, software can provide the perfect studio, I console myself, as I fire up Ulysses or Vim in a full screen terminal.

The spaces that writers most seem to crave are strategic retreats, half in and half out of the world, places where they can be alone or undisturbed. Ideally there might be a journey to this space, a symbolic transition from public to private world. It took George Bernard Shaw a full minute to walk from the back veranda of his house in rural Hertfordshire to his hut:

> *In some ways, the sanctuary resembled Doctor Who's flying police phone box: smaller-looking outside than within. And it gave the illusion of flying round the world since, with a couple of hefty shoves morning and afternoon, it could be made to revolve and follow the sun. And who would have guessed it contained so much technology? There was an electric heater, a typewriter, a bunk for Napoleonic naps and a telephone to the house which could be used for emergencies such as lunch: surely everything a writer could need.*

The space inside, like many writers' rooms, is small and cramped. Writers require legroom and dream time. Visual artists, on the other hand, need workshops, ateliers, almost industrial spaces.

I go back again to the Bacon studio. Writers' spaces are essentially neutral; it doesn't really matter to us where Joyce composed his sentences, but for visual artists studio and work seem part of the same continuum, and part of the attraction of this studio conserved for our inspection is that it makes the connection explicit. The museum suggests to us that this studio is a part of the artist's legacy, as legitimate an object of study as the paintings displayed in an adjoining room. And yet of course there is something deeply artificial about the room in its current location. For a start, the artist is missing; no one stands at the easel, no one is applying paint with cut-up dressing gowns or corduroy trousers. There's a ghostly quality about the paraphernalia; it's like peering into a tomb. The only reason we can stand here looking in is because it has been removed to a museum. And as we look at it we are aware of the extraordinary work that went into its assembly. In fact, the whole presentation of the room is designed to reinforce our awareness that what we perceive here as chaos is in fact the product of meticulous order. A panel informs us that the Gallery removed the contents of Francis Bacon's studio at 7 Reece Mews in August 1998, an operation which required a team of archaeologists to map the space, to tag and note the position of seven thousand items in the studio and catalogue them in a specially designed computer database. Our experience of the studio is simultaneously an experience of archaeology and technology:

> *Every item in the studio has a database entry. Each entry consists of an image and a factual account of an object. The database has entries on approximately 570 books and catalogues, 1,500 photographs, 100 slashed canvases, 1,300 leaves torn from books, 2,000 artist's materials and 70 drawings. Other categories include the artist's correspondence, magazines, newspapers and vinyl records.*

The windows allow us to drink in the contents of the studio as if we were right inside it. On one wall a kind of fairground telescope licences the voyeur in us to peer secretly into the interior. Our peering, our viewing and consumption of the space is part of the point: ours is a cultural moment which values biography, process, which likes to peer over the shoulder at the artist at work. Part of my reaction to the studio is to flinch at the kitschy consumerism to which it partly appeals, but this is overcome by the real pleasure in the space as a repository for the imagination at work. All those paint tubes, jars of pigment, paintbrushes, utensils, tin cans, pastel sticks, sponges, bits of cloth, the door painted on both sides, are images of the glorious materiality of the artist and work, and the whole experience reaches us back into the remembered and dreamed spaces of childhood.

There is a tradition of photographing artists' studios, which is part of the background of both the Bacon studio and Eamonn McCabe's photographs of the writers' rooms. Often these portraits show the artists *in situ* surrounded by their works: Cartier-Bresson's Giacometti in a blurry haste carrying a sculpture while one long thin figure seems to run with him and another looms in stillness above him, or Fernand Léger caught by Robert Doisneau leaning over one painting, with another behind him as backdrop, his head almost exactly level with a clown's, so that he seems to be embedded in his own painting. Both of these are mentioned by Stephen McKenna in his foreword to Amelia Stein's photographs of members of the Royal Hibernian Academy (*Amelia Stein, Photographs RHA 2009*, Royal Hibernian Academy, 2009). Stein is the first photographer to be elected to the academy, and her eye is very much that of a fellow practitioner. She has always been a remarkable photographer of resonant objects, as in *Loss and Memory* (2002), her series of black and white still lives of her late parents' personal and household objects: her mother's gardening trowel and hand fork, her father's gym shoes, her lipstick, his sports trophies, little china figurines, a clock. 'I am afraid that when their house is clear of these objects — objects that remind me of the minutiae of our last trips, exchanges and incidents — I may be unable to recall the details. I am trying to weave a safety net out of the threads of these memories, trying to make of it something more solid.'

These are implied portraits, portraits in the absence of their human subjects, and she has brought the same attentiveness to the physical object to the portraits of the artists and their studios. I say *and* rather than *in* their studios because although the artists are indeed photographed in their studios, the studios are also photographed separately and have their own distinct life. Often the images of the physical spaces focus on a single object. One motif running through the series is the empty chair: wooden chair, office chair, paint spattered plastic chair, cushioned, uncushioned, a jacket draped across the back or over the side. The prominence of these chairs functions as a powerful image of stillness and concentration, yet the chairs also strangely assert their independence, as if in their solidity and emptiness they embody the spirit of disinterested creativity. We expect to see rows and jars of brushes, canvases on easels; the chairs, somehow, seem more intensely alive and watchful. Some of the most powerful studio images, apart from the chairs, are those where the objects print their materiality on our eyes, like Rachel Joynt's chisels, pliers and scissors or Remco de Fouw's workbench and vice.

Likewise, though the portraits of the artists are wonderfully revealing, the most memorable human images are the photographs of hands, usually holding an implement — pencil, charcoal, pastel stick, chisel, file — as if the hands lived their own lives independently of their owners, or as if individuation were less important than art itself. Apart from the photographer in her own image of herself, only one of the artists is working in the photographs; he sits with his back to the camera in the act of drawing and his face is visible to us in a reflection. All of the others are posed in their studios. In some cases the suggestion is that the camera has arrived as an interruption to work which will soon be resumed, and the subjects sit or stand in work clothes, implements in hand like an extension of themselves; in others the artists are photographed at rest in poses of varying formality and informality. The actual art produced by the artists isn't foregrounded. As with the Bacon studio, and the writers' rooms, art is the mysterious spirit that animates the spaces, is the elusive quality the photographers and the constructors of the Bacon studio seek to reveal. Amelia Stein's own self-portrait in the RHA book shows her bent over the top-mounted viewfinder of her Hasselblad camera, looking at what might be the scene on the facing page, a chair insistently alone in a room bathed in the light from a partially opened shutter . . . a perfect emblem of the fierce elusiveness of art.

# Within and Without

Sir John Perrott decides to make a circuit of the walls of the city. It is 1585, he is the Lord Deputy of Ireland and a suspected son of Henry VIII. In seven years' time he will die in the Tower of London, convicted of treason. Fifteen years earlier he had come to Ireland as Lord President of Munster, landing at Waterford and conducting a ruthless campaign against the Geraldines, the heads of fifty of whom he fixed to the market cross in Kilmallock, *pour encourager les autres*. He hanged another eight hundred before he returned to England in 1573. He took up the Lord Deputyship in 1584, and here he is now patrolling the walls with military thoroughness, working his way round clockwise via Pole Gate, Geneville's Tower, St Nicholas's Gate, New Gate, Gormond's Gate, Bridge Gate and Prickett's Tower on the river side and up towards Isolde's Tower and Dame's Gate. You could rebuild the walls pretty efficiently from Perrott's circuit. He gives us the exact distance between each gate and describes the shape and conditions of the towers, the ramparts and the ditches outside the walls, and where the towers are not in the ownership of the city he tells us who they belong to; so we learn of Mr Christopher Sedgrave's tower, Sir William Sarsfield's tower, and 'the tower in Mr Richard Fagan's possession'. Some towers are both round and square, like Stanihurst's, 'round without the tower and square within'. He is thinking of the defensive capacity of the walls, so he gives us the thickness of walls and towers and gate-houses. He notes the ordnance available to the city, inspects the portcullis over New Gate, laments the absence of a portcullis and 'murdering hole' over the castle gate. You can see a visual representation of this walled Dublin in a wonderfully detailed drawing made by the architect and writer Leonard Strangways in 1904, the city running from the castle to Usher's Island and from Patrick Street to the river, the castle a walled and gated citadel within the city, and watching over it. You can identify the streets and imagine their inhabitants and their traffic. You can see where the butchers operated from, where the fishmongers had their stalls, where the taverns were clustered and where food was offered for sale. You can see and comprehend an entire encapsulated urban island.

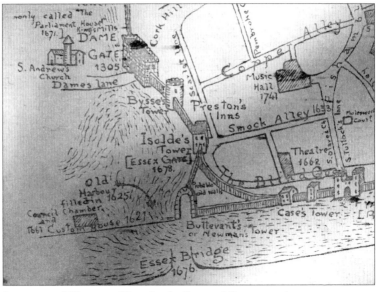

Strangways NE corner (Drawing by Leonard Strangways)

Perrott is a soldier looking to the defences of a garrison town, a town which mostly dislikes him, as it happens. He pokes around and notes down his details. Maybe action was taken, maybe tradesmen were summoned to insert a proper murdering hole above the castle gate. A woodcut from John Derrick's *The Image of Irelande*, published in London four years earlier, shows Perrott's predecessor, Sir Henry Sidney, father of the poet, riding out of the castle gate across the bridge over the Poddle which served as the castle's moat, his army crowding Castle Street, on his way to impose as much as he can of the Queen's will on the Irish. Just behind him, impaled on spikes above the portcullis, are the heads of three rebels whose fate is commemorated by the following admonitory lines:

> *Their truncles heddes do playnly showe, eache*
> *rebeles fatall end,*
> *And what a haynous crime it is, the Queene for to*
> *offend.*

In the little museum under City Hall they have made a model of this scene, adding the homely touch of a couple of citizens going about their business outside in Castle Street, paying no attention to the clatter of soldiery beside them.

⌒

I go to see a stretch of the old wall. There isn't much left of it but what there is is impressive enough, a stretch of thick grey stone wall with buttresses and battlements, running down Cook Street at the back of St Audoen's Church, protecting the city from, among other things, the ovens of this street of food shops and bakers. Once the Liffey came as far as here, and everything below this line is built on reclaimed land. The wall is now the boundary of St Audoen's Park, entered here in Cook Street through the last remaining city gate set in its impressive gate tower. You can see the steps into St Audoen's behind, but the gate itself is bleakly padlocked. I think back to John Speed's 1610 map; the tiny city on its hill enclosed by walls and entered by gates. Walled cities exercise a strong pull on the imagination. Antiquity is part of the lure; a wall is an image of the unreachable past, it implies glamour and danger. The walls of Jericho, Uruk, York, Avila, Babylon. There is the absolute definition of what is within, the pure zone snug behind the walls that can't be adulterated by sprawl. There's no need to ask where the city is, or the centre: it is unarguably here. No buses trundling from the suburbs with the mysterious, mythical destination *An Lár* blazoned on the front. And then there is the theatre of exit and entrance, the restrictions and tolls, the gates and gate towers. A walled and many-gated city is a serious place, a place of prestige and danger. The walls of Dublin protected the inhabitants from the ravages of the Irish who occasionally descended from the mountains to exact their own bloody toll. Later they become a statement of civic power and achievement: the city is that which is enclosed. It has its own charter, its own laws, its own exclusive systems and work practices, its rigid social demarcations, its closed-shop guilds and privileged merchants, its underclass of the unenfranchised and despised. There is within and there is without. The first suburbs are much more than suburbs, they are an alternative urban jurisdiction, the liberties, liberated from the writ of the city: anti-cities, in fact.

Back inside the walls the laws multiply, thought up by the municipality or shipped in from England in cargoes of parchment, written in Latin, French or English. Don't put your dung outside the door. Cattle shall not be eviscerated beside the river. Hides not to be salted in the city. A miller who steals fourpence worth of corn shall be hanged from the beam of his own mill. Pigs are forbidden within the city walls. Even so, they continue to rampage through the archives until the end of the eighteenth century, destroying gardens, fouling streets, even, in 1601, devouring an infant.[1]

The pig-warden, whose job it is to round up illegal pigs, is also responsible for clearing beggars from the city. In 1579 this is Barnaby Rathe, bellman, master and beadle of the beggars. His main problem is less the pigs and beggars than the slippery citizens who are supposed to be paying him fourpence per house per year for his labours. After a couple of years he asks to be relieved of the job, claiming that he can't collect his stipend. He asks instead for a room in St

John's, the poorhouse, but the aldermen are too canny for that. He's either very good at his job or beadles and pig-killers are hard to come by. They come back with a counter-offer: you can have the room but you have to keep the job. But it's no use, and even the constables assigned from the various wards to help him in the execution of his duty can't extract the necessary funds, and he eventually secures his retirement.[2] Unringed pigs snort in the records for centuries after.

You realize what a tiny place is enclosed by these walls. Many of the citizens are known by their first names: William the Clerk, Robert the Moneychanger, or by the place they originally came from: John of Notyngham, Wulfran of Bristol. Even the city charters are small, not the vast scrolls unrolled ceremoniously by heralds that you might imagine, but tiny micro-documents you could slip into a jacket pocket. Dublin's earliest charter, issued by Henry II in 1172, was a mere 6½ inches long by 4¾ inches broad. Tiny, self-contained, rigidly hierarchical — a typical medieval town.

Apart from the cathedral, a length of wall off High Street, and the longer section behind St Audoen's, and of course St Audoen's itself, and the older parts of the castle and its walls, there's not a shred of any of this left. The roads and the names are the same, but the epicentre of the medieval city is the yellow box junction between the top of Patrick Street and Christchurch, with its constant north and south-bound traffic. It's something of a leap to banish the frenetic rush of cars and step back into the different din of the earlier city, picking your way down High Street through the mess and rubbish and the marauding pigs.

Where would someone, descended from the distant future to make a survey of Dublin's boundaries today, begin and end? The walled city is beautifully simple; the city and its liberties and the northern stretches across the river are easily comprehensible. The later city, with its centre shifted eastward, and its broad streets and squares, is still a compact place. As is the city of Joyce. Suburbs have grown up in the nineteenth century but these themselves are distinct, satellite townships connected to but separate from the core city. But as time goes on and the car becomes the dominant form of transport and the dominant feature in the minds of planners, the core is increasingly dug out and its inhabitants deposited in newly created functional suburbs. Today, the commuter belt stretches north or west into Meath and Kildare and south as far as Wexford in an expansion driven by developers and property values that forced people ever farther from the old boundaries. These are cyclical events, money pushing and pulling the boundaries, dispersing and collecting populations.

Yet in some respects people's experience of the urban centre isn't that far removed from the medieval city. They journey to the core for work or for shopping. The latter tends to be confined to Grafton Street, Henry Street and their surrounding areas, a tiny geographical area whose boundaries don't really shift much. It's a peculiar feature of Dublin life that no matter how much the greater urban area sprawls across the map, the area properly recognized as the city or 'town' stubbornly refuses to expand. There's a kind of mental or psychic wall running from Stephen's Green north to Parnell Street, bounded to the west by George's Street and Capel Street and to the east by O'Connell Street. This is the area into which visitors, shoppers, suburban Dubliners pour in great numbers every day, giving it the flavour of an intense, carnival village. This is where the shops, cinemas, coffee bars, pubs and big department stores are. This is the area illuminated by lights at Christmas. This is the mysterious *An Lár*, at which all in-coming transport aims, and an area that can only effectively be traversed by foot. The limits of this city are also the limits of the pedestrian impulse. I remember how much of a challenge it was, when I worked in a cultural institution in Parnell Square, to lure people that far north for an event, yet Parnell Square lies at the top of the city's largest thoroughfare, O'Connell Street. It was as if the Gate Theatre, on Cavendish Row, represented the limits of the tolerable city after seven o'clock and a portcullis snapped shut outside the Rotunda, prohibiting any further northward progress. There was a certain amount of class prejudice embedded in that, but it's hard to imagine the equivalent distances in any other city generating the same unease.

People who live in big cities think nothing of traversing them constantly for work or play, but they have the subway, the *métro*, the underground, the *subte*, to do it. But Dublin is still a medieval town at heart, it doesn't really matter how big it gets, how far it sprawls, it still vests its sense of itself in the same historic core, the locus of its informal as well as its ceremonial life, the stage on which it acts out the drama of itself. Those whose families were exiled from the centre during the slum clearances of the last century still retain strong ties with the city areas their families moved from. The centre, and the districts to the east and west of it, are now full of new apartment buildings, and new generations of city dwellers will develop a strong relationship with the area between the canals. The suburbs are awash with shopping centres, coffee shops, restaurants, offering increasing competition to the centre, but they can never be really self-contained. The core of a lot of newer suburbs is a shopping mall — safe, secure, soulless. Nothing that we have built in a century has managed to house the urban soul which is why we hunger for the centre, why we take the bus into town, looking for the point at which the buildings and the accelerated life of the streets tell us we have arrived.

Perrott is busy making himself enemies. A man of violent temper, enmity comes easily to him, and he has a habit of attacking his associates. He decides that he wants to get his hands on the funds of St Patrick's Cathedral to endow a couple of colleges, earning the undying hostility of the Archbishop, Adam Loftus. Drink didn't help. On one occasion, in the council chamber, he struck Sir Nicholas Bagenal, the elderly knight marshal. Eventually he is replaced, and when he gets back to England his many enemies there are waiting to plot against him and ensure his ruin. The account of the circuit of the walls seems too calm, too disinterested a work to come from the hand of this rash and impulsive man. How likely is it that he did it? He would certainly have conceived and ordered it, but maybe it was some minion who actually walked around and took down the details.

～

From Cook Street the walls would have continued through what are now the bunkers of Dublin City Council on Wood Quay. The wall was in fact discovered during excavations when the offices were being built, after widespread protests against the destruction of a unique Viking site. The original plan was to demolish the wall and store it somewhere else but in the end it was left on the site. The wall is now part of the new Wood Quay Venue, but I discover when I go to see it that it has been incorporated into a private space for hire. There is a viewing platform on the upper level, part of a multimedia exhibition of the city, but when I go to it the blinds have been drawn as a meeting is in progress in the room with the wall. It is only available to view when there are no meetings and the security guards are unable to tell me when that is likely to be. The only way to get a close view of the wall with its stones numbered in preparation for the cancelled demolition, is to hire the room. Unless you have a purpose and a Powerpoint presentation, the wall is off limits. The guardians of the city, having built the wall to repel intruders and then smothered this part of it with its colossal bunkers, now exacts a toll from any of its citizens who want to examine it. I shake my head at the polite

Eastern European guards, leave the museum, and continue on my circuit of the mostly vanished walls.

⌒

When I lived in the area I always felt a psychic connection with its past; I was excited by the sense of the multiple layers of the streets, and by the various excavations that were being conducted at the time. The simple physical experience of walking through these streets was a link with everyone else who had walked them down the centuries. I felt somehow brushed by that past, implicated in it. It's hard to explain, exactly, but it seems to me that this constant murmuring from the past is one of the gifts of old cities. Dublin's past is, like that of many cities, complicated and cantankerous; many cities are embedded in it, many prejudices and factions, many exclusions. Perrott's circuit of the walls, whether personal or virtual, is a small reminder that for centuries it was a bastion of colonial privilege, designed to keep the natives out. Another city has long since arrived at the gates of the old and completely submerged it. Yet all the stages of the city require our attention. Living in a city is a relationship with what's not there as well as what is, with the demolished and buried as well as the brightly flourishing.

Now and again the citizens come out to assert their rights to their past. One of the most spectacular examples was the struggle over Wood Quay which brought more than twenty thousand to the streets. It might seem astonishing, given the level of the protests, that the Corporation nonetheless went ahead and built the Civic Offices on the prime site of Viking Dublin, but the civic bureaucracy moved, like all bureaucracies, with unstoppable force, impervious to argument. The historical geographer Anngret Simms remembers giving guided tours of Wood Quay during the summer of 1977, 'when thousands of people walked on the medieval stone wall and glimpsed for the first time the physical origins of their city . . . as a settlement along the waterfront'. Her worst memory of the site was October 1980, when she walked with some students up Fishamble Street and found that 'the medieval stone wall was being dismantled by a group of building workers, and bulldozers were moving on ground that, a short time before, had held the fabric of the first streets and houses of Dublin. The anger of the students was intense, probably because they instinctively realized that in a democratic society the preservation or neglect of historical monuments reflects fairly closely the cultural consciousness of that society'.

Thousands of people had come, unexpectedly, to find out about the origins of their city. No one had anticipated the level of public interest in the archaeology of Wood Quay, or the strength of the opposition to the city's intent to build its tower blocks on the site. Anngret Simms felt strongly that 'the national monument in the core of medieval Dublin should have been preserved as a symbol of the continuity of human purpose in the city'. That seems to me to be the key, the human continuity of the city. In all sorts of surprising ways people discover that the past, even, or especially, the remote past, is important to them.

This is the case, even or especially, when the past seems to have vanished. I was standing outside the apartment building in Christchurch Place recently, about to visit friends, when a tourist asked me the way to 'the Viking Quarter'. The visitor, to whom the past is most energetically marketed, expects it to be visible. The Vikings and their quarter have long vanished beneath the city and all I can do is make a sweeping gesture with my hands to indicate the geographical area where the disappeared past took place and, of course, direct the tourist to where it is recreated as a consumer 'experience', to the Civic Museum or 'Dublinia' with its ghoulish exhibits and kitsch concoctions. In a city which has outlived its past and carelessly swept it aside the past has to be kitsch, has to be a virtual product peddled for small change. For the citizens, though, the past is internalized, it lies quiescent somewhere in the back of the brain like a hidden map or an unused language until it's pulled to the front by an unexpected event or a threat of extinction; we know, and are, maybe, vaguely comforted by the fact that there's more beneath our feet than the pavement of the present . . .

# Please Touch the Exhibits

We park the car and shiver our way down to the members' entrance where I show the family card with the chimp on the front, more engaging than the faded ghostly image of member number 113728 on the rear. We are hardened zoo attenders. Today, though, is a focused trip, no meandering through the African plains, no noses pressed against cold glass trying to spot the grey wolves. We march straight into the reptile house, a low building with a central corridor on either side of which are the confined spaces where the reptiles gaze out at us. Here is the chameleon turning gold in the ambery light that is shining on him. And then we find what my daughter is looking for, the two coiled pythons splayed harmlessly on stone shelves, unmoving. Does our scent reach their tongues through the glass? We imagine their loosely hinged jawbones at full stretch over a rabbit or a sheep, but here in the flesh they are less frightening than the images we have seen on the computer, and which have driven us here in the first place. They are like still photographs of themselves, a long way through the glass. No intensity of our gazing will stir them to movement.

The reptile house is a monument to stillness. There are few visitors, and everyone is quiet with that half reverential, half skittish museum or church quiet, except for one giggling couple who seem to be besotted by the spectacle of their own visit to the zoo, as if the reptiles in their Sunday quiet were some outlandish, ironic outpost of themselves. Beside the pythons two greyish Nile crocodiles gaze out through us with dull eyes, utterly motionless, one with his mouth gaping open, as if he thought the glass might shatter and one of us fall in. Can he be real? He looks exactly like a stuffed model of a crocodile, his mouth waiting to snap on prey that will never come. It seems impossible that either of them could be alive. They are in a state of suspension, as if we had taken a wrong turning and stumbled into the Dead Zoo. In the next booth the monitor lizard lies on a branch, from which he is barely distinguishable. We study the information panel and watch one of the largest lizards in the world take his Sunday leisure. An absurd image comes into my mind, of Sunday expeditions to seaside carparks, lines of cars with newspapers spread out against the steering wheels, with occasional glances out across the grey expanse of the Irish Sea. The same feeling of the world deferred, its breath held, waiting for the next phase to kick in. On the other side one tortoise has climbed onto the back of another. Are they mating? Whatever it is, there is no hurry.

Beside the tortoises there is some swift purposeful movement, the turtles swimming in their small pond. They swim with an urgency absent from everywhere else, and we stand there a long time, watching them, glad that they seem to have worked out how to live animatedly in their tiny world. We turn to go, but there is one more task to perform. Near the entrance is a measuring board with a series of upright snakes and a crocodile. We each take turns to record our height, then, with a last glance at the reptile house, we leave.

The cold drives us from house to house. From the reptiles to Roberts House, named for the field marshal who was president of the society at the time it was built. As you approach this building with its elaborate decorative brick, its whiff of empire, you feel you have arrived in the heart of the old Victorian zoo. You expect to meet the old Council members in their beards and frock coats, their Gladstone bags full of accounts and breeding results and petitions to London for the loan of an elephant. The house was originally built to house lions and other carnivores, and I wonder idly if it was here that Cairbre, who roared his way to glory as the MGM lion, was born. There were other famous lions, of course, the Belgian lion Albert, for instance, who killed the popular lioness Flame not long after he arrived from Antwerp Zoo in 1951. The Zoo, presumably feeling that he had outstayed his welcome, gave him to the famous Dublin lion-tamer Bill Stephens, who named him Pasha — a definite improvement on Albert — but circus life seems to have appealed to him even less than life in the Park, and he mauled the lion-tamer to death in the Fossett's Circus winter quarters at Dunsaughley Farm, north of Dublin, in January, 1953. The event was actually witnessed by the Superintendent of the Zoo, C S Webb, who had brought some American friends to observe Stephens put three lions, Finn, Pasha and Sultan, through their paces. There was clearly a relationship between the zoo and circuses that allowed it to dispose of troublesome or surplus animals, but it seems astonishing that an aggressive animal with a track record of killing should have been released to a lion-tamer as a titillating public spectacle. Stephens entered the cage and somehow slipped, at which point Pasha attacked him. Webb raced to the cage, grabbed a pole and managed to beat the lion off and haul Stephens out, but the badly mauled lion-tamer was dead before he reached Richmond Hospital.

All the common elements of tragedy are there, the unwonted accident, the habitual precautions for once not taken. Stephens usually called one of the three Fossett brothers to stand close by and watch him, but on this day he hadn't done so. If one of his lions hadn't escaped in Finglas a couple of months earlier he wouldn't have been ordered to remove his animals beyond the city boundary and so wouldn't have been in the Fossetts' winter quarters. The plan had been to go on tour with the Fossetts when the season opened at Easter, with the largest pride of lions in Ireland. He was only thirty, but it wasn't the first time he had been mauled, or that someone else had been mauled by one of his lions. The previous November his lioness, Zalika, had escaped from her compound in Fairview and mauled a garage attendant. She wandered around Fairview for half an hour or so, pursued by the police who eventually caught and shot her. A few months after that Stephens had been mauled during a show in the Olympia, and again in Limerick.

The other two lions had remained quiet in the cage during the attack, though one of them was the same lion that escaped in Finglas and killed three pigs, so causing the exile to the farm. And Albert-Pasha, what happened him? A trawl through the *Irish Times* archive revealed that he was shot, at the request of the lion-tamer's widow. The execution was carried out in the yard of the police station in Finglas. It is always these details that stay, little independent republics seceded from the main narrative. The lion wandering around Fairview, the lion attacking pigs in Finglas, the lion in the yard in a police station in Finglas as the guns are loaded, the last lines in the *Irish Times* account of the mauling to death of Bill Stephens which report that 'Mrs Stephens, who had met her husband while he was in the Royal Air Force in India, spent the night with friends'(*IT*, 28 January, 1953), almost as if, that awful night passed, she might wake up and walk out to somehow resume a life uninterrupted by tragedy.

Easier to engage with, though bleak too in its way, is the fate of the lioness, Old Girl, who lived to the considerable age of fifteen. Old Girl, or Henrietta as she used to be known, had a record-breaking fifty-five cubs in thirteen litters over a period of twelve years. Among the first lions to be bred in the Zoo, she was born in 1859, but at the end of her days she lay feeble and diseased in her cage, troubled by the rats which crept through the bars at night and took lumps out of her. Someone had the clever idea of putting a small terrier into the cage to keep Old Girl company and put the rats to flight. The unlikely symbiotic companionship of the terrier and the lioness is a comforting, Disneyesque image. It's a bit like the scene in the Charlie Chaplin film when the tramp ends up in the cage beside the sleeping lion, and a skinny, busybody terrier comes racing up to yap furiously, as if to warn the lion of the intrusion. Still, if all you have to look forward to in life is a yappy terrier and a rat-free death, you might be forgiven for feeling shortchanged. In a little building at the back of Roberts House they keep the skins of dead lions and tigers, and one noble looking but mangy, stuffed lioness, beside which is a sign, cheerfully ignored by every child, that reads FRAGILE DO NOT TOUCH. It looks old enough to be Old Girl. Again, it feels like a slightly Victorian Dead Zoo-ish encounter in a half-forgotten, unreconstructed part of the Zoo.

The ghosts of lions may haunt the building, but we've come for the fruit bats and the birds which now live here. We look up at the soft leathery folds of the bats as they cling to the top of their cage. These bats are known as flying foxes, from their size and foxlike faces, and there aren't very many of them left in the world. If you close your eyes you can hear the folds and flittings above. When you look up it's the size that impresses, these heavy leather sacks with their foxy heads sticking out of the bottom, suspended in the gloomy light of the building. Through the door is the best part of the house, an outside-inside space, full of trees and greenery and free-flying birds and bats. We stand and look and listen. Is that a Great Hornbill perched on a branch? And here's a clutch of bluish pigeons just over the fence. There's an intimacy about this space that isn't replicated anywhere else. I remember that in the street around the corner from where I lived there was a house whose owner had built a makeshift extension onto the side of his house and filled it with a jungle greenery for his small monkey. I often glimpsed the monkey as I passed, gently swinging on the trees or just perched silently, looking out at the road. I think it was the space itself that fascinated me, more than the monkey — that undecided transition between indoors and outdoors exactly as here now in this old house, like a memory of old possibilities before the shutters came down on the cave and the curtains went up.

As we shuffle from building to building on this freezing January day we pass shivering family groups. A brisk father rattles out a series of orders to his two young boys and produces a packet of sandwiches. A harried mother runs after an escaping toddler. I don't know if there are statistical surveys on zoo attendance, but if there are, I'd guess the largest slice of the pie chart would be occupied by parents and children. I can't think of a single friend without children or whose children have grown up who has been to the Zoo in the last several years. How often did I come here myself before I was a parent? I was brought here as a child, I came here on occasional trips alone or with a girlfriend, partly out of obscure desire to see animals and partly to connect with those previous childhood visits, partly in that zone of erotic fervour that needs elaborate theatres of irony to parade itself in. The children here today seem poised between mild interest and boredom. Most of the kiosks are closed, and many are complaining loudly, ice-cream and sweets being a primary accompaniment to the viewing of animals. At least none of them is wreaking the kind of havoc I read about the other day, perpetrated by a seven-year-old in the Reptile Centre in Alice Springs who almost managed singlehandedly to destroy the place. He broke into the centre, picked up a number of small beasts and fed them to Terry, the three-metre-long saltwater crocodile. By the end of his rampage he had disposed of a turtle, four lizards, two bearded dragons, two thorny devil lizards and a Spencer's goanna, and the video cameras show him smiling delightedly through the whole enterprise.

We end our brief winter expedition in Haughton House, now a learning centre with video booth and a central exhibition, the altar of the temple, of the huge skeleton of an elephant with, beside it, the skeleton of a human for scale. This is what the dead look like, and this is what we look like under our skins, I tell my daughter, who likes the bones, and likes even more the exhibition which shows how much an elephant eats in one day and, in the brightly lit section underneath this, how much shit a single day will produce. The massive turds lie convincingly behind the glass, a solid incontrovertible weight. The final exhibits are arranged for our touch. PLEASE TOUCH THE EXHIBITS, the sign tells us, and we run our fingers along the treasure, exploring a mammoth's tooth, a tusk, and the great foot of an elephant. I think this might be all that's left of Sita, who stamped on her keeper in 1913 as he nursed her injured foot, perhaps this very one. He died instantly and the RIC, in another unfortunate incident in the relationship between the constabulary and wayward animals, were summoned to shoot Sita. The foot was kept for years in this house, so I suspect it may have been dusted off to assume its place in this little theatre of touch, proof of itself.

I'm surprised, in one sense, at how rare these incidents are. No matter how humane, well organized or spacious a zoo is, to a bird, animal or reptile it offers limitation, sameness, a treadmill of predictability. You're not surprised to hear about the disturbed polar bears, the monkeys, elephants or tigers locked in repetitive or depressive behavioural patterns. They pay a heavy price for our need to witness them, our need for evidence, proof of the worlds beyond our experience. I wonder if my daughter is better off for having seen the motionless pythons or crocodiles. She is greatly excited by whales, though she has never seen one. Her greatest moments of excitement here are the toys in the souvenir shop and the hot chocolate in the Meerkat Restaurant. Wolves are off the radar, unless I tell her again tonight the one about the wolves which jumped the keepers, took their uniforms and sauntered out of the zoo and down the long avenue into the city, where they took a taxi to a certain house ... Rhinoceroses aren't bad, but not half as interesting as the playground beside them. As for me, I love the Park, and the fact that the Zoo is in the Park makes me fond of it too. And I love the old buildings, the sense of all that solid Victorian endeavour. And more than all of that I love our going there, the little family expedition that, today, lightens a wintry Sunday. This is how parks, zoos, all urban amenities work; they offer you, ultimately, yourself. As we walk back to the car I put my finger in my mouth, touching a molar, remembering the mammoth tooth, running a finger along the afternoon as a small proof of the weight of our own lives.

# The Pleasure of Small Streets

The drawings show, in great detail, the junction of Gold-smith Street and Geraldine Street. They are architectural drawings, designed to pull us in to observe the specific details of the chosen scene. In the first we see a recessed doorway with a generous fanlight and the brickwork of the narrow porch ranged fan-like on the arch. There is a narrow garden outside and spiked, wrought-iron railings in front. Across the junction a row of similar red-bricked houses continues, a terrace made up of symmetrical pairs of houses, each with its elaborate door and single large front window. The houses are low, with a double pitched roof like two pleats of an accordion, each with its own chimney stack. The spiked railings continue around the end terrace, enclos-ing an area no more than a step wide. If you jumped up in the air a little you could see over the roof, or at least it feels like that. The tower of St Joseph's Church on Berkeley Road with its four turrets completes the view of the terrace. The second drawing foregrounds the end of a terrace, drawing the eye to decorative white bricks on the corner and the eaves-cornice that gives a clean finish to the façade. Around the corner we can see how the arch of the porch is defined by light-coloured bricks at its edges and centre, and the vertical splay of bricks above the parlour window. The houses were built between 1830 and 1860, and they are so typical of a certain kind of Dublin city street that they often go unnoticed. Yet here they are, these streets I know well from lunchtime strolls when I worked in the area, drawn twenty-five years ago, occupying pride of place in a special supplement on the city published by *The Architectural Review* in 1974.

The drawings are by Kenneth Browne, artist, architect and townscape editor of the *Review* who co-wrote the supplement with Lance Wright.[1] Why did Browne choose these streets? They were, apparently, chosen 'almost at random among hundreds of possible alternatives' to show 'the nineteenth century Dublin builder's racy adaptation on the idiom of the century before' and 'the skill of today's Dublin householder in picking out and colouring up the telling architectural detail'. The writers also comment that 'To walk among these little streets is one of the world's classic architectural pleasures.' It's an architectural pleasure because there's a certain formal coherence in this small group of streets that forms an island between the Great Western Way and the North Circular Road — Fontenoy Street, Auburn Street, Primrose Avenue, Geraldine Street, Goldsmith Street and O'Connell Avenue; the streets relate to each other meaningfully, and their aspect and details are pleasing to the eye.

There is too the human scale of streets and buildings like this which are far from the designed-for-show elegance of the visitors' city. If they take their stylistic cues from the earlier century they scale it down to a level where the less than lordly can enjoy it. It may be architecturally fascinating

to observe these features, but you don't have to be an architect to enjoy these things — they're part of the everyday
experience of living in a city. You walk through a residential
area you don't live in and have no particular business to be
in either because you're on your way somewhere else or
because you have chosen to enjoy a part of the city for its
own sake. You want to enjoy the particular urban mood that
the combination of light and soft red brick conjures up; you
enjoy the details, the workmanship, the sense of continuity
that comes from old buildings and streets that have been laid
out and undisturbed for generations. You enjoy the quiet of
places out of the clamour of the city. Part of the point of a
city is to cater for the spontaneous strolling pleasure of its
citizens. Dublin offers many streets like this, a quick walk
from busy thoroughfares, relatively unregarded or unvisited
spots.

It's also true that certain eras get all the attention. In
Dublin the period spanning the late eighteenth century and
the first decades of the nineteenth century is the undoubted
cock of the walk. The grander Victorian suburbs get their
share of attention too, but streets like these rarely figure on
the aesthetic map. Maybe it's just as well I think as I walk
down the equivalent of those streets in my own neighbourhood: Raymond Street, St Alban's Road, Greenville Terrace,
Washington Street. These were built later than the Phibsboro
streets — in the 1870s — but the idiom is exactly the same:
impressive doors with scaled down but still elaborate doorcases and fanlights, and the one window on the front lights
the tallest and grandest room, the parlour, which, when they
were originally built, would have been where all the social
aspirations were concentrated. Each house has a tiny area
in front marked off with wrought-iron railings. The area
enclosed is so small you might think it is hardly worth distinguishing the frontage from the pavement. But the point
of having the small area in front is to have beautiful railings
around it; it is part of the theatre of entrance and a way of
subtly differentiating each house from its neighbour. And,

although the houses seem to be the same, the closer you get to them the more you begin to notice the differences, the more each house quietly asserts its own distinctiveness.

Sometimes the house type changes, so that a large basement appears below the railing; often it's the smaller details that change. These are long streets — long, narrow and lined with trees, giving them a tunnel effect — and would have been built by different developers. But they would have used the same builders, the same craftsmen, and the templates were so well established that it would have been unthinkable not to work with them. Walking the street, observing the decorative brickwork above windows and doors, and the subtly different decorative touches, you begin to develop an affection for those craftsmen. Maybe this has to do partly with the fact that so much modern housing is built on replication, without difference or distinguishing feature, without any real streets or sense of a city as a series of coherent spatial relationships. All around this area, and in many other areas, in houses of this era, even the tiniest cottages have a richness of detail unimaginable in most modern builds; they are meant to be looked at and enjoyed. The artisans and craftsmen were working together in a public form; they had, you feel, a clear vision of the city as a meaningful space. And this is why, walking here, I feel a proprietorial warmth, as if all these bricks, fanlights, doors, windows and railings are intended for me as much as for their owners. This is another way of considering the success of a city: how much of it can be said to belong to all of its citizens — not just parks and public spaces, but the public aspect of the private dwellings where its people actually live. For much of the time we are conditioned by economic circumstance or a certain kind of obsessiveness to think of the city as 'property'; to only truly pay attention to a house when it is for sale. We are exposed to housing as a commodity in which we may or may not have a vested interest; we're encouraged to think in terms of the single valuable commodity rather than the townscape or cityscape it occupies. Our interest begins when the front door opens, and the street is simply where we park our cars. Privacy like this is where cities are lost.

⌣

I go back to Kenneth Browne and Lance Wright's view of Dublin in 1974. There's a specific context for their concern with Dublin: a sense of the exhaustion of 'the modern city' with its 'tall buildings clustered in the middle, fast roads leading up to them, the segregation of uses by "zoning", the dispersal of the community into one-class suburbs'. They call for a changed vision of urban possibility and they choose Dublin 'because she retains more of the earlier city pattern than any other metropolis'. They come to Dublin with a certain urgency since the city seemed at the time to be wilfully indulging in its own destruction. The city, at this point, seems to them to be at a critical point in its history, where it can opt to restore urban fabric and urban community and 'become the first truly modern city, fashioned on all that is best in Western experience' or, like Liverpool or Birmingham, 'reshape herself on the image which reflects the tycoon, over-centralized government — and the motor car'.

The subsequent and ongoing development of Dublin still struggles between those two extremes — the greater Dublin area expanded by over a quarter of a million people, most of whom live in the commuter belt of Meath, Fingal and Kildare — but it's fascinating to see how the city appeared to these writers nearly fifty years ago to embody the battle-ground between two opposed urban ideologies, one of which seemed to have the whole massed and irresistible force of modernity behind it. The disfigured Dublin that was evident in the seventies would fare even worse in the decade ahead, before its fortunes began to improve some-what in the nineties, and yet the final motive they give for their choice of the city was its persistent beauty which made it 'at once the most personal and the most surprising metropolis in Europe'. And, interestingly, they locate that beauty not only in the classical elegance of the eighteenth- and nineteenth-century legacy but 'in the Dubliner's own, continuing visual gift'. The aesthetic heart of this perception is in the nineteenth-century city, when the visual knowledge gained in the previous century was retained and deployed to good effect. Modest terraces of houses are prized because of the way in which they work together — seen as something typical of the Dublin 'visual sense':

> *time and again you find groups of [buildings] which, taken one by one, have no special claim to architectural quality but which, when taken together, produce an effect which is just right.*[2]

This is another definition of the ideal city: a place where, as far as the physical fabric is concerned, the different elements work together, where the visible city operates harmoniously. Yet attempting to describe a city can be fraught with difficulty. If this were a walk in the hills I might pause here to admire the shape of an ash or the smell of the bracken or listen to a wren or chaffinch and set it all down naturally in a language familiar and comfortable to anyone who might read it. The city, though, is always half imagined, and a great deal of its soul resists articulation. You can talk about buildings, you can say things like 'the stucco projects in front of the wall face and a cable-mould is added to it, the consoles are more deeply cut and are festooned with swags', but this is the language of the specialist, even the impassioned specialist, and our minds may not digest or retain or engage emotionally with the information. This is partly because we are not ever trained to experience the city; we don't have a tradition of careful and impassioned observation. Culturally, our sense of place is of rural places. The city, inevitably, eludes us.

The beauty of Kenneth Browne and Lance Wright's writing and photographs is the way they alert us to the familiar and encourage us to develop our own habits of noticing and maybe our own language to express it. To look at streets like Auburn Street in Phibsboro or St Alban's Road off the South Circular Road with their freshness and excitement is to recover something we might only have subliminally possessed. And it isn't simply about an architectural flourish or style — it's the sense of human pride and interconnectedness that gave rise to these streetscapes, a vision of the city as a series of small-scale interactions. All those Victorian builders and craftsmen draw us back, if we let them, to their quiet celebration of individual distinction and collective coherence and invite us to enjoy the city with their eyes: 'they offer a manifestation of a "popular" conception of architecture'. Popular architecture here means the dispersal of good architectural principles and visual elegance across a whole spectrum of workmanship. We don't quite know who did what in the hundreds of small Victorian streets around the city — there's no single voice that can be isolated in the chorus of craft. Trying to attribute the achievement is 'an art historian's nightmare':

> *Was it an architect? Or a builder? An architect copying a builder? Or a builder copying an architect? Or a householder thinking something up on his own and getting a blacksmith down the road to make it for him?*[3]

Whoever they were they probably didn't anticipate the extent to which market values would remove these houses from the reach of the kind of people who would originally have lived in them, or who were living in them at the time Kenneth Browne and Lance Wright were writing about them. The 1911 census shows the occupations of the residents of Geraldine Street as follows: two milliners, two tailoresses, a cooper, four seamstresses, two motor mechanics, a shirt maker, a slater, a pantry maid, a post office worker, two insurance agents, two draperesses, three cattle dealers, a horse dealer, three drapers, a typist, a van driver, three commercial travellers, four brass finishers, a furniture dealer, a chemist, an assistant chemist, ten dressmakers, a laundry packer, a sculptor, a charwoman, a stonemason, a cook, ten carpenters, a carpenter's apprentice, eighteen clerks, a cabinet-maker, a medical student, a draper's assistant, two nurses, an agricultural student, a bookkeeper, a distillery labourer, a telegraphist, a detective sergeant, three railway checkers, four general labourers, a police constable, two waiters, three brewers' labourers, three school teachers, a corset maker, a collar maker, a postman, a printer, a cycle mechanic, a hotel porter, an Irish lace examiner, a gardener, a confectioner, a brush maker, two messengers, three shop assistants and a Dublin Corporation inspector.

These were the houses of trades and crafts people, the solidly employed — only one person is listed as out of work. They could well have built the street as well as supplied most of the furnishings and a large proportion of them must have been direct inheritors of the visual knowledge that enriched the physical fabric of the city.

Market forces can cause a 'popular' architecture all too soon to lose contact with the generality of the populace. Still, though, we can at least hang on to the democratic vision of the art historian's nightmare; we can enjoy the streets into which so many skills have flowed, a river of energy and purpose, and try to incorporate their modest pleasures into our own sense of what a city should mean.

# Soul Rooms

The first time I came across Gaston Bachelard was in Thomas McCarthy's 1982 collection of poems, *The Sorrow Garden*. 'Bachelard's Images' and 'Professor Bachelard' mined images from Bachelard's pioneering works on the imagination, on childhood, reverie, and the magical spaces of houses:

> *Weary with physics he took the awkward*
> *road, the flooded pebble-lane to childhood*
> *where archetypes broke the backs of graphs*
> *and instruments couldn't gauge one's mood.*
> — Thomas McCarthy, 'Professor Bachelard'

Not long after, I got my hands on *The Poetics of Space*, first published in 1958 in French. Bachelard started off his working life as a postman and became a professor of natural sciences before turning to philosophy and eventually becoming a professor of philosophy at the Sorbonne. *The Poetics of Space* is one of those rare books that, once read, never entirely leaves you but keeps drawing you irresistibly back into its world. It's a hard book to describe because one of its joys is that it defies categorization. Poetry, philosophy, psychoanalysis, observation, memory all rub shoulders: the book is really an investigation of the soul by means of a grand tour of the interior landscapes of the imagination, with chapters on drawers, chests and wardrobes; the significance of the hut; nests, shells, corners. It would be hard to think of another writer who so intensely inhabits inner spaces and how they operate on the imagination. Childhood plays a large part in this since it is the child who is most aware and engaged with the spaces of home, and also because childhood, poetry, memory and solitude are all part of the same imaginative continuum. For a child the house is a dreamscape: 'The house we were born in is more than an embodiment of home, it is also an embodiment of dreams. Each one of its nooks and corners was a resting place for daydreaming . . .'

The book itself is a kind of poem; its mix of dense materiality and spiritual generosity reminds me of Francis Ponge, the great poet of things and 'thingness'. We think of Irish writing as preoccupied with place, with its tradition of *dinnseanchas* and the lore of placenames in Irish, but Bachelard offers us the lore of the micro-place, the primal shelter. He describes himself as 'a psychologist of houses', and I think the book helped me understand my own obsession with interior places, and with buildings and gardens both real and imagined. Some of it has to do with getting back to the perceptual state of the child. Childhood, Bachelard reminds us, 'is certainly greater than reality . . . It is on the plane of the daydreams and not that of facts that childhood remains alive and poetically useful within us'. He also saw the lure of the house as a search for stability. 'A house constitutes a body of images that give mankind proofs or illusions of stability. We are constantly re-imagining its reality: to distinguish all these images would be to describe the soul of the house; it would mean developing a veritable psychology of the house' (translated by Maria Jolas).

The intimate world Bachelard describes is to an extent pre-social, the world of solitary engagement or reflection. The minute you step into a street you enter the social world of the city, your footsteps join with those of the other walkers; you take your place in the living stream of the city. We have a different kind of relationship with the spaces where our family life takes place, or where we're on our own. If I think of the rooms that have left the biggest impression on me they are invariably solitary. I think of the attic in Victoria

Road where I spent endless hours reading or playing, surrounded by assorted junk: an electric clothes dryer, parts of
beds, abandoned cupboards, two tea chests from Rangoon,
the desk I sat at, forgotten toys. None of these was important, it was more the simple fact that the attic was the last
place in the house, the farthest from the control centres of
kitchen and living room, and that no one but I ever went
there. That, and the silence, the liberation that came from
the prospect of limitless uninterruption.

The room I usually work in is a little like that. Set back
slightly from the main activities of the house in an extension, it's tiny, and an appalling mess, crammed with books
both on shelves and in every available position on the desk,
on the floor, on the windowsills. Papers, memorabilia, a guitar, my daughter's paintings, discarded cables and key-
boards, and the two computers. It's like entering the cockpit
of a plane, uncomfortable and unmanageable until you sit
down. And then the mind can begin to find itself, the apparent chaos finds its order, and the work can start. I might
sometimes take flight as far as the kitchen table, removing
my mind from its habitual clutter, but nothing much ever
happens in the clean, well-lighted space of the kitchen. Some
routine administration, maybe, the occasional letter, but
anything creative reserves itself for the cramped hut-like
space of the workroom. Cramped-ness, mess, disorder seem
to be triggers, and I am very happy to spend long hours in
their embrace.

We carry rooms around with us, those that we currently
enjoy, but also rooms long since abandoned, that somehow
refuse to dissolve. One sloughed-off self is still pottering
around a dishevelled room in Merrion Square, headquarters
of the weekly newspaper for which I am labouring. I have
the room to myself mainly because the paper is so short-
staffed that almost all of the content comes in from free-
lancers. I remember almost nothing of the work I did, not
least because I wasn't much good at it, but the room itself is
still printed firmly on my mind. It was utterly bare, every

vestige of its former life, if there had been one, stripped from the walls and floors. Our occupancy of this middle floor of a dilapidated Georgian mansion was theatrically provisional, as if the enterprise was a prank, or an idea born during a long night's drinking given an impulsive but doomed reality. Every possible expense had been spared, from journalists' fees to typewriter paper. The paper we were granted came in giant rolls, enough to last for a year, and you simply ripped off the finished article from the roll when you were finished and handed it to the sub next door. The floor had a slight incline, so that the heavy roll tended to drift across the floor as I typed. To come back into the office and see the roll of paper resting against the wall on one side of the room feeding the typewriter on the other side used to fill me with gloom, an emblem of the Sisyphean production that lay ahead. We were a weekly paper and we went to bed on a Thursday evening, hoping that nothing too newsworthy happened between Thursday and Sunday, when we hit the stands. The tension in the building racked up as the working week continued. By Wednesday editorial outbursts about fuckers who didn't know the meaning of the word deadline began to fill the air. The horse racing correspondent performed his weekly ritual of locking himself in the toilet while the editor banged on the door outside, berating him. 'A few fucking races, that's all you have to do, and you can't fucking do it!' I cowered in my high-ceilinged room like a relic from a previous century, hoping nobody would notice I was still in the building.

The room had one other feature that was an actual relic of the past, an ancient telephone attached to an old cable that looked like braided cord, like a prop from a nineteen thirties film, the kind of instrument that Philip Marlowe might have on his desk or that some elderly mandarin of the Foreign Office might be barking orders into. It lay in a corner of the room, discarded, forgotten but bizarrely, still functioning. No bill ever arrived, no one in the Department of Posts and Telegraphs was aware of the line's existence, yet when lifted,

Peter Sirr

the headset produced a faint ringing tone, as if from under
water, or from some electronic past that had not yet entirely
faded. Late in the evening when the offices were unoccupied
by anyone else I would lift the handset and dial my girlfriend in her town in the north of Holland. We could barely
hear each other, and I don't remember a single word of anything either of us said, but the room, the phone, the shakiness
of our voices are all still there. Years later a sudden unexpected
phone call prompted the following poem:

Conversation

*I put down the phone
and the years go by.
Twenty years later your voice
is unchanged, as if
as we paused to catch our breath
or press the receiver closer
our bodies lurched from us
and half our lives
fell through the conversation*

*or we go back and forth
and now as you speak again
I'm sitting on the floor
in an empty office in Merrion Square
clutching an antique phone.
Daily I abandon the typewriter
and the continuous paper
and leave the world on the table*

*to sneak a call through the crackle
as if we stood on ships in wind
and swayed: our two cities swaying
with small news. My copy's due
my roll of continuous paper
has rolled to the other side of the room*

*and now, much later, years later*
*now that the paper's gone*
*and the line shut down*

*somehow the conversation continues*
*somehow we lie in swaying water*
*and never alter, somehow the line holds*
*and the years stretch, snap back*
*and we fall out, come to, send*
*our signals out, always*
*finished, unfinished, always*
*plugged in to a ghostly exchange.*[1]

# Shirts for Books

I stopped in Clare Street and stared. Surely? But of course it wasn't there, Greene's bookshop had vanished, even if there was still a corner of my brain that expected to see the green painted book barrows under the awning on the street outside the shop as I crossed over from Merrion Square. Instead, I found myself looking at expensive shirts: the lilac button cuff, the blue Cadogan, the Cavendish light blue stripe. Greene's was now Henry Jermyn, the London shirtmakers and court tailors, business shirts made from one hundred thread count Egyptian cotton, ties brought from raw silk to finished product in Como, Italy. Inside, where the books and post office used to be, you could see the neat shelves of business shirts. I found myself reluctant to accept the visible evidence of the new life of this shop. I could still see the bookshop so clearly in my mind's eye that the shirts kept receding to reveal the slightly chaotic downstairs section, with its small selection of new books and a queue in front of the post-office window and, in September, queues of harassed parents with their long lists of school books. There were no queues today, no fervent shirt buyers scanning the shelves. The death of a bookshop always hits hard. There are never that many of them to begin with and they are rarely replaced, so that one more opportunity to idle among familiar shelves disappears. I can't remember how many hours I spent in Greene's but I hardly ever passed it without going in. It was not a great bookshop in its last years, but the second-hand section upstairs always demanded to be rummaged through, just in case you missed something the last time or a few new books had come through. Maybe someone had died and their relatives had sold off the library; there might be a clutch of poetry or French novels of the 1930s or a dictionary of agricultural terms or an account of medieval travelogues you had to climb the ladder to pull down. Regular bookshops push their predictable lines of new titles by the currently favoured, but the real joy is the second-hand shop because, dingy and dull though their stock might often be, their true offering is surprise, the random encounter with a book placed there, you imagine, by some serendipitous god exactly so you should find it. These are where the unsought, life-changing books are stored, the books you would never have thought to search out. A book collecting friend was always finding treasures here, which was not always welcome news, but he committed more time to it and was, I suppose, entitled to his rewards. Even bookshops reward productivity. I was more usually than not disappointed but this didn't matter. The place itself was surprising enough. The massed paperbacks on the walls as you climbed the stairs, those three upper rooms stacked floor to ceiling. One of them was used by staff to parcel up books and send them out to customers. It all looked very Victorian, the big brown table, the rolls of brown paper, the patient labour. In that way of second-hand bookshops a large part of the point was atmosphere. What kind of books were they sending out? Who were the customers? Someone somewhere was waiting with interest for a brown parcel secured with twine and Sellotape. Before the internet I don't think I ever received a parcel of books. It seemed to belong to another era, when one wrote to one's bookseller with a list of titles and settled up at the end of the month. Now the postman brings me regular jiffy bags with ex Californian library editions of poetry, books from all over the world that I have, often rashly, bought after a bout of browsing when I should have been doing something more profitable.

Greene's, though, was more than a bookshop. It was a kind of cultural icon or beacon flashing dependably year after year near the end of Clare Street, an unmistakable part of the city. It had been there, after all, since 1843, and the Pembreys had run the business since 1912 when they first took it over. Now it operates as an online bookseller from an industrial estate on the southern edge of the city, so the business is still intact, dealing mainly in school and library supplies. Henry Jermyn sells online too, 60% off all shirts and blazers, yet I found myself rooted to the pavement trying to wish all these shirts away and coax back the shelves of dusty books from their sterile suburban storage. I feel a strong urge to go upstairs and have one more rummage. No cheap shirts in a barrow outside entice me in to the new shop. Shirts for books, it doesn't seem like a fair exchange. I think briefly of the other bookshops lost to the city. Fred Hanna's up the road in Nassau Street, the APCK in Suffolk Street, the Eblana in Grafton Street where I used to come as a schoolboy on Saturday mornings to worship at its altar of poetry titles. Parson's by the canal, of course, but now we enter the era of genuine nostalgia and literary history, 'where one met as many interesting writers on the floor of the shop as on the shelves' as Mary Lavin once put it. Not an entirely public space, there at the centre of bohemian Baggotonia, Seamus Heaney felt: 'Something told you that this was a slightly privileged zone . . . You were welcome but you were there to behave yourself. And the books for sale gave the same sort of message: they weren't exactly neutral products, but bore the stamp of Kingly and Flahertish approval.' There's a book about it, from which this information is taken, *Parsons Bookshop: At the Heart of Bohemian Dublin 1949-1989* by Brendan Lynch. I have only a single memory of it, having marched up Baggot Street and over the canal to inspect it towards the end of the era. I didn't encounter anyone, but sniffed for the ghosts of Kavanagh and Behan, had a quick scan of the shelves and sloped out self-consciously. The space was too small to hide in. There's an optimum size for a bookshop, I think, and below a certain square footage browsing starts to feel like intrusion. There's also, probably, a minimum number of bookshops, and especially second-hand bookshops, for a city, and Dublin has long since slipped below the crisis line. Where are all the browsers gone? Maybe they are at home trawling through Amazon or Abebooks; or maybe they've read enough and have settled down to watch their boxed sets.

The city still has plenty of bookshops but many are part of chains, and most stick to a safely commercial stock. They are retail outlets where the products happen to be books. Or there are antiquarian shops where books are slipped into plastic covers and converted into outlandishly expensive fetish objects. On the other hand, there is the civilized refuge of Books Upstairs which has journeyed from South King Street (the original 'upstairs') to George's Arcade to College Green and currently resides in D'Olier Street, or the Secret Book and Record Store in Wicklow Street, at the end of a narrow passageway past a doctor's surgery. Not that long ago the bookshop part took cash, but if you wanted to use a card you had to take your docket to the record shop man at the other end who appeared from his stacks of vinyl to apply the technology. Now we're getting somewhere, must and old books and half-forgotten music and a complex retail experience. A portal through which you can leave the city and the fixed trajectories of your life. This is something else which the shirts will never replace. Bookshops are mental spaces, they are places for thinking and dreaming; the best of them have an atmosphere that makes them seem like the outward embodiment of the inner life. The physical proportions, the disposition of the shelves and the smell of old books all seem like extensions of the imaginative life; they leave an impression that can be entered and re-entered long after you have left. They are part of what Susan Sontag in her introduction to *One Way Street* calls 'the geography of pleasure'. She was writing about Walter Benjamin who was a devoted collector of books whose books were also portals into the rooms, in Berlin, Naples, Danzig, Munich, Moscow, where they had been bought. 'Book-hunting, like the sexual hunt, adds to the geography of pleasure — another reason for strolling about in the world.' No one will hold a shirt in his hand and fall into a reverie about the shop it was bought in or will idle away hours in a department store browsing the socks and trousers. A wardrobe is not a library, no matter how well stocked. Bookshops are like parks or museums, spaces where public and private collide, where the inner and outer worlds become porous — to use a Benjamin term — and admit each other. And both are hospitable to the solitary wanderer; they are constructed to serve solitude. At one point in my life I used to fantasize about running a bookshop, reading books about it, gathering all of the technical information, thinking about stock management and computer systems. All of that was far too real, it was about retail, whereas what I wanted was a kind of private city, or an officially sanctioned privacy. So impractical was the impulse that I'm sure, had anything actually come of it, my wish would have been granted. It would have been a perfect licence for idle reverie. It is, though, one of the reasons I am jealously attached to the freedom of bookshops and why they are the first port of call in any city I visit. And it's why I am standing outside here now, trying to suck the shirts out of their bubble on Clare Street, lost now to all but the serious buyers of serious shirts.

The only problem is that most good second-hand bookshop dealers know their stock only too well; there may well be surprises, but few enough bargains. The ideal, I thought, as I looked through the window of Henry Jermyn, would be a bookshop operated by a shirtmaker. The shop didn't last too long, as it turned out. It went into voluntary liquidation in 2017 and is now a plant shop. The god of bookshops is up there somewhere waving a cautionary finger . . .

152

# 'Suddenly songs come upon us'

In the middle of the square is a Victorian railed park. What is it about these places? They have a peculiar magnetic pull, as if some part of their design contained an alchemical potion to sweep the observer into an irresistible nostalgia for an imagined past. Their genteel confinement, maybe, their neat parades of trees and grass, their gravelled paths hint at something barely contained, a serious Victorian passion. Something, some kind of ghostly echo or memory woken by iron railings and municipal warnings. A murmur of childhood . . .

The park sits at the centre of a grand square of tall red-bricked houses built in the 1880s, the last planned square of the nineteenth century. A place of serious, unthreatened prosperity, then as now. I used to come here a lot on foot or by bicycle, partly to enjoy the square itself, and partly for the park. Later my wife would join me, then my wife and dog, and later still wife, daughter and dog would make occasional visits. But that all stopped when the square was ripped out of its peaceable and prosperous kingdom and yanked into a story of tawdry modernity it could hardly have anticipated. The park, it seemed, didn't belong to the city, but to a descendant of the original owner of the lot and he sold it for a nominal sum to a rural builder who immediately announced his intention to convert it into a car park.

The first act of ownership is the locking of the gates. Private, after all, is private. It is the right of the private citizen to exclude all other citizens from his or her property, and nothing in Ireland is more sacred than property. And so it happens that the residents look out their tall windows one autumn morning to see the gates unlocked and a sign offering cheap all day car parking to the city's commuters. Quickly, some of them rush down to block the gates and shortly afterwards an embarrassed council, having somehow managed to lose a park, gets an injunction from the High Court to prevent the new owner from parking more than two cars on the affronted grass.

It is a calculated violation, this intrusion of the car into one of the few spaces in the city where you can expect to escape it; it is a clear gesture at the sensibilities of the residents and, by extension, to all city dwellers, but it is also a triumph of privacy over the public domain and as such it touches our ambivalence about the public, the shared and communal, and many commentators seem to relish the assertion of the ancient rights of the property-holding individual. There is also, sometimes, an assumption that the park really only concerns those who live around it. Why didn't they buy it themselves? some want to know, seeing the thing in terms of competing privacies. It takes me half an hour to walk here, yet I consider this space as much mine as Stephen's Green or Belgrave Square or Palmerston Park. Something of the soul of the city lies in these two acres . . .

It is, of course, a game, as is the gombeen theatre of a 'portable' tile showroom in a caravan, or the tents and generator that follow over the succeeding months. The real aim is to make money, and before long the site is offered for sale for a hundred million euro, or ten thousand times what the new owner paid for it. The story, then, is also a parable of the new Ireland — the Ireland of property developers and inflated values and the right to unlimited profit. To which can be added the whiff of class distaste. The owner is not a large scale billionaire developer, as the prestige of the site might have demanded, but a small scale businessman, a tile salesman. An account in *The Irish Times* at the time shows the extent to which he was affronting solid bourgeois values; it describes him sitting 'in his shabby, red, '97 registered Ford Scorpio' which he 'got for nothing off a friend of mine'. Apart from the horror of a ten-year-old car, he is 'armed with a lunch roll, a bottle of fruit juice and a big, Benny Hill-style grin'. It's hard to know which of these is the most distasteful to the newspaper. Meanwhile 'a large, unsmiling, monosyllabic lieutenant in a blue van is keeping guard on the right'. How many genteel breakfasts were troubled by that blue van?

A second caravan is installed in defiance of a Circuit Court injunction. Meanwhile, since this is an election year, the builder stands for election in the Dublin South East constituency where he gains twenty-seven first preference votes. Further excitement follows: the Circuit Civil Court seizes the assets of the tile company when he disobeys court orders relating to the unauthorized use of the two-acre park. Dublin City Council, meanwhile, rather than expose themselves 'to the possibility of a substantial and financially prohibitive award' back down from the compulsory purchase order and try a different approach, placing a Tree Preservation Order on the park and also including it as part of the designation of Dartmouth Square as an Area of Architectural Conservation. This effectively prevents the builder from doing anything with his property. Eventually a temporary resolution is reached. A resident of the square negotiates with him to maintain and run the park as an amenity for the locality, and the plan is that the park will be open to the public daily, and that events such as children's football tournaments, barbecues, plays and concerts will take place in the coming months. So the park will be returned not just to the residents of the square but to the wider neighbourhood, 'to anyone who can walk or cycle here', says the organizer, which is itself a pretty good definition of a neighbourhood — not a geographical entity but a space that can be negotiated easily on foot or bicycle.

So here I am, on the day that the park will be opened again, riding around the square and observing the silver poles with white flags that announce the return of this space to a temporary, provisional civic status. This afternoon locals and actors, artists and musicians will be here to mark the event. The builder, apparently, hopes the development will lead to artistic and entertaining events taking place in the square, but adds, characteristically: 'My long-term aim is to turn it into a car park that would offer the people of Dublin a secure place to leave their cars for € 5 a day while they go about their business.'

As I look around at the square's grand houses I remember how this used to be the kind of place an average citizen could afford to live in, in rented basement flats or rooms carved out of the original grandeur, and think too of its artistic associations. Luke Kelly, of the Dubliners, lived here, in number 7. Micheál Mac Liammóir and Hilton Edwards were in digs in number 30 before moving on to the Regency opulence of Harcourt Terrace. Paul Durcan was born in number 57, and not far from where I am sitting on my bicycle Michael Hartnett lived in a basement flat with his partner, Angela Liston. I remember the day that the poet Pat Boran and I arrived in a taxi to bring Michael to RTÉ where we were recording a CD of poetry about Dublin. Michael came out speaking enthusiastically about Heine, whom he was translating, and fretting about the glasses he thought he might have left in a pub the previous night. When we got to the studio he couldn't see the poem he was to read — 'Inchicore Haiku', written a decade earlier to mark his return to English after a period of writing exclusively in Irish, as well as his return to living in Dublin:

> *Now, in Inchicore,*
> *my cigarette-smoke rises —*
> *like lonesome pub-talk.*

An edgier Dublin than Dartmouth Square, in the middle of an economic slump, the poet alone, separated from his family, finding a new people to be faithful to. Faced with the prospect of not being able to go through with the recording, Pat took the poem to the photocopier and came back with a greatly magnified version of the poem which Michael managed, with difficulty, to read. I can't listen to the recording without seeing him through the glass, hunched over the four hundred per cent magnification of his poem. No plaque commemorates his stay here. Is any poetry being written this morning in the square, I wonder, as I look around? Is anyone working on a version of Heine, like Michael Hartnett in 1997?

> Songless, anxious, a long time —
> now I am writing again!
> Suddenly songs come upon us,
> like tears, like pain.

Maybe, somewhere in the square, there's a basement or garret space waiting for the push of pencil on paper or finger on keyboard. The patient cursor waits, flags still flutter in the unseen green, but this seems an unlikely fantasy. Artists flee the expensive, gentrified contemporary city for Leitrim or Berlin. The houses of this handsome square are as untroubled by art as by the rumble of a phantom generator and the flickering lights of a caravan filled with bathroom tiles . . .

# 'The Sentiments of my Heart': John Rocque Comes to Dublin

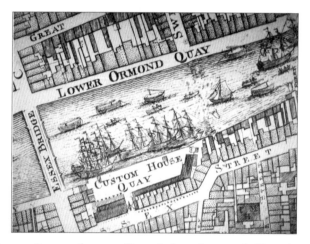

Cutthroat Lane, above a list of churches and directly above the engraved figure of the surveyor and his tripod, as if his view of the city might also be an inspection of its criminal underlife. The city obliges: Murdering Lane. Cutpurse Row. Dirty Lane. Dunghill Lane. Bedlam. Black Dog Prison. The names vanished now, though the routes are all still there. But also much that is completely familiar so that, if set down there, I could easily find my way around. The time traveller's machine lands in, say, Smithfield. He makes his way through the din of the cattle market and moves south down Arran Street and along Arran Quay until he comes to the old bridge, which he crosses. Assuming he has made it this far, assuming he has a coin to fling at Hackball, the King of the Mendicants, who guards the bridge like a troll, he climbs up Bridge Street and . . . a moment of confusion at

Wormwood Gate and Cook Street, he pauses, remembers his Latin, *Haec Ormondia dicitur, Hibernicis Orwown, id est Frons Momoniae, Anglis Ormond, et plurimis corruptissime Wormewood.* Corruptissime . . . He leaves Ormond, Urmhumhan, Wormwood Gate and veers south again down New Row and across Corn Market towards Francis Street. Familiar territory now, though the houses are unrecognizable. Head down, tries not to call attention to himself. The clothes, the stench! Across The Coombe into New Row South, turn left into Blackpitts and then . . . And then nothing, trees and marked-out plots of land, and the traveller's home a vegetable garden, and will be for a long time yet. Some of the fields have rows of posts and, if it's fine, he might see the woven cloths fixed to the posts with iron tenterhooks and stretched out to dry. Fifty years from now the weavers will get a purpose-built Tenter House so they don't have to rely on the Dublin weather. But for now they're here, looking balefully at the grey sky. Room in this corner for Andrew Drury, the mapmaker's engraver, to flourish his name.

North of here is crowded, dense, the houses and plots packed close together, a warren of tiny streets and narrow lanes with occasional open patches: Huguenot territory, Newmarket, Weavers Square. I cast off the time-traveller mask and settle down to some serious exploring. I begin greedily with my own patch of the city, hunting among Malpas Street, New Street, The Coombe, the vanished streets between The Coombe and Newmarket — Skinner's Alley, Cuckold's Row, or those which have been renamed, Crooked Staff (Ardee Street), Mutton Lane (Watkins Square?). Just north of the east side of Newmarket, right in the centre of this bustling area of weavers, tanners, skinners and butchers is the homely rectangle of St Luke's Church, and I feel an odd pang of nostalgia as I gaze at the avenue of trees leading up to its door. Where the avenue was is now the wide extension to Cork Street which cuts a brutal swathe through the area, and the ruined church sat on its hill behind ugly green railings for years before being imaginatively repurposed as an office in 2017, preserved from the wrecking ball by order of the same Council that built the road. The trees were gone at least a hundred and fifty years before that, so it's hard to account for the nostalgia, except that Rocque gives them such presence on the 1756 *Exact survey of the city and suburbs of Dublin*, all twenty-one of them lovingly sketched, that I can feel myself walking down the avenue. The headstones in the graveyard are also visible. Everything is visible, every stable lane, dwelling and warehouse, so that I can hardly force myself to hurry through this crowded neighbourhood.

I leave the trees and follow the curve of the The Coombe before turning up the broad expanse of Meath Street. All around me is the industrial heartland of eighteenth-century Dublin. At its northern extremity, where it meets Hanbury Lane, Meath Street narrows sharply before it joins the great thoroughfare of Thomas Street. Here's the Glib Market, with its meat and fowl, and here's St Catherine's Church, not yet the handsome current building but clear and substantial, its name in a pale band in the centre of its black bulk. Behind the church I can make out the individually marked gravestones. If I go back to the street and turn to the right, looking back towards the old city, I can see, just before Francis Street and Cutpurse Row, the long vanished Corn Market House, since demolished by the Wide Street Commission, much to the annoyance of the local traders. It may be 1756, we may be in a bustling industrial and trading quarter, and the abbey which gave the street its name — founded by Henry II to atone for his part in the murder of his troublesome archbishop — may have disappeared, but the Middle Ages are still everywhere. They're there in the narrow burgage plots stretching back from the great old street, in the route of the street along the ridge that slopes down to the river, the old *Slí Mhór*, the road to the west.

The street begins to appear on the ancient route in the twelfth century, on the outskirts of the walled city, a district unto itself, a traditional locus of dissent, the most famous icon of which is the print of Robert Emmet's gruesome execution outside St Catherine's in September 1803 after the disastrous insurrection, the executioner holding the head aloft, *'The head of a traitor'*, as the crowds seethe behind the massed soldiery with their backs to Bridgefoot Street and the pinprick onlookers stare from the windows and gables of the Dutch Billys in Thomas Court. The print is late nineteenth century, the event is 1803, the barbaric death a sinister medieval theatre. Hastily I flee from an image of an event yet to happen, cross the river and make my way up Queen Street and in behind the Blue-Coat Boys' School to another remnant of the Middle Ages, the shrinking expanse of Oxmantown Green, home of the Norsemen, rival to St Stephen's Green, once covered by a wood whose timber was exported to William Rufus for the roof of Westminster Hall. A carpenters' widow house on the north side. Every appearance of a site about to be developed. Where is it now? Oxmantown Green is a development of twenty-five luxury apartments, each tastefully furnished to the highest specification. After the Robin Hood gang broke up Little John came to Oxmantown Green to display his archery skills to the citizens of Stoneybatter, but the press of old habits was too hard and he soon went back to robbing until he was caught and hanged on Arbour Hill.

These old outskirts suck me in. Quick, zoom out, forget the medieval city, fly up and look down at the whole picture. I zoom out on both computer screens and look at the pattern of streets and the ships that come as far as Wood Quay. Then I abandon my machines and spread the Royal Irish Academy reproductions open on the table.

I take in the sweep of the city — the huge eastward expansion, the broad avenues and new squares, the signs of prosperity, of order and planning, the development of new urban estates. Great open spaces like Oxmantown Green and St Stephen's Green are encroached on. Stephen's Green is built up on all sides, with an open square in the middle. New quays and new bridges have shifted the traditional east-west axis of the city to a north-south one. As the eye travels east from Oxmantown it falls on the district radiating from Smithfield and, further east, a new suburb linked to the south city by Essex Bridge and centred around Capel Street and Jervis Street, bounded on the southern edge by Ormond Quay and Bachelor's Walk and to the north by Great Britain Street. A broad new street, Sackville Street, Luke Gardiner's masterpiece, with a central mall for the *beau monde* to parade itself in, stretches from Great Britain Street to Henry Street, linked to Abbey Street by the narrow southern extension of Drogheda Street. Here too is the other great street of the Gardiner estate: Henrietta Street, with its palatial houses, though not yet leading to James Gandon's King's Inns. On the southern bank of the Liffey ships stream upriver as far as Wood Quay. The streets of what we now know as Temple Bar flow from the bustle of Custom House Quay. Just north of Stephen's Green is a grid from Grafton Street to Kildare Street and from Nassau Street to Beaux Walk. At its centre are Dawson Street and Molesworth Street. South of Dublin Castle and west of Stephen's Green another clearly planned district appears, radiating from the broad Aungier Street. The old medieval city with its twisting lanes and streets contrasts with the new grid-planned estates to the north and south.

The map makes clear what we know from history, how in the hundred and fifty odd years since Speed's map the shape of the city was transformed by the development of large urban estates by the city and private landowners. The map also clarifies the character of Dublin as a port city bisected by a river. One of the reasons Rocque gives for his attraction to the city is precisely the order and solidity of its quays. This is a functioning, thriving maritime city well adapted for trade, full of prestigious buildings, spacious streets, gardens, walks. The smell of money and success is everywhere. Rocque has landed in a city proud of its accomplishments, economically successful, socially and culturally preening itself. The city of Swift, Goldsmith, Congreve, Sheridan. Handel's

*Messiah*. There's Smock Alley Theatre, not yet a church or a Viking experience or a restoration of its former self as a new theatre. A recent excavation of this site found wig curlers and oyster shells — a step up from popcorn kernels. A city of Ascendancy comfort and security. Rocque's map is the perfect mirror of all this success: it offers the city a detailed image of itself, a frozen image of harmony, order and industry.

This, of course, is how maps lie. They offer detail, information, above all an aesthetic experience. George II was so impressed with it that he hung it in his apartments. If he scrutinized it before he went to bed it probably wasn't because it offered him an insight into the social and economic conditions of his second city, but because it offered a tantalizing image of completeness. It offers the spectator every single building in the city. There are, estimates Patrick Fagan in his *Catholics in a Protestant Country: The Papist Constituency in Eighteenth-century Dublin*, (Four Courts Press, 1998), 11,645 houses. Maybe, on sleepless nights, the king climbed out from his bed to count his way down Sackville Street or to follow his little finger down the lanes of the old city.

We know that the map is both beautiful and deceiving. The city it portrays is both familiar and alien; its alienness is all the more unnerving because of the familiarity of the names and the geography. It is, for one, a Protestant city. Not in the demographic sense; the Catholic population swells throughout this century. According to Fagan's figures in 1700 70% of the population was Protestant and 30% Catholic, but a hundred years later those proportions were exactly reversed. But the institutions, the university, the churches, the parliament, the castle, the barracks remind us that we're in a colonial garrison. Catholics are actively excluded from participation in the institutions of the city, even from the officially sanctioned practice of their religion. A certain laxity, or rather a pragmatic acknowledgement of the facts, means that the priest-catchers no longer stalk the streets — remember the infamous Garcia, priest turned priest-catcher who lived safe

within the walls of the castle? — and that no serious attempts
are made to prevent Catholics worshipping in openly designated places. Too many fires, too many accidents and collapses
of upper rooms have taken place to continue with active
suppression without inflaming the ever-growing mob. Only
twelve years earlier, on the 27 February 1744, after the
authorities closed down all the mass-houses, the house in
Pill Lane where a priest was celebrating mass collapsed,
killing the priest and nine others. After this incident the
viceroy and magistrates decided it would be better to allow
the Catholic population their chapels than have people die
in this manner.[1]

Something of this can in fact be read in the map. Look at
the many churches — St Patrick's, Christ Church, St
Catherine's, St Michan's, St Ann's, St Peter's, St Nicholas's,
St Werburgh's, St Kevin's, St Mary's, St Thomas's. We know
that these are all Church of Ireland, that Rocque is carefully
paying his respects to the state religion. But he's not content
with that. He was, after all, born in France in the reign
of Louis XIV who, nineteen years before Rocque's birth,
revoked the Edict of Nantes, which caused the Huguenot
Rocque family to emigrate, first to Geneva and then to
London. And Dublin is also a city of fruitful dissent. His
mapping of that dissent is brilliantly illustrated by Kenneth
Ferguson in his essay 'Rocque's Map and the History of
Nonconformity in Dublin: A Search for Meeting Houses'.[2]

The map shows seventeen buildings labelled as Meeting
Houses — Presbyterian Meeting Houses (7), French Churches
(3), Quaker Meeting Houses (2), the Dutch Church and a
dozen 'Roman Chappels' marked with just a cross. Non-
conformism was legal by then, since the Toleration Act of
1719, but what it had in common with Catholicism 'was a
distinct want of parity with the Establishment'. The Church
of Ireland buildings that existed in Rocque's time have
mostly survived, and most were still being used for worship
into the twentieth century. The last surviving Quaker
Meeting House was the building that's now the Irish Film

Institute in Eustace Street. Just beside it, what's now The Ark
children's cultural centre, was a Presbyterian Meeting House.
Anyone who has been inside will appreciate its sense of
space and light, a fact not always appreciated by those who
observed it when it was first built. Kenneth Ferguson
observes:

> When new in 1728, a Quaker remarked of this
> building: 'Where there is so much vanity without,
> there cannot be much religion within.' The people
> who assembled here ... were headed for Rationalism.
> These were the 'new light Presbyterians' who would
> ultimately — here in Eustace Street about 1830 —
> become Unitarians.

Maybe the most interesting feature of Rocque's mapping of
Dublin dissent is that the Meeting Houses were usually
positioned discreetly in the city, out of general view, down
side streets or in laneways. Ferguson again: '*In a sense literal
as well as metaphorical, Rocque put the religious alternatives
on the map ... It was a riposte to the intolerance of his native
France, where a map with such information could not have
been compiled or published.*'

Ferguson notes that in the early eighteenth century Dublin
supported four Huguenot congregations, two on each side
of the river. These were further divided into 'conforming'
and 'non-conforming' congregations, the former of which
used the Book of Common Prayer in French while the latter
chose their own French models. There was however 'no ran-
cour between the congregations and their clergy co-operated'.
Rocque places three FC (French Church) symbols on his
plan: Peter Street, opposite the old Adelaide Hospital; Lucy
Lane or Mass Lane, beside what is now the Four Courts,
and the east end of St Patrick's Cathedral. The Lucy Lane
congregation buried their dead in Merrion Row, and the
cemetery is still visible today. Ferguson supplies some fascinating details about these congregations. The Peter Street

church, he tells us, 'was consecrated on 19 December 1711, and remained in weekly use until 1806', by which time the congregation had practically disappeared. The last pastor, Isaac Subremont, died in 1814, after which the building became a school, until 1838, when it was demolished. St Patrick's Cathedral had offered its Lady Chapel to the fleeing Huguenots and it was used by them from April 1666 until 1816.

Soho, 1738. In the background, the spire of St Giles-in-the-Fields. To the left a tavern whose sign proclaims *Good Eating*, showing the picture of a human head on a plate — John the Baptist, presumably. the body of a woman, but no head. On the far left a black man fondles the breasts of a servant girl, causing her to spill juices from the pie she is carrying onto a small boy standing beneath her. Whether because of the hot juice on his head or the plate of food he has let fall to the ground, the boy is bawling piteously. Meanwhile an urchin savages the fallen food. Upstairs in the tavern a row is in full spate. A man stands behind a woman who has taken a plate with what looks like a leg of meat and is slinging it out the window. Down in the gutter a dead cat lies surrounded by the stones that were presumably used to kill it. All is disorder, mess, un-virtue. The virtue is all on the other side. Out of the French Church spill *les grecs*, as these French Huguenots sometimes refer to themselves, since the church was originally used by Greek refugees fleeing Ottoman persecution. The persecuted inherit the persecuted. This congregation has come up in the world, though. Most are soberly dressed, as befits the followers of Calvin, but at the front stands a lavishly dressed couple, very French and fancy, with their equally stylish son got up as a foppish adult. It looks as if Hogarth, whose engraving this is, doesn't much like the French, and sides proudly with *les rosbifs* with their avid appetites and comic timing. The Huguenots don't look as if they're about to tuck into anything and only the fancy couple seems to find life amusing. Maybe he's fed up with all the French he hears on the streets — *'many parts of this parish so greatly abound with French that it is an easy matter for a stranger to imagine himself in France'*, writes the Scottish topographer, William Maitland, a year later — and would prefer if they all buggered off to France.

This is John Rocque's London, though how he feels about Hogarth's representation of his fellow Huguenots isn't recorded. He has other things on his mind. He's busy: he's a surveyor, engraver, mapmaker, map-seller and publisher, first from 'The Canister and Sugar Loaf' in Great Windmill Street, then to Piccadilly, before moving to bigger premises, first in Whitehall, then in the Strand. In his early years he's happy to describe himself as a *dessinateur des jardins*, surveying aristocratic gardens. One of his plans, his *plan du jardin et vue des maisons de Chiswick*, can still be seen in the Victoria and Albert Museum. What he really wants to do is to make maps, but mapmaking is an expensive business and you need patrons. The aristocratic connections he's made will eventually help. It's clear that there are no decent maps of English towns, but those in power, from merchants to military, are beginning to realize that a map is knowledge, intelligence, a means of control, and the necessary funds begin to be provided. Bristol, Bath, Exeter, Shrewsbury are all surveyed and mapped. But the big prize is London, which takes him nine years and is finally published, as the *Survey of London Westminster & Southwark,* in October 1746, on twenty-four sheets, for the price of three guineas. What makes it significant is the level of detail which makes it possible to study the growth and history of the city. Houses, churches, streams, ponds, paths, roads, tenter grounds, hills and rivers, even orchards and woods, can all clearly be made out. There are boats in the Thames, and the gibbet at Tyburn. I travel through the eighteenth-century city by means of a YouTube video of the map; I find an interactive online version and zoom around: Great Eastcheap, Little Eastcheap, Hounds Ditch, Bishopsgate, Spittle Fields, Black Eagle Street, Crabtree Lane, Snow's Fields, Five Foot Lane . . .

And then of course it hits me: what I'm looking at, what keeps pulling me back is *names*; the attraction of map travelling is not just the physical layout of the city and the painstaking survey of alleys, streets, courtyards but the thousands of placenames — more than 5,500 in the case of London — carefully recorded and preserved. And this work wasn't slapdash — because Rocque has the municipal authorities behind him, Beadles are provided to help collect and double-check the street names. Before publishing the map Rocque invites the public to his Hyde Park Road shop to examine the drawings and correct any errors — *No, mate, it's Bull Yard* — and so the city is frozen in its moment, the perfect ghost of itself. A great many of the names still survive; others, along with the streets they identified, have vanished. The whole place is smaller: it's intimate, traversable; the past seems more manageable than the vast contemporary megalopolis. That's maybe one of the satisfactions of a map like this, it offers a vision we can readily comprehend as opposed to struggling with a Tube map or navigating the city with Google Maps on a smartphone.

Rocque's London map is a big professional achievement. Not long after this, in 1751, as further acknowledgment of the importance of cartography, he is appointed Chorographer to the Prince of Wales. Business continues to thrive, and then, three years later, he's ready for another challenge. To the surprise of some he decides to go to Dublin. Nor was this a brief trip: he spends nearly six years in the city and produces several maps, of which the *Exact survey* is the best known.

Why did he come to Dublin? He was sponsored by the Irish parliament; he had some support from Dublin Corporation and as always he sought and received aristocratic patronage, but it was clearly also a congenial labour. He liked the city. A lot of the reasons he gives in his foreword to the public in his *Exact survey* have to do with the aesthetic pleasure offered by Dublin's buildings and layout. Not everyone agrees with his assessment. Many have tried to dissuade him from coming to Dublin, telling him the Irish city has nothing to offer. Yet we can see in the map, he tells us, that Dublin is one of the finest and largest cities in Europe. He singles out the quays:

> *After having executed the Plan of London and its Suburbs, I wanted only to do the same by Dublin, in order to have the Honour of having traced out two of the largest and most celebrated Cities of Europe. If I had given Credit to what I had been told of this City, I should never have had the Pleasure which I have enjoyed in this work. Several Persons had represented this City as not deserving the Attention of Strangers, not being remarkable for any Singularity, nor affording any Thing worthy of the Curiosity of a Traveller. But we see in this Map, that Dublin is one of the finest and largest Cities of Europe, as well*

*as on Account of its Quays, which reach with Order
and Regularity from one End of the Town to the
other, as on Account of a great many Buildings in
different Parts on either Side; for instance Kildare-
house, the Barracks, Hospitals, Parliament-house,
the College, and the Castle, which is the Residence
of the Lord Lieutenant, &c., and also on Account of
several spacious and magnificent Streets, the
Gardens, Walks, &c. Besides that, the Situation of
Dublin is very agreeable and commodious; being a
Sea-Port, it hath a magnificent Harbour, through
which a surprising number of Vessels are continually
passing up the River; which they cover from its
Mouth to the first Bridge . . .*

Maybe the intimate scale of the city appeals to his cartographer's instinct for completeness. One of the things that makes
his Dublin map different is that it's the only map of its era
with individual plots marked out, 'the ground plot of all
Public Buildings, Dwelling Houses, Warehouses, Stables
and Courtyards'. The city seems to be there in its entirety,
no building or plot unrepresented. Almost, but not quite
— the wealthier areas are all there, the poorer areas are
more likely to have their buildings guessed at rather than
observed and recorded, though the relationship between
money and cartographical detail is more apparent on the
map of London.

It's not hard to take in the four sheets of the *Exact survey*,
compared to the twenty-four sheets of the London map, but
one of the most enjoyable ways to experience the map is by
reading Colm Lennon and John Montague's *John Rocque's
Dublin: A Guide to The Georgian City* (RIA, 2010), which
reproduces forty extracts from the map and accompanies
each with a commentary. One of the most intriguing for
me was the Custom House Quay, where Wellington Quay
now is. The map shows the ships beside the dock and,
behind the dock, an archway leading to Essex Street. A series

of mysterious black dots near the edge of the street turn out to indicate 'the piazzas', a colonnaded walkway. We know this because a drawing by Hugh Douglas Hamilton, from 1760, shows a shoeboy standing in front of Custom House Gate while behind him another boy is busy shining the shoes of a man leaning against one of the columns of the covered walkway. We also see a dray on its way through the gate bearing a hogshead of whiskey or beer. The rigging of a ship and a weighing scales suspended from a tripod are also clearly visible.

I couldn't get the shoeboy out of my mind. That image, combined with my daily map travelling through the eighteenth-century city and a story of a boy abandoned by his father and sent into indentured servitude by his uncle, which I first came across in Maurice Craig's *Dublin 1660-1860 A Social and Architectural History*, sent me off on a journey that eventually ended up as a novel. I plotted my characters' movements carefully across Rocque's map, so much so that the publisher wrung his hands and said in exasperation, 'There are too many bloody streets!' I borrowed a lot of details from the edition of Hamilton's *The Cries of Dublin*, published by the Irish Georgian Society. The shoeboy's polish, I was glad to find out, was made of lampblack and rotten eggs; the shoes were shone with an old wig. And thanks to the *Hibernian Journal* the shoeboy's voice was recorded. Here's a taster from *The Shoeboy's Address to the Citizens*:

> We, da shoeboys of de city make a resolution not to clean shues less dan a pare a coppers de pare ... Dere is a great many people may wonder at us for raizing our price, but were we not as good as any oder trade? Havent we as good a right to it as de painters? Don't we handle the brush as well as dem?

Lennon and Montague's book is full of other treasures that add an extra layer to my own walks around the city. What went on in Goat Alley, Love Lane and Beaux Lane off Aungier Street? My own daily walks cross much of the territory covered by Rocque. Every day I walk down Long Lane and as I approach Clanbrassil Street I glance across at a house some friends once lived in, on a plot shown as an unnamed garden in Rocque's map but which, thanks to this book, I discover was actually Naboth's Vineyard. In the Old Testament Naboth owned a garden coveted by King Ahab but which he refused to sell to him. Queen Jezebel arranged to have Naboth murdered and thus the land was acquired. Jonathan Swift's ironic naming of the plot derived from his own cheerfully admitted cheating of a neighbour to get his hands on it. I imagine the peaches, nectarines and pear and apple trees flourishing where the terrace of houses now stands, and the Dean's relish as he samples his ill-gotten fruits.

I think, too, of the ubiquity of maps in our lives. For a while now, if I have to go on a trip somewhere, I've been in the habit of looking up the destination in Google Maps. Sitting in front of my computer or glancing at the phone I plot the journey like an ancient navigator with his charts. Most of the time I don't really need to do this. There are signs, after all. You get off the motorway at the right exit and follow the road. But a combination of anxiety, curiosity and an over-developed need to control my fate means that I am there virtually wandering through Newbridge, Athy, Waterford, Killarney, staring at the building I have to find, looking for the car park, noting the locations of petrol stations, coffee shops, bookshops, parks, imprinting the streets on my brain, and later, on arrival, laying the real street and houses down on the grid already established, letting the town confirm its virtual self. And it's strange how vividly a car park or arts centre will announce itself, as if to say, *Look, the world is real after all, here we are!* Often, I spend more time on the map than on the actual place, so that the map is the more intense reality. More sinister is the realization that all my movements are tracked. I look at my phone and see that Google has a timeline of all my movements going back several years. Every step I've taken, every mile I've driven, every shop or restaurant I've visited has been plotted and mapped. *What did you think of Avoca? Are there restrooms in the Adare Tourist Centre? Can you rate your experience here, there, everywhere?*

There's no street view or timeline for the past, no little icon to be pulled down into Sweeney's Lane or Mill Street to reveal the bricks of the long vanished Dutch Billys, the cut of a coat or the shine of a coach, nothing to hint at the lives that might be led there, yet here I am, sitting in front of two computer screens with the blown up *Exact survey*, plotting the journey as if I might step out of my front door and walk down two hundred and fifty years. Or else I'm just gazing at the map, taking it in, enjoying it, standing in front of it as if it were hanging in a gallery . . .

If all of this suggests anything it's that to contemplate a map is complex. Yes, it is an insight into the past, the continuity and endurance of a place; an aide to imagining the lives that occupied these streets and houses, that worshipped in the chapels, churches and meeting houses, that paraded in finery or struggled to keep body and soul together. In itself the map is pure, abstract; its city is idealized. It's an image. I think again of the story of Rocque's Dublin map appealing so much to George II — maybe he just liked it. The link between cartography and art is long established, and indeed explicitly acknowledged by Rocque. Look at the elaborate cartouches, with nymphs, goddesses, Anna Livia, Hibernia with the harp on her shield, or the image of the surveyor himself in agricultural land south of Cutthroat Lane, that take up a decent part of the map. They speak, surely, to the aesthetic gaze of the beholder. Rocque is a dramatist, they might be saying, and the map is his stage.

Cartography had long lodged itself in the creative imagination before Rocque applied his chain and theodolite to London or Dublin. In 1665 Madeleine de Scudéry designed a 'Carte du pays de Tendre' (map of the land of tenderness) for her novel *Clélie*: a map of an Arcadia whose geography is determined by love. And visual artists have continually been drawn to maps as subject and method: Jasper Johns' 1961 representation of the states of the United States in 'Map' comes to mind, or 'The naked city' by Guy Debord and Asger Jorn which consists of nineteen fragments cut out from a travel map of Paris, in order to make '. . . an urban topography into a social and affective landscape'. Debord coined the term 'psychogeography' which considers how geography, usually urban, can impinge on the affective life. Closer to home I think of Kathy Prendergast's 'Black Map' series, which uses printed motorist maps almost entirely obscured with ink, or 'Atlas', an installation consisting of paintings made using over one hundred copies of the *AA Road Atlas of Europe*. Maybe somewhere, somebody is busy cutting up the *Exact survey* and converting it into a tender map, a psychogeography of dark desire.

I think, though, I should leave the last word with Rocque:

> *But what contributes yet more than either Nature or Art, to the Embellishment of Dublin, is the Temper of its Inhabitants, obliging, gentle and courteous. The Irish keep up the most amiable Society; are frank, polite, affable, make it their Pleasure to live much with each other, and their Honour to treat Strangers with Politeness and Civility. They are particularly remarkable for a Lenity and Mildness which Justice is executed, almost unknown except in this Country and in England. They endeavour rather to discharge a Prisoner and soften his Punishment, than to condemn him. I am extremely surprised that the Author of the System of Geography has given so different a character of this Nation. He is ill-informed, not to say any more; and his Articles of Dublin and the Irish are entirely false, and can make no other Impression upon the Reader, than of his Impertinence and Boldness in venturing to forge a Descrip-*

*tion without Foundation, and without Probability. For my Part, I have had the Pleasure of being in Dublin above two years and have all that Time to be acquainted with the Genius and Temper of the People, and in the Picture I have drawn of them I have only expressed the Sentiments of my Heart and paid to Virtue the tribute that is her due.*

*Footscrapers*

Sometimes all I see is a line of down pipes and footscrapers, a dog's eye view of the world, long red terrace and the ghosts of uplifted feet.

# 'O commemorate me where there is water'[1]

What is a neighbourhood exactly? A network of places, amenities, social relationships. It may or may not have some or all of these, but in a city a neighbourhood can be defined as much by choice as by geography; you make your own mental map as you close your front door behind you, and decide how much of the available possibilities you make your own. You can stay close to home, or you can follow the thread of an elective affinity and stride off as the mood takes you. If you walk or cycle to work that journey can be incorporated into your sense of neighbourhood, or the extension of the neighbourhood. Likewise, with a bus or tram journey, both of which involve you with the journey in a way that a car can't really achieve. A car is its own inviolable neighbourhood.

In this sense, maybe, all neighbourhoods are virtual. Today as I walk along the Grand Canal from Portobello to the basin and back again I realize that I look at this thin slice of the city as part of my neighbourhood. It takes me no more than a few minutes to get to the canal from my house. I usually come at it through the streets behind the South Circular Road. Once I'm on Portobello Road I'm pulled forward like a barge and wouldn't think of veering off. Although I do use it as a route into certain areas of the city, usually, if I'm here, it's because I want to be here. There's something about a body of water in a city that's hard to resist. Once it was busy with traffic; now it exists as thoroughfare and for pleasure, as a horizontal park, so part of the attraction might be to do with its removal from the bustle beyond the banks. But even if it was full of slow-moving barges 'bringing from Athy/ And other far-flung towns mythologies' it would be just as powerfully attractive. Apart from the little boat that comes to clear out the litter not much moves on the canal these days apart from the odd kayak. The swans, ducks and moorhens have it mostly to themselves. They are themselves part of the attraction, along with the other birdlife, the starlings, magpies, sparrows and the odd heron lurking on the bank. Any body of water gathers its own life around it, and the combined effect of trees, grass, reeds, water and living creatures creates an ecosystem quite distinct from the rest of the city.

If there were more than just the two canals in the city, the Grand and the Royal, they would be stitched seamlessly into the fabric of the city, like Amsterdam or Stockholm, and they'd be less distinctive, less noticeable; we'd simply take them for granted. Here, part of the pleasure comes from the fact that the canal and its banks are both part of the city and, especially if you travel for any length along it, quite distinct from it. It's more a series of islands, divided by locks and bridges which occur at busy intersections, so there can be a lot of dodging and weaving to get from one section to the next. And of course it also marks a border, traditionally dividing the inner city from the first suburbs, a division maybe subtler now than it once was, but still very much there. To walk along it is to travel between two versions of the city, conscious of both. North of the canal lie the busy urban districts, south is leafier, more residential. These are broad distinctions — the districts aren't all equal. The canal itself is not a single entity either. Each section has its own distinctive flavour and atmosphere.

Today's journey starts a bit unpromisingly, with a pair of fat rats scuttling out from the reeds on Windsor Terrace. Whatever they're living on, though, at least they're thriving on it. Their purposeful hurry is echoed by the joggers streaming down the narrow towpath. More leisurely are the dog walkers, the dogs, like my own, stopping to examine every tree. Further down the scale of activity is the possibility of standing completely still: every few yards there are designated fishing stands, though it's rare to see anyone actually fishing. But the metal numbered stands in the shape of fishes are pleasingly optimistic. This section of the canal is a back garden for Portobello, or a front garden for the terraced cottages of Portobello Road which look over the canal. There's an Italian restaurant which has been here for several years now but still has a provisional look, its wooden sign not quite obscuring the name of the previous business on the brickwork. When the sun shines the banks are crowded with people taking their ease, drinking beer and reading newspapers. Outside the college at the Rathmines end is a plaza skateboarders have taken over. Some of the Asian students from the college have taken to playing cricket there and there is some tension between them and the skateboarders who don't seem interested in sharing the space. I walk this stretch so often that I hardly see it as any kind of distinct space anymore, it's effectively my local park, along with the Iveagh Gardens. I start to see more as I leave for the other side, taking in the red-painted iron of Portobello Bridge with its beautiful central lamps.

On Charlemont Mall all I want, to begin with, are the willow trees hanging their heads in the water by the short boardwalk. And then to look across at hidden Ontario Terrace on the other side. At the end of this section is The Barge pub, where on summer evenings drinkers sit on the bank and on the arms of the lock or stand in animated groups on the road. The farther east I go the more I like the canal. As I dodge my way across Charlemont Bridge and head down under the Luas bridge I pause to look at the barge that operates as a floating restaurant, taking diners to what I still want to call the Grand Canal Theatre at the end of the line, a journey that takes about an hour and a half. I have always been obsessed with barges and narrowboats, part of a strange lifelong affair with a kind of genial confinement. Huts, cabins, treehouses, caravans, tents, yurts, caves, enclosed womb-like spaces of all kinds I find deeply attractive.

I think if I owned a barge I would be less interested in navigating it than in simply lying still in the cabin enjoying the cramped cosiness. It is a desire for retreat, I suppose, the desire to stay still in a fruitful space. The attraction of a barge or a houseboat has to do also with settling on the sway of water, as if the self might somehow move more freely there, unshackled to bricks and mortar and the sense of being in permanent, unalterable habitation. I think of the book I'm currently reading, Alastair Reid's *Outside In*. Reid is a poet, translator, memoirist and inveterate traveller who perfected the art of travelling light, often choosing to house-sit friends' apartments, and live out of two bags. His nomadism was made easier by having an office at the *New Yorker* where he could keep his books and do his writing. For a time he lived in a houseboat in Chelsea where he was visited by Pablo Neruda who immediately decided to throw his birthday party there. Only one poet fell into the river, a Ukrainian, but they managed to pull him out of the Thames mud. Reid describes an arrangement that he had with different friends whereby every now and then they would exchange places. The friends would come to live on the houseboat and he would move to their houses, thus getting to experience living in different parts of London. 'We all relished these unlikely vacations, since we left one another elaborately written guidebooks, and we could take in another part of London — markets, greengrocers, pubs, restaurants.'[2]

He wonders, as indeed do I, why more people don't do this. Every time I wander around the city I imagine what it might be like to live in a particular street or district, and find myself chafing against the notion that my address is permanent, fixed, unalterable. That, of course, is a privileged point of view in a city many can no longer afford to live in. The periodic shifting of addresses is one of the ideals of Thomas More's *Utopia*, but in that case it's to stop the inhabitants getting too attached to their properties, whereas my fantasy is fuelled by a mix of restlessness and curiosity, a desire to experience multiple spaces in the city. I think what Alastair

Reid is describing is a fundamental restlessness or nomadism that lives under the skin of the habitual accommodations we make with our lives. In Ireland, especially, there is often a great hurry to fix the trajectory of a life. Reid was a son of the manse, and he deliberately arranged his life to avoid the stony permanence of that life and found that provisionality has its own poetry:

> *In our travels, my son and I occupied rented houses and apartments from Barcelona to Buenos Aires. He came to remember every one of them in detail, down to its sounds — the creak and shudder of the houseboat as it rose off the Thames mud on the incoming tide, a house in Chile with a center patio cooled by the cooing of doves, a cottage in Scotland in a wood of its own, guarded by a cranky tribe of crows, and the small mountain house in Spain that was our headquarters. Moving was like putting on different lives, different clothes, and we changed easily, falling in with the ways of each country, eating late in Spain, wearing raincoats in Scotland, carrying little from one place to another except the few objects that had become talismans, observing the different domestic rites — of garden and kitchen, mail and garbage.[3]*

I move on down the canal, pausing to look down Harcourt Terrace and across at the affluent red brick and greenery of Dartmouth Square. At Leeson Street Bridge I stop to stare down into the deep lock chamber and make a brief film of the roaring water. Ross and Walpole Engineers, Dublin, 1907. From here, Leeson Street has the look of a country village that has been set down accidentally in the city. Where the road forks a homely block of houses, painted pink, white, blue and cream, faces the city. Joe Byrne's betting shop, Natural Interiors, The Canal Bank Café, Pizza Hut. The heavy traffic dispels the illusion. This is a major route south, part of the N11. Across from these houses is O'Brien's pub, an old favourite.

I return to the canal and continue down Wilton Place. This is the real heart of the city canal. Mature trees line both sides; across, on Mespil Road, a terrace of Georgian houses is reflected in the water. We're in Baggotonia, although I doubt anyone calls it that anymore. The name was less a geographical designation than an evocation of a Dublin bohemia of the fifties and sixties, reflecting the fact that many writers and artists lived in the area. One of the most celebrated is Patrick Kavanagh who is commemorated here by John Coll's bronze sculpture of the poet sitting on a seat on the Wilton Terrace side and by a bench on the opposite bank. This was his beat, this was where he loafed and invited his soul during the hot summer of 1955 after his lung operation and is the site of some of his most famous poems, 'Canal Bank Walk' and 'Lines Written On A Seat On the Grand Canal':

> *O commemorate me where there is water,*
> *Canal water preferably, so stilly*
> *Greeny at the heart of summer.*

His biographer gives us a very precise account of his occupation of the canal bank:

> *He stripped off his jacket, socks and shoes and lay*
> *there. . . in what he described as 'an ante-natal roll'*
> *with a hand under his head, sometimes raising*
> *himself on an elbow to contemplate Lesson Street*
> *Bridge. He could be utterly idle for hours on end*
> *without any sense of guilt, and this he thought*
> *hastened his cure. The canal bank, with its dry wiry*
> *grass, was like 'a little sample' of the fields of*
> *Drumnagrella or Shancoduff.[4]*

Looking at the statue and the bench across the canal it's hard to comprehend the official indifference in which Kavanagh generally operated. In his memoir *The Pear is Ripe* John Montague offers a telling glimpse of Kavanagh at a reading given by Robert Frost at UCD: 'The contrast between the silver-haired, Horatian, gentleman-farmer poet and the crumpled figure of Kavanagh who, unlike Frost, had actually been born and bred on a farm, was heartbreaking.'[5] Needless to say Kavanagh was not invited to the various formal events afterwards, including a reception in Áras an Uachtaráin. In another incident, the last public event that the poet attended, the unveiling of Edward Delaney's 'Wolfe Tone' sculpture, Kavanagh was asked to leave one of the special seats 'because he looked so strange and shabby'.

Kavanagh, though, always had a complicated relationship with Dublin. It had, in many respects, failed him. It had failed to take him seriously when he moved there as a young man in 1939 with his first book of poems and a volume of autobiography, *The Green Fool*, under his belt. Unfortunately, Oliver St John Gogarty took exception to a remark in the book — 'I mistook Gogarty's white-robed maid for his wife or his mistress; I expected every poet to have a spare wife' — and slapped the poet with a libel suit. The book was withdrawn and the incident marked an inauspicious beginning to the poet's relationship with the city, the nadir of which reached some years later in another libel suit, this time taken by Kavanagh himself against a journal which had featured an irreverent portrait of him written anonymously by another poet, Valentin Iremonger. Kavanagh lost that suit, and the city had its entertainment at his expense. The poems he wrote about Dublin are often harshly satirical — the satire of a proud man who felt himself unjustly neglected, but who also held himself aloof from the city's literary cliques and writers whom he felt were still mired in the conventions of the literary revival. To the urban intellectuals who gathered in the Palace Bar — the Malice, as Kavanagh called it — he was too rough around the edges, too much the country bumpkin. Something of the flavour of Palace wit can be inferred from the fact that Brian O'Nolan's great career as Myles na Gopaleen actually began as a series of mock letters to *The Irish Times* by himself and two friends from UCD days, lampooning Kavanagh's poem, 'Spraying the Potatoes', which had appeared in the paper. The correspondence so amused the editor, R M Smyllie, that he offered O'Nolan a regular column which became the famous 'Cruiskeen Lawn'.

The cranky isolation of Kavanagh's Dublin life is perfectly caught in the lines of 'If Ever You Go To Dublin Town':

> *If ever you go to Dublin town*
> *In a hundred years or more*
> *Inquire for me in Baggot Street*
> *And what I was like to know.*
> *O he was a queer one,*
> *Fol dol de di do,*
> *He was a queer one*
> *I tell you . . .*

A poem from around the same time looks back ironically at the hopes Kavanagh had when he first came to Dublin:

> *Show me the stretcher-bed I slept on*
> *In a room on Drumcondra Road,*
> *Let John Betjeman call for me in a car.*
> *It is summer and the eerie beat*
> *Of madness in Europe trembles the*
> *Wings of the butterflies along the canal.*
> *O I had a future.*
> — 'I Had A Future'

Although he prowled its streets, bars, cafés, betting shops and bookshops, the city is less subject matter than theatre for Kavanagh, the backdrop for his own dramatic self-projections. He's not a flâneur, in the Baudelairean sense of someone who walks a city in order to experience it or write about it, but it's still the place where he situates himself, where he lets his poetic self wander, and in this sense he's a classic urban poet. By the time he writes the canal poems or 'The Hospital', Kavanagh has given up his material expectations of the city; he is content to sit in this quiet haven and celebrate both physical recovery and spiritual rebirth, and he is perfectly content to let his eye fall where it will, 'to wallow in the habitual, the banal' or to study 'the inexhaustible adventure of a gravelled yard'.

Yet it shouldn't be thought that Kavanagh was alienated by the city. It was, in many respects, his natural element. He had, after all, left his Monaghan farm to seek out the comforts of the city — companionship, the company of the like-minded, conversation. He found all of these, and he also constructed for himself a self-contained rural village across the canal in Baggot Street. I take a detour from the canal to inspect Upper Baggot Street, the business end of Kavanagh's village, which has always been one of my favourite parts of the city, for reasons that aren't completely clear to me. Maybe it has something to do with the distinction between the lower and upper streets. Lower Baggot Street is largely Georgian, or Victorian still dressing as Georgian, and once you get past the city end it has a certain stateliness about it. Upper Baggot Street on the other hand vaunts its Victorianness, and the northern end of this street has fine red-bricked buildings with impressive gables. The most beautiful building on the street is the hospital with its brick and terracotta façade which I pause to photograph. There's nothing particularly interesting about the street, a few generic shops and a supermarket, but there are plenty of good pubs and restaurants. It has something, though — a sense of a lively and distinctive neighbourhood where it's still possible to find old flats with reasonable rents. This is the beginning of Dublin 4, after all, and the place could have been entirely gentrified.

I continue south to inspect the tall houses of Pembroke Road with their huge staircases to the first floor. Here is

where Kavanagh lived, in number 62. Not far away is Raglan
Road where he also lived briefly and where he first saw the
woman who inspired the poem 'On Raglan Road'. She was
Hilda Moriarty, a twenty-two-year-old medical student; he
was a broke forty-year-old poet. They had a mild dalliance
— mild, that is, on her part. As the poem suggests, Kavanagh
was deeply smitten. He converted his passion into a ballad,
with a specific tune in mind: 'The Dawning of the Day'. The
writer Benedict Kiely, who worked with him at the time on
the *Standard*, claims to be the first person who heard it.
Kavanagh produced the pencil written poem from a pocket
and enlisted his help in singing it in the office. He was keen
that it should be sung and frequently pressed it on people
who had good singing voices, but nothing came of it until
the day he gave it to Luke Kelly in The Bailey. From that
point onward the song's life changes, and it enters the lore
of the city. Luke Kelly sings it with a fierce tenderness no
one has equalled since. By now the song has become a
cliché, guaranteed to be roared out at the end of a night, and
usually best avoided. Its romantic rhetoric needs a hard clear
voice to steer it from sentimentality. And the song has also
become a defining moment in the legend of the poet. It fits
the image of a poet so perfectly, the helpless, unrequited
passion, the dark-haired beloved, the sudden *coup de foudre*
on the street — as if the city itself was participating in the
romance. The lovelorn poet loping from Raglan Road to the
Green, the recuperating poet reclining on the banks of the
canal, the fractious poet holding sway in The Bailey — these
are the images the city retains.

In one sense his life makes clear what a slender hold the
poet had on the city. His Pembroke Road tenancy was
always shaky, he was perpetually broke, his involvement in
the cultural life of the city was as a permanently disgruntled
and vituperative critic. Kavanagh was the quintessential outsider, in his Monaghan youth as much as in his later Dublin
life, and, as often happens, the very qualities that made his life
difficult — the irascible, overbearing, prickly yet enormously

vital personality — are what charge the poems and make the best of them unforgettable. At the same time, for all the sustaining antagonism, Kavanagh was part of the visible cultural fabric of the city. Whether holding forth in pubs, drinking tea in Mitchells tea shop in Grafton Street, addressing students in UCD, jobbing on the *Standard*, or appearing in an ad for Odearest mattresses in bare feet with his battered hat and horn-rimmed glasses — even if pictured in a field near a farmyard — he was part of the iconography of the city. The differences between country parish and city, particularly a city like Dublin, are not always as great as might be imagined, and it's not hard to see why Dublin functioned as 'an enlarged version of Inniskeen', in Benedict Kiely's words. Whatever about the city as a whole, for Kavanagh this neighbourhood was like a country town; it had, Kiely observed in a radio documentary[6] about the street, 'everything Paddy needed to make him think he was walking up and down the main street of Carrickmacross on a market day'. Anthony Cronin makes the same point: 'This was his village. It contained what he would have regarded as the necessities of life — three or four pubs, a couple of bookmakers and a bookshop. And he patrolled this area, he knew everything about its life, he knew all the people in its pubs, all the gin-drinking landladies in The Waterloo lounge, all the Baggot Street irregulars, all the soaks, all the girls who were in digs round there he'd stop them in the streets and ask them questions about their progress in exams or their boyfriends or their jobs. There can hardly ever have been an area of a city so intensively patrolled.' And equally, of course, they knew him. The same documentary contains an interview with his grocer who sold him bottles of milk and eggs 'which apparently he would eat raw', and for which he'd sometimes pay in stamps.

A great deal of Kavanagh's life was public and visible in a way that would be true of fewer poets or artists today. This has a lot to do with the personality of Kavanagh himself, but the city itself has changed, and the role occupied by the artist is in some respects greatly improved. There are institutional supports, awards, grants, organizations, buildings, festivals. Arts and culture sit down at the cabinet table and, even if there's a good deal of lip service, the fact that the artist has any status in the official sphere would doubtless astonish Kavanagh. But the kind of bohemia that sustained him has also pretty much disappeared. The pub has lost its centrality in the cultural life of the city, its functions as talk shop, office, workspace, forum as well as refuge taken over by more sedate and controlled equivalents: the reading, the festival event, the launch reception, and you can't help feeling that if someone now was as visible in his or her neighbourhood as Kavanagh was, the reaction would be somewhere between bemusement and suspicion.

In 2010 Dublin was designated UNESCO City of Literature. I went to the inauguration at the basin of the canal, in the shiny new Grand Canal Plaza, in the shadow of the Liebeskind-designed Grand Canal Theatre (now the Bord Gáis Energy Theatre). There were speeches by the Minister, the Lord Mayor, a representative of Dublin City Libraries, which was the prime mover in the initiative. There was an atmosphere of general good feeling and a sense that whatever may or may not happen in the future the accolade was the least the city deserved, given its rich tradition of writers both past and contemporary. This note was struck again and again, in the comments from writers, in press releases and in commentary in the press. The editorial in *The Irish Times* was in no doubt about the literary importance of the city: 'The submission to UNESCO goes straight to the point when it states that "Dublin's chief credentials as a City of Literature lie in the historical body of work that has come from its writers over the centuries and from the equally acclaimed contemporary output of writers native to, or living within, the city's confines".[7] But it did go on to acknowledge that relations between the writers and their city, or the country whose capital it is, were not always cordial, and gave a list of escapees: Richard Brinsley Sheridan, Bram Stoker, Wilde, Shaw, O'Casey, Beckett and Joyce. It offered a compensatory list of those who stayed — Mangan, Yeats, Behan, Flann O'Brien, Kinsella and Austin Clarke — and also referred to the many writers who migrated to the city and 'enriched its literary DNA', like John McGahern from Leitrim, Brendan Kennelly from Kerry, Seamus Heaney from Derry. Yet all of this, and indeed the event in the Grand Canal Plaza, left me a little queasy for reasons I couldn't quite articulate. When asked by a newspaper what I felt about the designation I mumbled something about not being sure what it meant but that if it resulted in practical initiatives that promoted literature then it would be a good thing. But even as I spoke the words I felt as if I had taken a mouthful of corporate chewing gum. It was as if the weight of official approval, of municipal and ministerial good cheer, was somehow too much. Maybe it was the implicit notion that writing was a kind of collective enterprise, an industry directed towards good, or economically quantifiable, ends. There was a sense that writing represents a moral good, an alternative to venality. 'Dublin is being seen as a literary city as opposed to the very crass city it was during the boom. It's a reassertion of literary values,' one novelist commented, though another, the author of the satirical Ross O'Carroll-Kelly books, disagreed. 'Having made my living from the crassness of the Celtic Tiger, I'm afraid it's all over for me. Now, it's all about values.'

I suppose I resist the idea that writing shines like a beacon of good in a nasty world, or that writers, of their nature, add an exploitable lustre to a place. It was almost a relief to read in a follow-up article that hardly any tourists in Dublin were aware of its literary mightiness, past or present. 'Neither father nor son, Frank and Thomas Seidl, from Graz, Austria, can come up with the name of a single Irish writer or book. When asked what they'd expect from a UNESCO City of Literature, Frank suggests, "To be able to visit birthplaces of writers. And to have more big libraries like this one,"' he says, indicating the Long Room behind him. Maybe another element in my resistance was the emphasis on prizes and awards: the Nobel winners, the contemporary prize-winning novelists. Most of these prizes are awarded outside the country and in most cases the rewarded writers are published in London and New York rather than Dublin. We still depend on validation from abroad, it seems, even in the midst of this celebration of cultural prowess. The emphasis on prizes by the various speakers is actually an indication of just how difficult it is to incorporate writers into the municipal self-image. It might be difficult to celebrate amorphous concepts like writing or literature, but everyone can identify with success and success is what the city badly wants in this low economic ebb. Rock stars, athletes, Nobel and Booker prize winners are what it wants. Not every writer, though, will be a medal winner, and some may not even want to enter the race. Some will be happy to choose invisibility or opposition; 'writing', after all, means nothing in itself, everything depends on the particular product of a single imagination working alone and not necessarily for anyone's benefit.

So what, then, is the proper relation between a writer and a city? As I walk back along the canal I think meanwhile of the many writers who got on with their work near this stretch of urban water. This is one definition: a place where writers live and work, where literature happens. The city offers inviting physical evidence of creative habitation: within minutes I find myself glancing up towards the shining curve of the new stadium to salute the shade of John Berryman in Jack Ryan's in Beggars Bush. Berryman wasn't drawn to Dublin by its beauty or its literary tradition; he chose it because it was cheap and English-speaking, as good a place as any to disappear into his own head, let the 'Dream Songs' combust and converse with the major Irish stroller in his mental neighbourhood, Yeats. Although he met many writers and gave a famous reading he didn't really engage with the place or its writers — 'are there any Irish poets of interest?', a diary note wonders. A troubled, ferociously intelligent, brilliant poet, he reminds us, maybe, that relations between writers and places can often be ghostly, that a writer can inhabit a place without being inhabited by it.

A little later, still alongside the canal, I'm outside 15 Herbert Place, looking up at the window of Elizabeth Bowen's childhood nursery with its watery light from the canal, and picturing, downstairs, the 'shapely Sheraton chairs, tables, cupboards, mirrors and sideboards that had been the work of Cork cabinet-makers in the eighteenth century'. Cork inside, and a cut-down Dublin outside, a micro-city, all rich 'red roads' and Ascendancy politics. She spent her first seven winters in that house — spring and summer were for Bowen's Court when 'Dublin seemed to be rolled up and put away' — and gives an account of the period in her 1943 memoir *Seven Winters*.[8] Dublin was her father's idea. The family had always lived in County Cork but Henry Bowen wanted to practise law and was called to the bar in 1887, three years before his marriage. His daughter inhabited her small winter world intensely, and exactly because it was always winter when she was there the place took on a slightly severe aspect. The canal itself provided daily drama, a mix of joy and terror as she watched a barge sink down into the lock and finally appear again on the other side. It's as if the lock were a kind of hell, an underworld from which the barge would only just escape. I'm reminded of a line in an essay about poetry by a psychiatrist. He asked a patient to distinguish between a river and a canal and immediately got the answer, 'A river is peace, a canal is torment.'

Bowen's city was, inevitably, the south city; everything north was *terra incognita.* 'I took it that Sackville Street had something queer at the end.' She describes her walks with her governess on the south side of the canal, 'Across here, one had a sense that the air lightened: the whole scene might have been the work of an artist with much white on his brush.' (*SW:* 20) She was impressed by the sense of secrecy which seemed to veil the mansions of the 'red roads' like Raglan Road and Waterloo Road, and her various governesses were awed by their wealth. 'Between my mother's stylish contempt for rich people and my governesses' patent regard for money I

was divided and unsure which way to feel.' (*SW:* 21) Bowen
has a real sense of the canal as a dividing line between city
and *banlieue*. The city behind Herbert Place with its trams
and barrel organs, and Stephen's Green, was a strong attraction. Sometimes, as she walked around the Green with her
governess, she would see her mother on the bridge over the
lake, looking for them, and then lighting on her daughter in
her scarlet coat almost with surprise. In one way the city is
backdrop to Bowen's curious relationship with her mother.
She is constantly patrolling around the city with a succes-
sion of governesses whose role is in part to regulate her
mother's affection for her by creating a distance from which
its intensity can be contemplated. Her mother's most
intense moments throughout her life were solitary, she tells
us: 'She often moved some way away from things and people
she loved, as though to convince herself that they did exist.'
(*SW:* 27) She didn't want to have to scold her only child as
it might somehow imperil the relationship, 'So, to interpose
between my mother and me, to prevent our spending the
best part of our days together, was the curious function of
every governess.' (*SW:* 27) And yet when her daughter was
with her governesses her mother thought of her constantly,
'and planned ways in which we could meet and be alone'.

So she journeys through the city and its streets and atmosphere make a big impact. Her walks often take her through
the classic streets of Georgian Dublin and her child's eye
view of these streets in the early years of the twentieth century is a striking feature of the memoir:

> *The perspectives of this quarter of Dublin are to any
> eye, at any time, very long. In those first winters they
> were endless to me. The tense distances that one only
> slowly demolished gave a feeling of undertaking to
> any walk. Everything in this quarter seemed outsize.
> The width of the streets, the stretch of the squares,
> the unbroken cliff-like height of the houses made the
> human idea look to me superhuman. And there was*

*something abstract about this idea, with its built-up
planes of shadow and light. (SW: 29)*

She shows a remarkable sensitivity to the mood of these
buildings, to how their complexion 'humanly altered from
day to day' (SW: 30):

> *The neighbourhood seemed infused with a temper
> or temperament of its own, and my spirits, on morn-
> ing or afternoon walks, corresponded with this in
> their rise and fall. . . . Some days, a pinkish sun-
> charged gauze hung even over the houses that were
> in shadow; sunlight marked with its blades the inter-
> section of streets and dissolved over the mews that
> I saw through archways. On such days, Dublin
> appeared to seal up sunshine as an unopened orange
> seals up juice. The most implacable buildings were
> lanced with light; the glass half-moons over the
> darkest front doors glowed with sun that, let in by a
> staircase window, fell like a cascade down flights of
> stairs.*

Her awareness of social nuance is very acute in someone
so young. She recognizes that these grand houses have come
down in the world, no longer the playgrounds where her
Anglo-Irish forebears 'had made merry with a stylish half-
savagery' but adorned with brass plates that signalled the
arrival of the professional classes, doctors, barristers, judges,
accountants. To the attentive child the brass plates are not so
much a commercial necessity, but seem a kind of flourishing
of the life within, a proud announcement that someone is
living there, equivalent to the gravestone's 'Here lies . . .'
When, for the first time, she sees a grand house without a
plate she's baffled, even hostile, and when she first encounters London she is saddened by the vista of 'street after
street of triste anonymity' (SW: 32). For her Dublin is the
template of the city, and London the aberration. The city, or

the micro-city which she inhabits, should be intimate and familiar; otherwise it appears unreal. One of my favourite moments in the book is when she remembers how she would come back home to Herbert Place, where I'm standing now, and, as she waited for the governess to open the door, would trace her father's name on the wall at the top of the steps, because her fingers moving on the brass plate gave both her father and herself 'an objective reality'.

Evidence, I'm thinking, maps, plaques, proof of the print of imagination. Here is Shaw as a toddler in Synge Street. Here are Wilde, Kinsella, Behan, here's Mary Lavin hunched over a story in the National Library, here's Máirtín Ó Cadhain correcting the proofs of *Cré na Cille*, here's the young Eavan Boland starting out on her poetic journey, and here, where fact and fiction intersect, is the house where Leopold Bloom lived 'in the imagination of James Joyce'. Here is the molecular transference by which posterior and bicycle saddle are united. To which could be added the succeeding generations. It's getting crowded . . .

And yet, I think, all of this adds welcome layers to the city; a city, after all, is as much a mental as a physical space. It becomes a map of achievement and everybody is free to construct their own version of it. All the more free since, in a sense, a literary city doesn't exist, any more than a composers' city or a visual artists' city. Writers and painters and composers and playwrights and makers of video installations exist. The literary pub crawl is a crawl through writers' heads, the clickable map is a virtual reality. And there's no absolute literature, no one version of literary truth. For some writers, though, the city does have, or did have, absolutist functions, as an arbiter of taste, a seal of approval, offering itself as a kind of club, a collegiate conviviality, a beacon of the imaginative life drawing the best to itself, and a place, ultimately, where the hierarchies were settled: the minor, the lesser, the pretender and the king slugging it out in The Palace, The Pearl, McDaids, The Bailey. Here's Kavanagh trying to get McGahern to go across the road to fetch him cigarettes like an errand boy, here's Behan frightening the life out of Kavanagh. Here are the famous remark, the ultimate put-down, the libel trial. A map of a particular kind of competitive maleness. The literary Dublin of the posters and the brochures was a male kind of city, hard-drinking and cordially vicious. 'I am so at home in Dublin, more so than in any other city, that I feel it has always been familiar to me. It took me years to see through its soft charm to its bitter prickly kernel — which I quite like too.' This observation by Louis MacNeice features on a bookmark for the literary website *Dublin Review of Books*, chosen, maybe, because it perfectly catches the familiar strangeness of the place and reminds us that a city can hold a mind even if it won't 'have me alive or dead'.

For many writers the city is an irrelevance; it may provide them with jobs or sustenance but *la vraie vie* is elsewhere, on the Aran islands, in a Connemara graveyard, on the streets of Boston or the villages of Maine. A literary city doesn't always feature in the list of characters. But for others the place itself is always part of the story, the city's print on the imagination is heavy and the writing unimaginable without it. And the visible presence of writers themselves can also lend an extra dimension. In her biography of Kavanagh Antoinette Quinn quotes the diary of a young engineer-cum-poet who lived in an apartment in Pembroke Road with his wife. He had missed the presence of the poet in the street when Kavanagh was on one of his doomed expeditions to London and had written to him when he returned to tell him he was glad to have him back. Why was it so good to have him back? She quotes his diary: 'it honours the city: it promises life'.[9] Maybe that's as good a way as any to think about it.

# The Librarians and the Nightingales

I lock my bike in Leinster Road and go up the steps of Rathmines Library. How long have I been coming here? I used to visit after school to raid the children's library and later consumed as much as I could of its fiction, history, travel and whatever else took my unsystematic fancy, later still gravitating to its poetry section. Before it was renovated in 2011 what used to strike me was how little it had changed. The issue desk was in the same place, the novels were in the same place; history, geography, travel all stood to attention on the same brown shelves under the same classification labels. I think part of the reason I used to come here had nothing to do with books but because it seemed to be a still spot in time, a place which was not subject to the same alteration as everywhere else. I simply wanted to sit in a chair under one of the high windows and contemplate the books.

Not that I was ever here early enough to get a seat. Every available seat was occupied by someone furiously pecking at a laptop, and one of the major ancillary functions of this space was to provide not books but the silence that books confer, the promise of a quiet place to sit. You sensed that the librarians themselves were in several minds about this. They couldn't actually prevent people coming in with their laptops but there were not very many places to sit and, upstairs, in the reference library, the desks were those diagonal workspaces excellent for consulting large volumes or for a spot of scrivening like a Victorian clerk, but useless for the positioning of a laptop.

As I look around at the high ceiling and the comforting brown shelves I realize there's a certain ambivalence in the relationship, an affection laced with guilt. I borrowed some books fifteen years ago from another library and forgot to return them, then lost them. Computerization eventually caught up with Rathmines and exiled me from the ranks of borrowers. I could just pay the fine and have done with it, but even now that the city libraries have declared an amnesty on fines and all I have to do is produce the book I keep snagging on some kind of institution-induced sloth, and now if I borrow I use my wife's card, shuffling uneasily before the desk, preparing to be challenged. I think guiltily of another breach of library morals — my copy of Yves Bonnefoy's poems, taken from the Centrale Bibliotheek, Amsterdam, in June 1989 and still on my shelves. I was leaving the country and the book found its way into the movers' boxes. I console myself by telling myself no one had borrowed it in the previous ten years. Now in Rathmines I look at the library flap in one of my own books, just to make sure no one has been borrowing it. A few years ago I tried to use the photo on the back cover of one of these books as identification, but it didn't count as a valid photo ID. 'We need a driver's licence or a passport,' the librarian told me, looking at me as if I might not be all there. How could I have imagined writing a book, especially an unborrowed one, would entitle me to join a library?

I did, though, work in libraries . . .

⌒

I stumble into the greyness of Kilmainham Courthouse. The court is in session and the hall is heaving with solicitors and their clients. The library headquarters is upstairs and I hurry up, groggy and late. I enter a tall light-filled and smoke-heavy room and take my place at a large table, and the task begins. Each of us has a pile of books on the desk, and our job is to put the protective plastic covers on them. This is not as easy as it sounds. The covers seem to be designed not to fit any known book and the paper back must be slit down the middle and then sellotaped together when the cover is flush with the book and the edges don't show. At another desk sits the inspector of book covers, a severe woman to whom we carry our piles of books and who subjects them to a scrupulous examination, deciding whether or not our work will be allowed to enter the branches of the Dublin County Libraries. Mostly not, in my case. For the first couple of weeks I work there almost every book I cover is deemed unworthy of further advancement and I slope back to my space to try again.

All of this happens in a thick pall of blue smoke. This is still the seventies, and to look back is like watching old black and white films where smoke is the unacknowledged but ever-present supporting actor. I light up another Rothmans and cut through the backing of a cover, determined that the next book will look as though machine-fitted with its sheet of cellophane. For years after when I handle books in a Dublin library I find myself wondering if the cover might be my handiwork, if some small part of my labour has entered or even prolonged its life for the length of its allotted span. How long do books survive in libraries in any case? I think of the systems, strict or lax depending on the available shelf space or the energy of the librarians, that determine the fate of the books. Is the author still alive? Has the book been borrowed recently? Has the book ever been borrowed? Are the pages intact? Has the cover come off? Is this book, yellowing and unloved by anyone apart from the author or the author's ghost, already halfway to oblivion?

We sit at our long table and chat and smoke. We're a ragged bunch of students and permanent employees, in our Victorian workroom, toiling away like doomed clerks, desultory and vaguely disreputable. At the end of the day, counting the minutes until release, someone opens the ancient clock and moves the large hand forward and we bolt for the door like school kids. But we're also firemen, waiting for an emergency in the county, waiting to be summoned to Clondalkin, Tallaght, Walkinstown, Dundrum, to fill in for stricken librarians. If our grim headquarters offer an inkling of our lowly station in the system the full realization of our abjectness is withheld from us until we enter the branches. A cloud seems to descend on us the moment we cross the threshold and shuffle up to the desk to offer our services. It seems a particular disdain is reserved for the temporary relief, as if we were barely to be trusted with returning books to their shelves or mastering the complexities of the issue desk. In the old libraries in the solid suburbs we look messy, sweaty and bedraggled after our epic bike rides from Kilmainham; we are unpresentable, a blot on the county.

Some of the libraries are still footholds in new communities, provisional buildings in the chill of bleak housing estates. In due course I find myself adding to the legends of relief incompetence. It starts in a Portakabin in the south county where I find myself hovering ineptly over terraces of tickets in their wooden slots as the librarian watches in disbelief. 'What's the problem?' The problem is I can't find the twenty-fifth of July, or the fourth of August or in fact any of the due dates where the tickets are filed, because, it turns out, however eagerly present I am, my eyes are some way behind, in their own dimly apprehended reality. I'm shortsighted, have been for years, but have somehow managed to miss the obvious signals. The edges of the world blurred so gradually that when everything seemed to have a kind of mist over it, it seemed entirely natural, so that when I eventually get a pair of glasses, the sudden clarity of everything is a shock. Where did all those edges come from, all those sharp distinctions? The world crowds into the eye with a profusion of unsuspected detail. One day I return to the Portakabin, startled at the vividness of the grass and mud around it, suddenly able to read the spines of the books on the shelves, and when my turn comes to issue the tickets I march confidently to my place where the dates and the blue ticket cards leap out from their compartments and announce themselves. The librarian looks at me quizzically, then shakes her head.

Peter Sirr

Apart from myopia my other failing as a relief library operative is reading the books. It's a bit like the drug dealer using his own drugs, or the betting-shop assistant busy filling out his own dockets and ignoring his customers; it's a serious breach of the employment contract. Often, when shelving, I can't help stopping to read. In Dundrum it's Auden, in Walkinstown it's *A Crucial Week in the Life of a Grocer's Assistant*, in Tallaght it's Graham Greene. In all cases it's ended by the hot breath of the librarian on the back of my neck and an angry remonstration. In *The Library At Night* Alberto Manguel recalls the words of the librarian in Robert Musil's *The Man Without Qualities*: 'The secret of every good librarian is never to read anything of all the literature with which he is entrusted, except the titles and the tables of contents. He who puts his nose inside the book itself is lost to the library!'[1] It's probably sound advice. 'You're better off as a customer,' the librarian tells me on my last day as he buys me a pint in the Submarine Bar. The dream of a librarian's life is only finally killed off a couple of years later after I apply for a job in the National Library. I am interviewed by a team of grave librarians and suddenly a lifetime of quiet industry in Kildare Street beckons enticingly, until the gravest of the librarians leans forward and asks me neutrally what I think of the Dewey Decimal Classification System, compared with, say, the Bliss Bibliographic Classification. I can think of nothing to say in reply. I travel up and down the stacks in my mind, trying to match the numbers with the appropriate books. Nothing happens. It's as if the books have fallen off the shelves of every library in the world. No insight into the human need to assemble and classify enters my mind, no witty speculations about the correlation between decimals and the universe of knowledge, no mantras about ease of access and retrieval. 'They're both very useful,' I begin, 'where would we be without them?'

Organizing books is, of course, what libraries do, whereas what I had dreamily envisaged was a life of haphazard reading. When I marched in to Rathmines Library after school it was never with any particular sense of purpose, but simply to go rummaging or to sit and think. This, for me, has always been the point. The greater the library, the greater the rewards of idleness. When I got my reader's ticket for the National Library years ago I was grilled by a panel of librarians who wanted to know exactly what I would be using the library for and I had to concoct a range of fake scholarly interests in order to be allowed into the building. You had the sense of being reluctantly admitted to the treasure trove of the nation, an organ of state, and everything, from the difficulty of getting in to the penitential state-issued toilet paper and the dry demeanour of the librarians, had the whiff of a sanctum of the civil service about it. Things are more liberal now. There are no interviews and less of a sense of the library as fortress or citadel. Yet I always felt that in my own case they had actually got it right, had somehow smelled out the purposeless idleness with which I would fill my desk in the reading room, the frivolity with which I'd browse the catalogue in its series of huge ledgers into which the details of the books and their call numbers had been pasted in thin strips. It was like consulting a book of spells. It was as if they knew that as soon as I got there I would order up books I had no intention of reading and leave them open on the desk while I got on with my own work. Part of the pleasure of writing in libraries is the slightly illicit sense of infiltrating a place of serious advancement for your own chancy purposes; but the real pleasure is stitching the private creation into the civic, public space as if to imply, or invent, a connection between the two. Or at least it's an attempt to bring the city into your head; writing or reading is intensely solitary, but doing them in the public space of a library almost feels like a collective act, a conscious alignment of the spirit with the other occupants of the space, past and present, but also somehow with the building itself and ultimately with the fabric of the city. This might sound fanciful but buildings profoundly influence our mood, and there's nowhere more conducive to the expansive absorption of reading or writing than the light- and book-filled space of a library.

Today I can consult the catalogue of the city libraries as well as those of Trinity and the National Library on my laptop before entering the buildings, and as often as not a trip to Google Books or the online journals in JSTOR means I can postpone leaving the house. Every time I do this I realize our relationship with knowledge is changing, and that the time will eventually come when most of everything is online. Part of me welcomes what could amount to the ultimate democratization of knowledge, but part of me also recognizes that copyright restrictions will limit the availability of vast amounts of books, including the ones I'm most likely to be interested in, and that all digital power over knowledge, apart from the closed online resources of institutions, is concentrated in the hands of a single monopoly. Yet for all these reservations I would still love to see digital access for everyone to the sum of human knowledge and creativity in a way that is fair for everyone. Universities are restrictive, closed off to all but their students and staff, and not everyone can get to a public library — and not all public libraries are worth the visit — or to the beautiful domed reading room of the National Library. And I don't see any contradiction between this and the desire that public libraries should be promoted, encouraged and better funded. We need both, in other words. Sitting at a laptop, for all that our curious fingers flit across cyberspace, confines us to our private space. We need the opportunity to wander and discover and be let loose among the materiality of paper and physical buildings.

Increasingly this feels like a visit to the past. Most people don't visit libraries, and the numbers of those who do are declining steadily. As I write this there is controversy in Britain about the closure of libraries. One of the justifications for the closures is under-use, the fact that people are staying out of libraries in their droves. Many who justify the closures and the cutting of funding to libraries argue that the various forms of digitization make libraries redundant. But Kindles, iPads and smartphones position reading firmly in the domain of the private. You can't share your downloaded book with a friend, you won't leave it behind in the rented cottage or donate it to Oxfam. You won't be leaving it on your shelves for your children to read and pass on to their friends. Electronic consumption is a closed circuit, a communion between the single individual and the source of knowledge. On the other hand the printed book itself is still thriving, and one of the reasons for under-use of libraries is the growth of book purchasing, especially from online suppliers. People are therefore making a conscious choice to consume books the same way they consume any other product. It's only when the economy dips that people start to drift towards public libraries again, only to find that their absence has left a library culture depleted of resources and under continuing threat. Does this matter? I think it does. Ancient manuscript and modern print culture has always depended on the intersection of the public and the private. The decision to gather books together and make them available is one of civilization's defining ideas. As opposed to the keyboard's combination of guesswork and algorithms, it offers a systematization of the current knowledge together with access and ease of retrieval. It's also a public celebration of the achievements of literate humanity, and a constant invitation to discovery. The ancient libraries were important social centres and intellectual hubs, with dining areas, meeting rooms, lecture halls and gardens as well as reading rooms. And the physical building of the library, the solidity of the shelves with their weight of scrolls or books offers an assurance that what is contained there will go on being available, unlike the movable feast of the URL or the shifting sands of the search results. That solidity, that continuous availability encourages us to stop and read deeply, whereas the Internet invites us to hurry and skim and search again, appealing to the restless, questing side of the brain for which the pursuit is all.

I think of Callimachus poring over his *Pinakes*, a bibliographical survey of all the authors whose books were held in the Library of Alexandria, the first such list of the contents of a library. Working on his own Callimachus came up with a system that allowed a user to find out if the library stocked a particular work, how it was categorized and where it could be found. Alexandria's other big idea was the requirement that every visitor to the city had to hand over any scroll they happened to be carrying. The library kept the original and sent back a copy to the visitor. It's a wonderful image of cultural taxation, the city constantly enriched by the traffic of visitors, but also of the hubristic, though doomed, ambition to amass the entire body of knowledge in the world. It may be that nothing of the library, or of Callimachus' tables remain, other than the gesture, the ambition, but they're powerful enough to haunt our imagination as images of an ideal completeness harnessed by an ideal order.

Despite the supreme achievement of the *Pinakes*, Callimachus himself seems to have had a troubled career in the library. He never made it to the top, his advancement possibly blocked by his rival librarian and poet Apollonius of Rhodes. A row between librarians might not seem that exciting, but the stakes in this case were high. It was in effect a row about two opposed aesthetics, two radically different conceptions of the role of the poet and poetry. Callimachus is one of the famous poets of the ancient world, a major influence on Catullus, Ovid and Sextus Propertius. Part of the reason for his influence lay in his rejection of the epic mode — *mega biblion, mega kakon* ('big book, big evil') was his mantra. He felt poets should avoid the Homeric and concentrate on brief forms. He claimed to have been visited by Apollo who advised him to 'fatten his flocks but keep his muse slender'. The younger Apollonius, on the other hand, author of the *Argonautica*, the only surviving epic of the age, strongly disagreed. Evidence of a bitter feud between the two has come down to us and thanks to a fragment of papyrus we know that Ptolemy II passed over Callimachus and appointed Apollonius as Chief Librarian. It's unlikely to have been the first time in history when rival poets slugged it out, or when worldly ambition and artistic vision mixed in a bitter potion, but at least the shade of Callimachus can find consolation in the livelier posthumous reputation. His distaste for epic didn't inhibit a prodigious rate of production — the Byzantine encyclopaedia *Suda* credits him with eight hundred papyrus rolls of prose and poetry. All we have is six hymns and sixty-four epigrams, enough to supply a convincing flavour of this mandarin perfectionist with his distaste for *hoi polloi*:

> *I despise neo-epic verse sagas: I cannot*
> *Welcome trends which drag the populace*
> *This way and that. Peripatetic sex-partners*
> *Turn me off: I do not drink from the mains,*
> *Can't stomach anything public.*
> *Lysanias,*
> *Yes, you're another who's beautiful, beautiful — and*
> *The words are hardly out of my mouth, when Echo*
> *Comes back with the response, 'Yes, you're another's.'*
> — Translated by Peter Jay, *The Greek Poets,*
> *Homer to the Present,* WW Norton, 2010

For me his most affecting poem is his well-known elegy for Heraclitus, in which the poet consoles himself with the thought that at least his friend's poems will live:

> *When I heard you were dead, Heraclitus,*
> *tears came, and I remembered how often*
> *you and I had talked the sun to bed.*
> *Long ago you turned to ashes, my Halicarnassian*
> *   friend,*
> *but your poems, your Nightingales, still live.*
> *Hades clutches all things yet can't touch these.*
> —Translated by Edmund Keeley, *The Greek Poets,*
> *Homer to the Present,* WW Norton, 2010

His faith in the longevity of Heraclitus's poems was optimistic, as it turned out, and only a single epigram has survived, a poem which describes the discovery of a fresh grave and gives us the words inscribed on the tombstone:

> *'Stranger, I am Aretemias, my country Cnidus. I was the wife of Euphro and I did not escape travail, but bringing forth twins, I left one child to guide my husband's steps in his old age, and I took the other with me to remind me of him.'*
> — Translated by W R Paton in *The Greek Anthology*, Loeb Classical Library, 1917

I'll finish with a snapshot from a few years ago. My daughter and I enter the small red-bricked library in Kevin Street (now also recently refurbished). This is a fixed part of the weekly ritual. The library is small but the children's section is disproportionately large, and my daughter settles down happily to a clutch of picture books while I wander over to the main section. For both of us there's a certain quiet drama about the building; once we enter the hush a concentration seems to waft out from the combination of books, shelves and the silence of other borrowers, and we sink ourselves in it and settle down to the examination of books, time passes quickly. This is in a way the least tangible aspect of the library experience, but also one of the most important. It's the library as the locus of spiritual refreshment. You can't take your child to the Internet, after all, but you can take them to a building like this and let them loose on its treasures. As we check out our books the librarian gives us the address of the book search site that holds the catalogues of all the local libraries, and tells us that at least a third of Kevin Street's business is the boxes of books that arrive each day, summoned by the fingers of browsers on their computers. This seems like a fair bargain, the meeting of technology and physical encounter; this is a future I could live with. I jot down the address of the site for future reference, as my daughter shyly hands up her books to be checked out. It's childhood, I realize, looking at her, and looking around at the books and the musty desks, that wave of well-being that washed over me as I came in the door has washed down the years from Rathmines, a wave of pure absorption that might, even now, even as the tide of literacy seems threatened, gather her too into its ancient folds. But even as I allow the warm glow of that thought to wash over me I think of its opposite, the library-angst, library-terror brought on by the funereal array of so many books, as if reading, even as it draws us in, has to contain its counterlife. I think of Luis Cernuda:

> *Don't let reading be for you, as it is for so many people who frequent libraries, an exercise in dying. Shake that barbarous intellectual dust from your hands, and leave this library, where your own thought could one day end up stored and mummified. You still have time and it's a perfect afternoon for going down to the river, where young bodies are swimming in the water more instructively than most books, including yours, Oh, to redeem the earth, whole and self-sufficient as a tree, all those excessive hours spent in reading.[2]*
>
> — Luis Cernuda, 'Library', in *Written in Water: The Prose Poems of Luis Cernuda*, translated by Stephen Kessler.

# Eastward Ho!

The immediately likeable thing about Pearse Square is that it has seceded from Pearse Street so completely that not a trace of that wide trafficky thoroughfare with its atmosphere of subdued depression leaks in through either of the two entrances to the square. The first thing you notice, apart from the pleasant aspect of the terraced houses, is the silence. The square is three sided with a leafy park in the middle and the north end is closed off so that the west and east terraces provide the only entrances to the square. This greatly increases its intimacy — you have no business being here unless you live here or wander in to have a look. The only external occupants today are myself, a girl sitting on a bench in the park, and the drizzle. I walk around the square admiring the narrow squashed down fanlights that look as if someone had sat on them. On the east corner a blue wall promises an all-day breakfast but the café is closed and the last sausage and black pudding have long since left the frying pan, the last teabag yielded its watery tea. There's an apartment for rent, I notice, and through force of habit I note down the details. The square could have drifted over from Rathmines or Donnybrook or any of the townships created in the nineteenth century to provide the prosperous with better air and more space. To move from it to Pearse Street or back is to shift between worlds. The difference might have been less noticeable when the square was built in the early nineteenth century, but as time has passed the street outside has become a major artery with a constant din of traffic. Pearse Street is emphatically a street of the clamorous present; the square lags several decades behind. Even the parked cars don't seem to belong entirely. You expect a few stately Humbers, Triumphs or Morrises. It must be strange to live here and pass daily through the membrane between silence and noise, a raw city clamour and motion and an island of stillness. One foot in the city and the other in the suburbs . . .

There's another sense in which the square inhabits a double zone. It's built on reclaimed land, on an area that was part of the river until the eighteenth century, when the Liffey was enclosed within a wall and quay. There's no hint of water now but we're in river country nonetheless, in a place that the city claimed for itself to accommodate its relentless eastward expansion. Between the square and the river it has turned its back on are signs of further expansion. The glass and steel of the tall office and apartment buildings of the new city loom over the square to the north and east, yanking it out of its quietest reverie, and it's to this city I now make my way, moving up along Pearse Street and looking at Alto Vetro, the skinny sixteen storey apartment building that stands at the top like a herald of confident modernity beside the Grand Canal Basin. *Welcome to South Docklands*, it seems to say, *look around and be amazed*. A little farther ahead Boland's Mill is in the process of being transformed into 'three new signature buildings whose tapering forms are designed to be read as a composition within the skyline set by Millennium Tower and Montevetro and whose coloured tones will complement the brick surrounds and limestone walls of the existing stone heritage buildings' (docklands.ie).

Grand Canal Square's east-facing aspect gives it a sharp edge; it's grey now but on even the sunniest evening the sun will have migrated to the other side of the city. As if to compensate for this greyness, the square, a huge expanse, has been given a spectacular design. The centrepiece is the two-thousand seat theatre designed by Daniel Libeskind, side by side with 45,500 square metres of office and retail space. Everything in Docklands, you quickly realize, is big. Big signature buildings, large public spaces, vast office and apartment complexes. The theatre looks like a tilted hangar lurching over the square, a massive and self-consciously theatrical gesture. The building, according to Libeskind 'is based on the concept of stages — the stage of the theatre itself, the stage of the piazza, and the stage of the theatre lobby above the piazza, illuminated at night. The theatre becomes the main façade of a large public piazza that has a five-star hotel and residences on one side and an office building on the other. The piazza, all 10,000 square metres of it, acts as a grand outdoor lobby for the theatre. With the dramatic theatre elevation as a backdrop and platforms for viewing, the piazza itself becomes a stage for civic gathering.' The physical building is certainly powerful, but it's a corporate kind of power. A place this big was never going to be about risk-taking or innovation, but about importing large, expensive international productions, the ballets and musicals that have proved themselves elsewhere. *Swan Lake. Les Misérables. Motown: The Musical.* The boldest gesture is the building itself. The design, the scale, and the ambition are utterly Docklands, yet I rarely darken its door. It opened in 2010 and is currently on its third owner, and doing pretty nicely, with a profit of €683,000 in 2017, when half a million people saw a show. Thanks to — what else? — *Les Misérables*, that figure would be increased for 2018.

I walk by the big red lopsided poles that extend from the front of the theatre along a red 'carpet' that runs right out into the basin, as if to welcome the boats that might bring the audiences from the river or the Grand Canal. The vision was Boston-based landscape architect Martha Schwartz's. The red 'carpet' is made from a bright red resin-glass material and is completed by the glowing red angled light sticks which are intended 'to mimic the "bustle" on the red carpet'. A green 'carpet', with seating on the edge of large planters, connects the new hotel and office developments. The square is be crossed by a series of narrow paths that 'allow for movement across the square in any possible direction while still allowing big activities such as markets or fairs'. Schwartz saw the new square as 'an urban magnet with twenty-four-hour activity'.

Both Schwartz and Libeskind saw their projects reflecting something already inherent in the city. Libeskind's composition 'creates an icon that mirrors the joy and drama emblematic of Dublin itself' while Schwartz envisioned her design for the square as an 'accurate interpretation of Dublin's energy'. Likewise, the hotel beside the theatre complex, by the young Portuguese partnership of Francisco and Manuel Aires Mateus, was inspired by the 'telluric, primordial geology' of the Giant's Causeway, though the final chessboard model result seems far from the original conception. The descriptions of these projects may be the necessary international design rhetoric grafting on the city's involvement with what are international gestures in the same way that Santiago Calatrava's bridges happen to span the Liffey but could as comfortably and interchangeably traverse a dozen other rivers. Docklands inhabits an international urban realm nowhere better exemplified than in this vast and busy square, but it's less the internationalism that strikes one than the reliance on the global brand leaders: we're very much in the realm of the starchitects and designers who flit easily between cities across the globe, so that Docklands' true neighbour is not the rest of Dublin but other dockland developments or urban sites in Berlin, Seoul, Denver, Belgrade or Boston. The hotel looks at the moment more like a giant cubic chessboard, white granite blocks alternated with black glass through which the guests can peer out at the activity below.

When you walk around any urban area you tend to take it for granted; it's here, it seems always to have been here. But it's instructive to pause here for a moment just to consider the sheer scale of the reclamation that underlies Grand Canal Harbour. This was where the gas for the city had been produced since 1830, which meant that the soil was full of contaminants. That in turn meant the site lay deserted for many years. The Dublin Docklands Authority, which ran from 1997 until it was dissolved in 2015, had to spend €50 million to decontaminate the ten-hectare site. An underground wall had to be built into the soil to prevent any of the pollutants from leaking, then the site had to be excavated to a depth of four metres and the groundwater pumped out to a treatment centre. Dangerous soil was exported to various EU countries, the rest was treated on site. 134,000 tonnes of material had to be removed. The process took five years. It's a reminder of the sheer ambition this area represents and of the huge powers that determined it.

I walk down around the dock looking down the newly

created streets, narrow channels between large apartment blocks. At Grand Canal Quay there are shops, cafés, Dublin Bikes, a Viking bus on the basin. At Hanover Quay, more restaurants and apartments. Yet as I walk around what strikes me, as always when I'm here, is how quiet it is, how empty the spaces are. It's like walking around a distant suburb except that there are no prams, no parents with toddlers, no evidence at all of children, no schools, no evidence of a complex community here in South Docklands. It has the appearance of a densely occupied urban zone but in fact, given that there will eventually be almost thirty thousand workers in the office buildings here, there's a serious shortfall of housing, with space for a maximum of 6,500 people. So one in four who live here might be close to their work, the other three will have to commute, which seems like a lost opportunity.

I pass some original dock buildings as I walk past Blood Stoney Road, called, apparently, and maybe a little disappointingly, after the Port engineer Bindon Blood Stoney who designed a diving bell. Here, until it was demolished, was the wall covered with graffiti by U2 fans. *Germinal loves Lucia. U2 are magnificent. All I want is you Larry. Engie was here.* After a tussle with the local residents, and slightly lower than originally planned, the U2 Visitor Centre has recently been approved. When it's finished several hundred thousand pilgrims are expected to flock here every year. In the meantime preserved parts of the wall are on view over at CHQ on Custom House Quay.

Down at the waterfront, along Sir John Rogerson's Quay, all is quiet. Office buildings, pedestrian walkways and cycle routes along the river. This part of the area will, like the companion area on the opposite bank, become an extended linear leisure area with trees and benches. Every time I come here I remind myself how unusual it is to see anything here, how not much more than fifteen years ago few who didn't live here would have ventured this far east. The Ferryman pub marked the limits of the navigable city for many and walking westward past the Custom House you always had the feeling of returning into the (relatively) safe embrace of the city. This part of Docklands is still eerily quiet. A large glass office block presents the spectacle of quiet industry to the waterfront: men and women hunched over computers and photocopiers, their desks surrounded by large white cartons. Legal files, maybe. Solicitors, trade mark advisors, business and management consultants, fund managers, debt recovery specialists . . . all engaged in their mystifying professions. A coffee kiosk operates on the quay with no takers at the moment. I sit on a bench and look across at the angled glass tube of the Convention Centre. What would it be like to live here, I think, in one of these apartments? Who, in fact, does live here? Most of the apartments around here are occupied by young, high-salaried professionals working for the likes of Google, Facebook, Airbnb. Many of the individuals who bought apartments here and were then stung by the crash and ended up in negative equity have now sold on, and most of these have been snapped up by investors. A recent estate agent's report gives a flavour of the current occupants:

> *Only 19% of our tenants are Irish though this is an increase on 2017. We are noticing more Brexit related demand and the average salary of our tenants has increased to €117,095 compared to €57,000 in 2015. The outlook for this year is very positive. Given there is enough office space planned or under construction to accommodate 40,000 workers in the greater Docklands area and the various schemes planned that will further cement Docklands as the most sought after city quarter in Dublin, I am confident capital values will increase in the region of 5% this year. The supply/demand mismatch in the rental sector will continue for another couple of years so I predict rental values will increase at least 8% this year and I believe improved rental yields will encourage more investors to buy.*

Well, it's one Docklands dialect. Part V of the Planning and Development Act (2000) specifies that 10% of a development of ten or more units must be used as social housing. This itself is down from the 20% included in an early Docklands development plan agreed with local residents. There is some social housing in Docklands. Of the 187 apartments built in Clarion Quay, for example, 37 were set aside for public housing. The mix of public and private occupancy was a deliberate strategy, termed 'tenure mixing', aimed at preventing the kind of stigmatization that can arise when poorer residents are all grouped in a single development. Stigmatization can happen anywhere, of course, and can take many forms. A recent study referred to the lack of interaction between the private and public sections of the development: 'None of the private residents of Clarion Quay who were interviewed for this study reported ever visiting the home of, or knowing the names of, any public renting neighbours. The former did not think this unusual but public housing tenants found this situation odd and unsatisfactory.'[1]

It would be possible to make too much of this. Lack of interaction with other residents is, for many, the point of apartment living. More revealing, maybe, is the tension that emerged over different perceptions of public space. Residents share a single communal space — a grass courtyard in the centre of the complex. The private residents, apparently, viewed the courtyard as a 'visual amenity' rather than as a space to be used for activities. We are, of course, in the familiar realm of class conflict here.

They also considered unsupervised play in the courtyard (almost entirely by public housing residents' children) as *de facto* problematic and raised questions about noise levels, children's safety and the quality of parenting. Public housing residents had a contrasting interpretation — they viewed the courtyard as a space which could and should be used and believed it was not only normal but inevitable that children would play there. So they couldn't understand objections to their children's play and interpreted these as a form of stigmatization.

Children. Play. *Unsupervised* play. Another reminder that we're in a planned world, with guidelines for everything. Smart lighting, smart bins, the city as code and data. At a conference on The Programmable City one of the participants spoke of Docklands as the new Ardnacrusha, showing a slide of the famous Seán Keating painting, but if it is it's the Ardnacrusha of neoliberalist Ireland, the triumph of silicon economics and profit-led development.

And what's happening the Part V social housing? The City Council is saying that it is being priced out of the area and cannot afford to acquire apartments for the 10% social housing provision. Therefore developers will be able to offer sites in other parts of the city in lieu of lucrative Docklands sites. In the Kennedy Wilson apartment development, Capital Dock, for instance ('Offering superior living accommodation with exclusive, private on-site access to a range of five-star residents' amenities and unrivalled dedicated concierge team, including on-site professional management, chef's kitchen, cinema room and 24-hour security to respond to your every need'), where rents will be almost €4,000 a month, the developers intend to provide their 10% social housing quota in Rialto, far from Docklands, a decision described by Labour Senator Kevin Humphreys as 'social cleansing'. There are currently eleven places in Docklands where developers are planning to build but a report from Executive Housing Manager Anthony Flynn confirmed that 'Some off-site units have been identified in the electoral area and deposits have been paid to acquire these units'. In April 2019 *The Irish Times* reports that in the case of three developments, 6 Hanover Quay, Boland's Mill and 8 Hanover Quay sites for social housing have been acquired off-site. The apartments at 6 Hanover Quay are expected to generate €800,000 per unit, and the Council has agreed with the developer to acquire 13 units at Castleforbes Square in Dublin 1. The Boland's Mill development, sold last year to

Google, will have 28,000 square metres of office space, 46 apartments, cafés and cultural space, but rather than acquire apartments at the site the Council will buy three units 'within the electoral area'. Likewise, with the Reflector Building, 8 Hanover Quay, where Airbnb and LogMeIn are based, none of the 40 apartments are being set aside for social housing and four will again be acquired 'off-site'. All of this, of course, negates the original intention of mixing tenure types and means that, in terms of housing provision, the area will be a ghetto for the affluent.

There are plans for most things in Docklands. It is a planned city state whose overarching plan is the attraction of wealth. The cold order of money is apparent everywhere. But communities, and cities, thrive on disorder, on unplanned organic growth, on various kinds of civic spontaneity, and maybe most of all on the conjunction of difference: different communities with differing levels of wealth living alongside each other and colliding on the streets, in the shops and cafés and in the educational and cultural institutions. Otherwise there is sterility, segregation, indifference. What Richard Sennett said of large cities applies equally to a mini-city like Docklands, that it takes 'dense, disorderly, over-whelming cities', to give us an idea of the real complexity of life and human relations.

If the social elements of Docklands feel tacked on or underdeveloped it's because the place is driven primarily by money. In the sixties the original docklands were badly affected by the containerization that removed the need for dockers. At the time the government response was to encourage families to move out of the area into the suburbs, which was the policy for much of the life of the new state and which resulted in a considerable thinning of the inner city population. The engine of the current incarnation was the Irish Financial Services Centre which was largely the brainchild of the financier Dermot Desmond and personally supported by the then Taoiseach, Charles Haughey. It was specifically designed to attract international investment; it provided a tax haven with quick access to European markets and a low corporation tax rate of 10%. It's unlikely that the government anticipated the staggering success that would reward the initiative, the hundreds of millions of tax revenue, the hundreds of companies attracted by the IFSC terms, the hundreds of billions of international bank assets located in Dublin, the thousands of jobs created.[2]

The very success of Docklands as a financial enterprise tended to push everything else aside, and the initial development around the Custom House Docks was entirely developer and investment-led. There was little sense of it having a meaningful relationship with the troubled and disadvantaged community around it. It showed all the classic signs of urban gentrification the world over. One of the starkest images of the social apartheid that characterized the first phase of development is the wall dividing the Custom House Square apartments from Sheriff Street. Effectively, all the local community got was a view of the new wealth crowding into the area, glimpses of smart new apartments they could never afford to live in. The original state agency for the development of the docks, the Custom House Docks Development Authority, was content to follow the model of dockland developments elsewhere and provide investment opportunities for private developers.

In 2012 the Strategic Development Zone (SDZ) for North Lotts and the Grand Canal Dock replaced the 1997 docklands plan, and the Poolbeg West SDZ was announced later, but there's no sign that priorities have shifted. They fast-track planning, but only a very specific kind of planning that favours business and capital. Plans to build 3,500 homes at the former Glass Bottle site on the Poolbeg Peninsula, including 900 affordable homes, were stalled for years, but this April (2019) An Bord Pleanála finally announced the development of an 'urban quarter' that will include almost 900 social and affordable homes at the site. Plans for the site include 350 units for social housing, while a further 15% — or 525 — of the residential units are designated for 'social and affordable housing purposes', which will bring the total to 875. The plan will also deliver 860,000 square feet of commercial development as well as school sites and community space. It will be very interesting to see if this plan is delivered.

Some, including former Trinity geographer Andrew MacLaran, have criticized the narrow focus of the development zones: 'the very delineation of this Strategic Development Zone is problematic to me, because it zones out Sheriff Street, East Wall, Ringsend and Pearse Street'. Elsewhere MacLaran has gone as far as to call the Docklands site a delimitation, 'clearly gerrymandered to exclude concentrations of poor indigenous Docklands residents'.

One new intervention, in poorer city centre locations, has been the investor-led luxury student housing schemes aimed at the forty odd thousand international students the Government wants to attract. These are relatively cheap to build, with more lenient planning guidelines and without the need to provide parking. One of these is in Sheriff Street. Gerry Fay, chairman of the North Wall Community Association and community activist, welcomes the arrival of young people into the area but deplores the lack of local housing provision, citing, in a recent *Irish Times* interview, 'broken promise after broken promise'. Of the 2,369 households on the area's housing list few are likely to end up there. 'There's no land left to build housing,' says local Workers' Party councillor Éilis Ryan in the same piece. 'Every site has been bought and you can be sure no developer is interested in social and affordable housing. The big profits are in hotels, student accommodation, offices and luxury apartments. The vast, vast majority of people on the list will have to leave the area.' City planners often favour purpose-built student accommodation precisely because it is built in 'depressed' areas of the city and, supposedly, brings life and money into the area. I'm not sure what the evidence for this is. I think of the large units in Blackpitts, near where I live. What was supposed to be a public courtyard through which the local community might pass is now shut off by an iron gate so that

Peter Sirr

the complex is effectively a closed-off compound, in defiance of the planning permission, while none of the promised 'retail, restaurant, event and social spaces', so prominently displayed on the billboards, were ever built.

The disparity between the needs of the existing community and the vision of a shiny new cosmopolitan district designed for high earning executives is hardcoded into the various editions of the Docklands vision. There is, you feel, always going to be a difference between what the dreamers of the dream actually want and what they are impelled to accommodate. This is most obvious in the early publicity material that came from the Custom House Docks Development Authority. Niamh Moore quotes a telling example in *Dublin Docklands Reinvented*:

> *It is a warm, calm September evening. The highly paid executives in the Financial Services Centre are still at work — their VDUs giving out the latest on Wall Street. At the Liffey's edge the tanned and fit members of the Custom House yacht club are tying up their craft and are strolling leisurely to the dockside pub for a pint or a G&T. The kids are not yet back in school. The culture vultures are on their third museum — in the Dublin section they are still not over the shock of what the city was like when it had vacant sites. At the heliport a Ryanair courtesy helicopter arrives with some more tourists. A limousine whisks them to their luxury hotel. In the apartments a successful young barrister has just arrived home via a vaporetto from the law courts up the quays. She sits on her penthouse balcony admiring the spectacular view of the mountains. As she sips her Campari soda she wonders if the Buñuel movie is playing at the Screen on the dock.[3]*

That was 1987 and if you remove the local references it could have been the blueprint for any urban gentrification. And many of those elements are still very much in the mix. We might have to swap the vaporetto for the recently re-introduced No. 11 Liffey Ferry, and the Campari for craft beer and complicated gin, and replace the barristers with the Facebookers and Googlers, but the picture isn't that different. Divisions between the original and the newly arrived inhabitants begin to seem a necessary part of the dynamic. These divisions are often expressed physically: walls, gated compounds, security guards, the ever-present CCTV cameras. Many apartment buildings offer 24-hour security and security is regarded as an essential ingredient of docklands life. The presence of security and surveillance highlights another aspect of docklands life: the blurring of the boundaries between public and private space. In the early days there was a strict policy on photography, particularly in the vicinity of the IFSC, and an expensive permit had to be applied for. You were allowed to take photographs outside the IFSC and private buildings but a spokesman for Docklands specified that 'we would like to be informed when and where someone will be photographing'. Today we take surveillance, control and exclusion for granted, but then this is part of a growing worldwide trend, not only in new areas that are heavily privatized but also on public transport, in shopping centres or central city areas as part of crime prevention or anti-terrorist policies. Cities everywhere are increasingly governed by fear, and docklands developments around the world with their ubiquitous cameras and security guards have been particularly blighted by an obsession with draping their urban landscapes in protective blankets of privacy.

It's often argued that 'social regeneration' often regenerates very little but simply builds new complexes and ignores what was there before. This is a criticism often levelled at London Docklands. Yet it shouldn't be thought that the DDDA's efforts at social regeneration were fruitless. The interaction between the authority and the local community did yield some tangible benefits in education, housing and jobs. The local community fought hard for a Local Labour Charter which secured some construction jobs. The DDDA did work closely with the local Docklands schools and the communities and many educational development projects were implemented at primary, post primary and third level. There were programmes designed to increase the skills of local residents, such as the Apprenticeship Programme and the Community Training Workshop. Under the Schools Job Placement Programme locals with the Leaving Certificate were given jobs by IFSC and other businesses in the area. Since it started in 1997 more than 300 young adults have been placed within the IFSC. A quota of places in the National College of Ireland in Mayor Street is reserved for inner-city residents and Pathways to Employment guarantees locals who finish courses jobs in financial services. The NCI's Discover University programme brings young people from the Inner City Docklands area to take part in summer courses to give them experience of student life. And, as we have seen, a certain amount of affordable homes were built, with more planned, but nowhere near the original target of 20% which the local community managed to get into the 2003 Master Plan.

Docklands, the DDDA. But what are these things exactly? I feel like a host at a conference who has forgotten to introduce the keynote speaker. Everything you see in Docklands is the result of a decision made by the now-defunct Dublin Docklands Development Authority. The DDDA was a state agency, its funds were state funds, its gains or losses were the taxpayers'. It was created by the Dublin Docklands Development Authority Act 1997 'to lead a major project of physical, social and economic regeneration in the East side of Dublin'. It was responsible for 1300 acres of land. It had a fifteen-year development period (1997-2012). Every five years a new Master Plan was issued, the most recent of which was Master Plan 2008. At the top of the organizational tree sat the Department of Environment, Heritage and Local Government. Beneath this was the Executive Board, and under this was the Council which was made up of representatives from the public and business sectors and the local community. A staff of around fifty people was deployed in finance, marketing, architecture and planning, project management, legal services and social regeneration.

This is all clear enough but, as always, it's when you begin to follow the money that the clear structure starts to become shrouded and the DDDA begins to take its place in a very familiar Irish nexus of power, money and cosy relationships. As property values shrank and developers went broke the authors started to come under close media scrutiny. It emerged that directors had been financially involved in Docklands sites. Questions were asked about possible conflicts of interest. The Irish Glass Bottle site in Ringsend had been purchased for €412 million, then the highest price ever paid for land in Ireland. After the crash the value of the site, which was so toxic the DDDA had to spend millions cleaning it up, fell to about €60 million.

The DDDA story was always short of glorious. A chairman of the DDDA stepped down following his appointment as chairman of Anglo-Irish Bank. His successor survived for less than a month, resigning when details of a complicated tax avoidance scheme he was involved in were published. In the words of the leader of the Labour Party, the chairman 'legally avoided the payment of Capital Gains tax by the convenient means of transferring the shares to his spouse, who then transferred herself to Italy for the best part of a year to qualify as a tax exile' (*The Irish Times*). In 2012 the Comptroller and Auditor General found serious shortcomings in the conduct of the DDDA's planning and development functions, particularly in relation to the Glass Bottle site purchase, prompting the then minister, Phil Hogan, to announce that the DDDA would be abolished and its powers transferred to Dublin City Council, and the same year the site passed into the control of the National Asset Management Agency (NAMA).

Little of this might have come out if the fall in property

values had not been so catastrophic. Without rehearsing every detail of the saga, what became clear was that this vast area was controlled by a small group of financiers and developers, and that everyone involved was playing a hugely risky game for giddying stakes. A single bank was the primary lender, and its clients made millions in profits determined in large part by the decisions of the state agency. A small group of developers, most of them bankrolled by the same bank, were the main builders. It seems pretty remarkable that a state agency such as the DDDA would gamble so recklessly in a speculative deal like the Ringsend site. Towards the end of its reign a new chair, Professor Niamh Brennan of UCD, was appointed, a specialist in corporate governance and forensic accounting, and she oversaw inquiries into the activities of the authority during the boom years. One of the things she found was that key records of the DDDA had gone missing: 'We understand that under the previous regime, it was not always the policy to ensure proper minutes of discussions and decisions were taken at subcommittees of the board,' she said at the time. 'As a result, we understand that there are a number of meetings where there is no proper record of what transpired. We are also aware that there were instances where minutes were kept but are no longer accessible. Clearly this is an unsatisfactory situation. It is now policy that all meetings are now minuted.'

Paul Maloney, who was chief executive of the authority from 2005 to 2009 and was central to the disastrous investment in the former Irish Glass Bottle, told the Dáil Committee on Public Accounts in 2013 that he had 'watched aghast' for four years as Ms Brennan 'issued report after report on DDDA without ever offering an opportunity for those involved to present their views or have a say'. He vigorously defended the record of the DDDA but the fact remains that the loss to the authority, following the transfer of loans associated with the Glass Bottle site deal to the National Asset Management Agency, was €52 million. Professor Brennan in turn objected to what she called 'inappropriate and personal attacks' made on her under evidence at the PAC by other DDDA officials. She disputed claims by one DDDA official that she had questions to answer as to how she carried out her functions. The truth is that the history of Docklands is a labyrinth of claim and counter-claim, of incomplete investigations, complex money trails, shifting policies and governance, and it will take a comprehensive study to tease out the detail of the making of this new urban quarter in all its gnarly intricacy.

As I walk down the quay I stop to admire the Samuel Beckett Bridge. We have the James Joyce Bridge, the Sean O'Casey Bridge, and now the Samuel Beckett Bridge. What would the writers make of their incorporation into the civic infrastructure? Samuel Beckett was imported from Rotterdam. At home on my computer I watched its stately progress through the Dutch port, laid on a huge barge and hauled by an impossibly small tug. Then I watched it coming up the Liffey through the East Link bridge. The bridge, a Calatrava, is a cable stay bridge that fans across the river like a lyre. Looking at it is another reminder that there is plenty to look at in Docklands. It is a visually fascinating urban space. I cross the Sean O'Casey Bridge, for me the most attractive of Dublin's new bridges, and enter the CHQ building on the other side. This is what used to be known as Stack A, a large nineteenth-century tobacco warehouse with a spectacular iron roof, built over stone vaults designed to store wine, famous for hosting the Crimean War Banquet in 1856, celebrating the return of 3,000 Irish soldiers.

All kinds of proposals for a cultural use of this historic building were made: a science museum, a Museum of Dublin, a gallery of modern art, a maritime museum, a transport museum. The architects who restored it were given a brief to convert it for use as both retail space and museum. London has its Museum of London Docklands. Rotterdam has it Havensmuseum in Waterstad, the heart of the harbour; Toronto's docklands will house an ambitious multicultural Toronto Museum Project. All of these make an explicit connection between their maritime location and the heritage of the docks. CHQ, for all the attractiveness of the building and location, has struggled to make an impact. The Grade One listed building was redeveloped by the DDDA in 2005 for a cost of approximately €45 million but struggled to attract tenants. 82% of the development was vacant when it was put on sale in 2013. It was bought by Neville Isdell, a former CEO of the Coca-Cola Company for €10 million and now houses the usual run of generic cafés, sushi places, office space and EPIC: The Irish Emigration Museum, which tells the stories of Ireland's emigrants 'who became scientists, politicians, poets, artists and even outlaws all over the world'. ('What is Rihanna's Irish surname?', 'Where was Ronan O'Hara born?', 'Which Irish-born author wrote *The Chronicles of Narnia*?' ask the bright green posters outside.)

Culture, it has to be said, doesn't feature heavily in Docklands, as the Master Plan admitted back in 2008: 'To date there has not been a significant provision of arts and culture infrastructure in the Docklands.'[4] It's as if Docklands doesn't want to link itself culturally with the surrounding community or, particularly, with Dublin. It was quite happy to vest its cultural interest in the two signature venues, the O2 and the Grand Canal Theatre, a few art galleries and some public art, including another giant but ultimately ill-fated commission, the proposed 48 metre high Antony Gormley sculpture close to the O'Casey footbridge ('almost as tall as the Statue of Liberty', 'nearly as high as Liberty Hall', 'bigger than Rio's Christ the Redeemer') which would, in the artist's words 'allude to the human body as a dynamic interconnected matrix evoking the collective body'. This project was, inevitably, doomed by the crash, which is possibly no bad thing.

Other than that there was the usual bland rhetoric about 'developing the arts identity of brand Docklands' and actively promoting 'the sustainability of the arts in the future'. There is also talk of seeking to 'explore the feasibility' of a maritime museum but, given what happened with Stack A, it feels a little hollow.

A few years ago as I left the old CHQ I paused to take a photograph of a Luas coming down Mayor Street. Within seconds a security guard came running up to stop me. 'This is private property,' he said, 'photography is strictly forbidden.' Did he mean this street, or this area? 'No, the whole Docklands area is private property. If you want to take a photograph you can go to Amiens Street.' Dublin ended at Amiens Street, it seemed. When I asked why Docklands objected to photography he explained that the 'clients' don't like it. The 'clients', whoever they were, were the real occupants of Docklands. The rest of us were visitors. Today I take out my phone and snap away unaccosted and yet as I cross the expensive bridges and walk up and down the quiet pedestrian walkways it still has the feeling of patrolling a private district, a corporatized park at the edge of the city, in search of a heart to call its own.

# Occupations

For as long as I could I clung to the feeling of being newly arrived, to being foreign, surprised, ignorant, even while plunging into the language, history and architecture of the city. And if they were emotionally and imaginatively accelerated those first few months were also a return to childhood. Learning the ropes of a new culture and language is, for a long time, weirdly infantilizing. Apart from the wide-eyed wonder there is also the childlike stumbling to understand and articulate, the desperate pointing at things one can't name, the change-filled hand abjectly proffered to the fruiterer or fishmonger because the effort to understand the price is too much, the foolish smile which becomes an indispensable part of the learner's grammar. In my first week in Amsterdam I went out to buy a loaf of bread, having rehearsed the phrases for a half, sliced, wholegrain loaf so that there could be no possible ambiguity about what I wanted. The bakery was busy and I had to wait in a queue, edging slowly and nervously closer to the counter, repeating my sentence in my head. Eventually my turn came and an assistant raised an inquiring eye. '*Ik wil graag een half grof volkoren brood, besneden.*' Immediately I produced my request the customers burst out laughing and the bakery staff held their sides and turned to each other. I stood there shamefaced and baffled, knowing only that I had somehow added to the folklore of linguistic incompetence. I grabbed the bread and shuffled out of the shop and back to the flat where my girlfriend explained that I had asked for circumcised, rather than sliced, bread. *Besneden* instead of *gesneden*, a single slipped consonant was the difference between a satisfied desire and humiliation. There was plenty more of this kind of comedy to be endured. My girlfriend lived in the northern city of Gröningen, her family in a distant village, so that I was very often in situations where English wasn't an option, and where I could either forever remain a child patiently plied with coffee and biscuits, or get to grips with the language and enter a kind of adulthood. So I learned the language and tried to lean a little closer to the country I found myself in.

Bussum. I have moved to this small town halfway between Amsterdam and Hilversum with reluctance, having failed to find anywhere to live after the lease on my flat in Javastraat ran out. I have found a job in the international section of a large Dutch school, the Alberdingk Thijm College, in Hilversum. On the night before the job begins I move my belongings from Amsterdam to Bussum by means of several train trips back and forth, stuffing everything into large suitcases and plastic bags until there is nothing left. Bussum is an upmarket dormitory town, deathly quiet, and with very little to do after the supermarket closes. My flat is the upstairs portion of a house in a quiet terrace; my *hospita* lives downstairs. I am her first experiment in property letting and my tenancy seems somehow to trouble her. On my first night she visits my rooms and notes with alarm that I intend to use the biggest of the three rooms as my sitting room. This, I discover, is because my rental includes heat, and the gas fire humming merrily and dispensing heat throughout the spacious room is the source of concern. It is not, though, the only one. In the smaller room there is a set of bookshelves partly filled with books in Dutch, alongside which I have placed my own books. My landlady surveys this scene, her face clouded with anxiety. Then she leaves the rooms, disappears downstairs and returns bearing a ruler. She bends to the Dutch books, which occupy the lowest shelf, and measures them with the ruler. There are, it seems, fifty centimetres of books. Six months later, on the eve of my departure, she returns with the ruler, measures her books, and finds several centimetres unaccounted for. This loss is quickly translated into an accusation of theft. Patiently I explain that I have not taken any of her books, and it is possible that her initial measurement was inaccurate. Eyes blazing, she glares at me. Liar. Thief. Unscrupulous intruder. I realize that my entire residency here has been a barely tolerated act of trespass. I should have been warned. In the early days of my stay there she told me several times about the nearby municipal swimming pool.

'It's not far from the house,' she would remind me. 'You could go there in the mornings.' For a while I am puzzled. Why is she so keen that I should swim? And then it becomes clear. 'They have showers there.'

The price of hot water. Of course. As winter approaches she suggests a supplement to the rent to allow for the extra heat I will consume. The rent is already excessive. I will have to go.

I will in fact be very glad to leave this town with which I have formed no connection, in which I have begun to feel oddly invisible. Even my landlady sometimes forgets that she has rented her upper floor to me and bolts the front door from the inside before leaving by the back door, so that when I return from my teaching I can't get in and have to while away the hours in the local library until she comes back. And yet at the same time she is generous, kindly. She invites me for dinner and sometimes I do the same. We get on well until she decides she's had enough of being a landlady.

Winter, in fact, is what keeps me going, suspends normalcy, charges with life. It's the coldest winter in a decade. Canals and rivers have frozen over, allowing the *Elfstedentocht*, the race on ice around eleven towns, to take place. Skaters in bright suits, their bodies bent double, flash by on TV sets. Rain freezes as it hits the street; I can feel icicles in my hair. Once, the train from Amsterdam that bears me to work in Hilversum is prevented from running, bringing delicious freedom, the promise of chaos. My clothes freeze on the veranda, irretrievable because the cold has jammed the door.

I remember it was winter when I first came to this country, three Januaries ago, on a reconnaissance trip. I met my girl-friend at the airport and we rushed to get the last train to the city in the north where she lived then. The train station at the airport was connected with the arrivals lounge by a series of tunnels and walkways, so it was only when we finally emerged three hours later from the snug carriage onto the icy platform that I felt the sharp bite of the sub-zero weather. A canal ran parallel with the station, frozen over, fringed with lime trees. Ice hung in the trees where the rain had frozen, so that they looked like bizarre sculptures, pinky orange in the glow of the street lamps. One young tree, crushed by the weight of ice in its branches, had toppled over and lay sprawled on the mud path beside the canal. We hurried through the narrow streets to the small terraced house near the railway tracks.

When I move again, this time to Hilversum, winter has receded and the prospect of chaos begins to be replaced by routine. Bussum and Hilversum were steps downward, away from the lure of the urban into the nullity of the sub-urban, the dormitory, the tamed, where people came to your door and told you your windows were dirty or wondered aloud why you were cleaning them on the Sabbath. They also represented a retreat from excitement to a more pedestrian reality, to the details of a life and livelihood. Semblances of permanence crept in quietly; the bike in the hall, my name on the gas bill, tables, chairs, a painfully assembled bed. The house I lived in was near the station which was, for me, its major attraction. It was a brick house in a brick terrace surrounded by other brick terraces enlivened by grocers, bakeries, a Greek takeaway. The longer I stayed there the more terrified I became of that enclave of brick houses and paved streets, by their silence, by the dark furniture that loomed at me out of windows as I passed. This was made worse by the fact that the relationship the house had been intended to house, and that had brought me to Holland in the first place, had ended. Solitary, disconnected, I felt I was living someone else's life. I couldn't quite believe the house I lived in, or the life that laboured to occupy it. I can still remember distinctly the feeling of walking along a street on the way to the school and thinking suddenly as if I had just woken up inside myself: 'What am I doing here?' This was not because my life there was unpleasant. I was surrounded by pretty villages, controlled green spaces, cycle lanes, little lakes. I could cycle with friends to Lage Vuursche and eat pancakes heavy with syrup, drink beer in a village *kroeg* with carpet on the tables. Yet I don't think I have ever lived more remotely from my life. It was as if I had gone to sleep and woken up in exactly the kind of Dublin suburb I had left Dublin to avoid, except it happened to be somewhere else. It was a kind of aftermath, or an afterlife. I think in any life periods of psychic wakefulness and sleep alternate at irregular intervals. After a year in Holland something fell asleep in me that didn't wake up until I left. But I do really believe that some places are more scarily soporific than others. If you live in a city of any size you can step outside into a current of life that at some level takes you with it and outside of yourself. Even solitary activities (and for me the quintessential urban experience is always a solitary one) are lapped by waves of the social, of other lives, other noises. To walk in a crowd, to sit in a café or pub, browse in a book-shop or record shop is to be socially private, or privately social — you take a dip in the social pool, you participate, even at a subliminal level, in the communal life and have a sense of skeins of connectedness from the self to the city. You are constantly being woken out of yourself. But in a place like Bussum or Hilversum or their equivalents any-where there was only the sleep of the private life, the life led within long defined circles of social and familial ties free of the accident and surprise of the urban.

I am, of course, being unfair and partial. I haven't done any kind of justice to the realities of these places, and I don't suppose I ever will. One of the perils of writing about places you have lived in is the tendency to generalize a personal pathology into an oracular truth. The truth was that I had constructed a place in my own head, a city resting shakily on wooden piles driven deep into the soft sand, a monument to provisionality. I loved to gape at the exposed sand when workers lifted the flagstones in Amsterdam. Maybe I loved this more than the city itself; I loved its temporariness, or rather, my own brief transit through it. I liked the feeling of being adrift, skating along its surfaces. I had no idea how long I would stay there; I was at a stage in my life when I simply wanted to be elsewhere, and the actual place I ended up in was less important than my shallow rooting there. Having no real connections there, no powerful reason to be there as opposed to somewhere else, I was simply privatizing the city, incorporating it into a personal narrative. Not that the city cared a hoot. But even that indifference was grist to the mill. The dormitory towns, however, didn't afford the same shifting backdrop for internal drama. They were too real, too permanent, and they produced in me a sense of dislocation, of being distanced from myself. It was as if I had been catapulted into a version of my own future, and been frightened by it. Certain kinds of travel, it may be, are an extended adolescence, and I wasn't ready to be a grown-up in Holland. Eventually, hungering for surprise, for another arrival, I decided to leave.

The way to leave was to go to the hiring fair, held every year in a hotel in the grounds of Heathrow Airport. Here, clutching the CVs that held the promise of a new life, supplicant teachers queued in front of desks at which the principals of desirable schools sat like tribunes or provincial satraps bored with their duties. Interviews were conducted in the hotel bedrooms. Bogotá was a British school which went in for uniforms and imperial grandeur, paid meagrely and liked its sport. Tokyo was a Catholic girls' school run by nuns. Istanbul was a genial conversation about the difficulties of the Turkish language after it became evident that there was, in fact, no job on offer. The following day brought Kenya, a fruit plantation, a houseboy, and the requirement that, on arrival, I would purchase a jeep from the school to the amount of a year's salary. Fine, I said, that sounds great. I must learn to drive I told myself as I left the bedroom. My final, last-hope interview was with the principal of an American school in Milan, a huge, shaggy man with an unsmiling face who seemed to be going through the motions of interviewing me in case, at some distant point in the future, all of his staff having been consumed by a plague, he might reach a sufficient pitch of desperation to want to hire me. Tell me, he said to me as he contemplated the floor, your five worst qualities. I groped around to encapsulate my failures as a human being, the ones I could reveal to him that would show me in a good light. I work too hard. I give too much of myself in the service of others. I am overly submissive towards authority. I don't remember what I did say but whatever it was hadn't seemed to make much of an impression for it took my interrogator a long time to retrieve his gaze from the carpet and force himself to utter the next question on his list.

It was with some surprise, therefore, some months later, all other options having expired, that I picked up the phone and heard his voice offering me a job at his school. His first choice had let him down, and his second choice had contracted a rare illness. I wasn't too concerned about the details as I stepped off the plane into the August glare of Linate airport. I was glad to be somewhere else, looking at new faces, listening to a new language. Something inside me was soaring, was *home*. Even years later I can't disabuse myself of the feeling that some part of me will always be at home in Italy, and my family has had sufficient injections of it that I think they feel the same. As I write this I hear my wife at her Zoom Italian class, part of a determination to get back there again.

The work was demanding and often fractious; the school was an island of Americanness and although most of the pupils were the children of the affluent Milanese, the atmosphere, the system, the ethos were firmly American. There was a peculiar doubleness to each day as I moved from one unfamiliar culture to another, tending, unfairly, to regard one as the necessary tax on the enjoyment of the other. The students were ferried to the school by their chauffeurs or by the fleet of school buses which were also available for teachers. Unwilling to face a busful of kids, and wanting to get at least an hour of Italy into my system before the bell rang, I would wake up, clamber down the stairs of the fourth floor walk-up I had found, eventually, in the city centre, bolt into a bar for a shot of coffee, jump on a tram crowded with Italians on their way to work, run for the bus to the suburb where the school was housed, enjoying the clamour of the Italian kids on the way to their school a few doors down, and then walk, trot or run from the bus stop until finally I slid past the team of *carabinieri* on permanent guard outside the gates, into the world, vaguely familiar from high school movies, of home rooms, hall passes, spot quizzes, advanced placement, eleventh and twelfth graders, the arcana of American high schools.

I live here for two years, slowly piecing the city together, arranging the tram stops and metro stations in my head, finding shortcuts from my apartment to the crowded theatre of Piazza Duomo, the massed baroque magnificence of the cathedral squatting, in D H Lawrence's disenchanted eye, like a great hedgehog. At the beginning of each month I make my way to the nineteenth-century building around the corner from my flat, and hand an envelope stuffed with cash to the *portinaia*, along with a pre-prepared receipt for exactly one third of the amount, for the benefit of my landlord's tax returns. I am foolishly proud of my first Milan flat, a very small fourth floor walk-up off the Via Ripamonti, not least because it was so difficult to get. Your relationship with a city where you intend to spend time is determined hugely by the search for accommodation; it's then that you begin to discover a little of how the place works and sneak a glimpse of its soul. If some cities are hospitable to provisionality, reserving tracts of the available accommodation for the flighty — shabby bedsits, sublets, modest spaces you can stay in for a few months, collecting your mail from a pile on the hall table and putting up with the damp in the bathroom, the hole in the floor, the surly landlord who comes once weekly for his cash rent — Milan is not one of them. Milan is a solid city; it assumes that if you are here for any length of time then you must have a very good reason to be here, and a solid family behind you. It doesn't take easily to the transient, the undecided, the lightly encumbered. In my first few weeks I scour the papers for flats. Whenever I get as far as the interview I seem to make a bad impression. Single men are, as ever, a threat to property, and single men from the bad end of Europe, pale, shifty, prone to violence like all *anglosassoni*, are even less welcome. When, eventually, I find the flat I spend my first year in, I am almost delirious with happy relief. I am invited to dinner in the home of my landlord and, though conversation doesn't exactly flow, I seem to be approved. And then things begin to go wrong. Although my landlord and I are engaged in a traditional commercial relationship certain niceties of the relationship elude him. He begins to make secret visits to my apartment when I'm at work and rings me up to tell me that I am untidy and would profit from a maid. He becomes obsessed with the idea that I have an electric guitar which is consuming vast quantities of electricity and, since the electricity is included in the rent, he begins to fret that he is the victim of an anglosaxon *inganno*, a sting designed to bankrupt him. This necessitates more secret visits to the flat. There is no guitar to be found. Where can I be concealing it? The neighbour has reported distinctly electronic sounds coming through the walls.

By the end of the year we no longer speak but this is such a familiar progression it seems no other would ever be possible. There is a single template which can never be departed from. A couple of years later, in Dublin, I will be pursued by yet another landlord seeking the return of his salad crisper. I have only the dimmest inkling of what a salad crisper actually is — though it sounds like a good idea — but it is a valuable enough contribution to humanity to take a sizeable slice out of my deposit.

In my second year in Milan my girlfriend and I took over the apartment of a teaching couple who had left for Germany. The landlord, however, has decided he doesn't want any more couples, so this year I don't exist; this year I am the invisible tenant, sloping in and out of the building like a secret agent or an illegal immigrant. There is a strange appropriateness about this. It's a sudden decision to move in together; we do it because it seems right, but also because we can, because the situation has arisen and the apartment is available. If we sat down and analysed it, it wouldn't take us long to count the reasons why this might not be the best idea, but we don't do that; my girlfriend signs the lease and I move in when the landlord has gone. Even if we make light of it the apartment, and the city, have in a way made a couple of us. We travel the length and breadth of the city and the country together on trams, buses, trains and in our ancient and not quite legal Alfa Romeo Giulietta, and our experiences deepen the bond in ways I don't think I realize until much later. Our relationship with each other and with the country merge seamlessly.

Here we are, in the Via Washington, up the road from Leonardo's 'The Last Supper', assembling our Ikea furniture, every frail stick of it an insult to the city's solidity, making the space habitable. The flat never acquires the sense of permanence that a committed life would give it; it remains ramshackle, haphazard and vaguely accusatory, as if to remind us that we are not trying hard enough, that our lives amid the sparse, improvised furniture are not real. And, of course, the flat was right, the furniture was right. I was the one who didn't take that life seriously enough, and I was the one who, in the end, walked out of it. I was, I think, fixed on provisionality then; I didn't want a permanent address and, with a selfishness that looks pathological in retrospect, I assumed relationships could be disassembled as easily as a bed or wardrobe. And so the day came when we left Via Washington, when that life slipped off us like an old coat we would never pick up again, and we took our planes to different countries.

How neat that sounds. The hurt, the mess, the pain of that parting have slid off the page. I can't undo any of them. I remember stupid things, the two us wandering around the Kafkaesque labyrinth of the telephone company head office, attempting, unsuccessfully, to cancel our account and return the handset. I remember our last days in the empty apartment where we lay in each other's arms unspeaking, as if we were at the beginning, as if we had just arrived in the city and met each other for the first time. I think I must have thought that our connection was a gift of the city, a sort of tenancy that would endure as long as our occupation of the city and then simply unravel, dissolve. It was only in the wrenching grief of the airport that I realized what I had done, and that there's no easy unpicking of love, but by then it was too late. I had spoiled the city's gift, and the damage spilled over into the city I returned to. Maybe the relationship I developed with that city in the years that followed had an element of reparation in it, as if you might live more innocently or more purely in the external life of a place, in its brickwork and patterns of habitation and history. Maybe this has always been one of the functions of a city, to rescue its citizens from themselves . . .

# Three Houses

It doesn't take long to dismantle a life.

The heavy sitting-room cabinet lies on its back in the front garden. My brother-in-law hits a spade against the shelves and works them apart efficiently, then jabs at the hinges of the fold-down table section. In a few seconds the whole thing is dismantled. I watch him, half admiring the calm thoroughness, half appalled at the violation of a piece of furniture so solid, so heavily rooted to its spot it was impossible to imagine it had not always been there, an outgrowth of the wall. We carry the remains into the garage to wait for the skip. How long was it there, in its corner of the sitting room? Not far short of forty years. It doesn't seem possible that it was once chosen, bought, installed. It's still planted firmly in my mind: I see the photographs, dictionaries, unread books received as prizes in school. Inside were glassware and silver, never touched, bundled from their darkness to the equal darkness of our attics. The wallpaper that the cabinet had hidden is shabby and discoloured. The table and chairs have gone, the TV, DVD player and video machine have all been carried off and disposed of. A box of Audrey Hepburn videos lies on the top of the otherwise empty mantelpiece. Anyone want them? No one has a video player. The sun spills in on the swirls of the carpet.

What was this room like the first time I saw it, when my parents first moved in here? It must have looked something like this: different wallpaper, different carpets, a more hopeful emptiness. We hadn't moved far. The old house where we'd lived for the previous six years was only two streets away. It felt farther, it felt like we had left the city and moved to the suburbs, crossed an invisible but definite border between sober red brick and a wide white road of semi-detached houses. I'd been very attached to the old house, so felt little excitement about being in this one. Some places get under your skin, but I never really felt at home here — the dreaming spaces, the places to which memory would persistently return, were elsewhere, back in childhood. Adolescence is always a suspended escape: by the time I arrived in this house I'd already begun my slow departure from it. But my sisters had lived here much longer, and the house was my mother's for nearly half her life, and she has only begun to realize that she won't be returning here. It's her life that lies here, her furniture littering the hall, her clothes in the wardrobe, her utensils in the drawer, her crockery in the kitchen cupboards. These are the objects of her world from which she's now permanently separated, her horizons shrunk to a small room in a nursing home, a semi medicalized space free of all but the most essential furniture, a room exactly like all the other rooms in the building.

A few hours and the house is returned to itself, a neutral space rinsed of memory, a place the new owners will enter and gradually occupy. We sit on the remaining chairs and sort through photographs and documents. Marriage certificate, my father's death certificate, a photo of his headstone. Graduation photos, a wedding album, my skinny parents in black and white outside the church in 1959, less than half the age I am now. I could slip into that photograph and stand behind them on the church steps, a smiling uncle looking forward to the reception. I go upstairs to what used to be my room. It's empty, it's been empty for years. I can still see the bed I used to sleep in, the modified sideboard I used to work at, the wardrobe I kept my clothes in. I can see the old record player on top of the sideboard, and my stack of vinyl, some of which is now in the hall with the other clutter, the other violated objects in the first stages of their permanent exile from this space. Back in the room I run my fingers along the keys of the Brother typewriter that was my proudest possession. The image vanishes, the room returns to itself.

⌣

Whenever I dream, or daydream, it's buildings I see, or some configuration of buildings and light, interior and exterior space. Houses, hallways, corridors, alleys, streets, gardens, courtyards, trees, the sun brightening brick or looming through a blind. Some of the buildings and scenes are real, most are imagined. The real ones are more than real, they're remembered, which is to say they're in that space between memory and invention. I think of the magical properties of interiors, of drawers, chests and wardrobes evoked by Gaston Bachelard, who quotes André Breton:

> L'armoire est pleine de linge
> Il y a meme des rayons de lune que je peux déplier
> *(The wardrobe is filled with linen*
> *There are even moonbeams which I can unfold)*[1]

I keep thinking about these lines until the only thing to do seems to be to make another poem out of them, a kind of fusion of Breton and the house I'm standing in now — or not really this house. It started that way but another interior slipped in, a heightened or skewed version.

Poem Beginning with Two Lines by André Breton

*The wardrobe is filled with linen,*
*there are even moonbeams I can unfold.*
*The roof has slipped back on the gables,*
*old trees march in from the cold.*

*The wardrobe is filled with linen,*
*the beds are slept in again.*
*Out of the air spill table and chairs,*
*the wine has crept back to the rim.*

*The wardrobe is filled with linen,*
*the drawers are packed with days.*
*The cabinet lies unsmashed in its corner,*
*there's a harvest of sun on the floor.*

*The wardrobe is filled with linen,*
*the shadows come back to the wall.*
*They've gone to collect the children*
*from the strangers who stand in the hall.*

*The rooms are empty and cold,*
*the drawers are littered with bones.*
*The wardrobe is filled with linen*
*no one can touch or unfold.*[2]

Not long after that I'm cycling past the house and seeing the door open and the new owners inside, realizing I would probably never be in this street again, and that the link with the neighbourhood is severed except in memory. In a city, where do you really belong? I think briefly of all the houses, flats, apartments I've lived in over the years. I carry bits of these around with me, parts of rooms, shafts of light, a lampshade, a table, bookshelves . . . I build a clumsy sort of composite dwelling, plant the various selves who inhabited them so they can be like neighbours, bumping into each other, borrowing cups of sugar from each other. This is the building that memory improvises, a ramshackle place, full of gaps, provisional furnishings, places that you're already departing from as you cross the threshold. I had coinciden-tally been reading a piece by Neil Powell about the English writer Ronald Bythe's *At the Yeoman's House*, a celebration of the house in the Stour Valley in Suffolk where he lives:

> *I particularly love the chapter called 'Floors'. It opens*
> *with a Crabbe anecdote which I greatly regret having*

*missed when I wrote my biography of the poet: while courting his future wife, Sarah Elmy, at Ducking Hall near Framlingham, where there were proper brick floors, he heard his prospective mother-in-law shout at a new servant, 'What, the likes of you scrub bricks like these!' She meant that the floor was too good for the servant, so she promptly got down on her hands and knees and scrubbed it herself.*[3]

His own house has a five-hundred-year-old brick floor:

*Now and then I feel them shifting under a rug like living things, this time soundlessly. I should get them fixed. But there comes a time when mending stops. When I brought some house failure to its previous owner, his answer was always the same. 'It will see me out.' This is what the farmhouse did for five hundred years, see its owners out.*[4]

What must it be to live in a five-hundred-year-old house with a five-hundred-year-old brick floor, to sit in it and listen to the bricks shifting under the rug? Ronald Blythe is an expert at staying put: he was born in Suffolk; his family has lived there for centuries; even his surname comes from its river Blyth. He has never left East Anglia for more than a month at a time. Little wonder that he can devote an entire book to a single house. Part of me envies that rootedness, that concentration on the near at hand, that sense of a house seeing its owners out generation after generation through the centuries.

Sold

*Imagine staying still,*
*rooted to the spot,*
*to the five-hundred-year-old*
*brick floor of a house*
*in a quiet valley, listening*

*to the bricks — I feel them shifting*
*under the rug, like living things —*
*to the years gather*
*in the darkening room.*
*Unchanging valley,*
*neighbourhoods of grass*
*but breath by breath*
*the bricks see out their owners,*
*there's nowhere*
*doesn't work its slow removal:*
*lean back*

*into yielding grass, the long*
*tree-lined avenues, take root*
*in the brick whisper, the flight*
*stored in the furniture,*
*the key as you turn it*
*slipping from hand to hand;*
*hesitate, linger, take what you can*
*from the opening door.*[5]

It is of course possible for an urban life to replicate that
rootedness, but it's unlikely. People who live in cities have
to look farther than their houses for a sense of belonging.
They will not usually live all their lives in the same house or
the same neighbourhood, so their allegiance is frailer, more
complex. An allegiance to immediate family, the immediate
networks of friends, community, schools, shops, all of
which are subject to change as time passes. Change is the
engine of urban life. The greater entity, the city itself, hovers
over this, but the city is abstract, ungraspable — buildings,
traffic, history. I walk around the streets of my neighbourhood every day, and in the walking and observing, in the
enjoyment of the physical pleasure of streets, I approach
some idea of allegiance. Or I sit in the small room I write in
and watch the smoke drift from my neighbour's chimney
and want to be off somewhere. I don't attend to the soul of

the house, but maybe it lives more intensely in my daughter, whose dream place it was and maybe still is, the place she came to consciousness in, the place that might linger in her imagination longer than the many other places she might get to live in.

⌐

I go back to my own first place. Only parts of the house remain. There is a great green door at the top of a short flight of stone steps, there is another entrance at the side, through a wooden door that leads in to a laneway, a private path only used by the occupants of the house and by our neighbours who can get into their back garden from the lane. I often go in there to play with the children who live there. In the garden there's a smooth plank of wood we sometimes stand on, we know that if we stand there long enough we'll be transported to another realm, somewhere remote and fantastic. We believe this absolutely, so much that we don't dare to put it to the test, and jump from the plank after only a few seconds, holding it in reserve. At the end of the laneway a door leads into the garden of the house where our flat is. The door doesn't open but there is a raised area beside it with trees strong enough to provide branches to help me over the wall and down into the garden. I'm now at the orchard end and am not supposed to go any farther. This is the limit of tenancy; the orchard and its fruit are for the owners. I slip in anyway. I don't care about the fruit; for me the real prize is the river at the end of the orchard: forbidden territory, where the land slopes down to the wide stretch of the Suir as it enters the city. Seas, river, lakes, canals — all bodies of waters pull us powerfully towards them, as if they were our real element and the land merely a temporary resting place. I sit by the bank of the river, staring at the dim industrial lands on the other side, imagining what it would be like to set off on a boat for the island a little upstream. I set a whole novel in the environs of this house, garden and river, in large part because I couldn't get them out of my head and wanted to populate them with a mix of the real and the imagined.

I sometimes stare at the house on Google Maps, a grey double-fronted Georgian building with the gate and laneway entrance exactly as I remember them. It's a mistake, though, I realize. The house, my house, belongs in my memory, with its edges blurred, safely out of time. I pass the other tenants in the hall, on the stairs, in corridors I'm not sure I haven't dreamed. The Guard, the Drummer and the Drummer's son Carlo, who pushed me off my bike in the garden. Didn't he? Upstairs, my father turns the television on and we sit and watch the tiny pinprick of light gradually wash over the screen until we behold the test card.

Back at my desk I listen to Max Richter, *The Blue Notebooks*, a musical response to Kafka's notebooks, parts of which are read by Tilda Swinton. I respond to this in turn, poemifying some of Kafka's prose, because it seemed to say what I'd been trying to say about childhood and memory:

The Trees

*The night after I heard*
*they'd long since bulldozed*
*the house where I was born,*
*that not a thing survived*
*that even the name had gone*
*and the garden was destroyed*
*that sloped gently to the river*

*I fell asleep and dreamed*
*that I went back there,*
*my wings outstretched*
*above the sunlit brick*
*and the heart-bursting*
*infinite garden.*
*I saw that the trees*

*were higher than they'd ever been,*
*that in all the years*
*since they'd been cut down*
*they'd kept on growing.*
*I woke to find*
*the leaves still scattered in my room.*[6]

Remembered buildings, just like Kafka's trees, keep on growing. My parents sit here in their young lives, innocent of the harm that will befall them. Doors open and close, an ongoing theatre of exits and entrances; straw leaks from the black rocking horse, I can taste the strands on my tongue. This is childhood's grip: nothing has happened yet, we're still safe.

⌣

How much do buildings condition how we relate to them, how much do physical spaces impinge on our emotional lives in some way separable from what else is happening? Or is it only in memory and therefore also necessarily in imagination that these spaces are infused with emotion and mystery? What could be more neutral than bricks and mortar, or more disengaged than sticks of furniture? Yet we don't experience them neutrally. The places we pass our early childhoods in will always be interfused with that childhood, impossible to separate from it: they become the containers for emotions we barely apprehend anymore, they hold on to the selves we left behind. In that way they are stubborn places, they offer their own resistance to the present.

Renewing the Contract

*In the old house*
*childhood negotiates its terms,*
*light clatters into the hall*
*and the tenants shift in their flats.*
*Here's a hat*

on a permanent lease, here's
the pattern of a dress. Blankets tumble
and stars gather above the orchard.

A door opens and closes, trees
open and close, the great wept willow
collapses and rises, you can touch
the hair of the rope of the swing and fly.

You can listen, year after year,
to shufflings and footfalls,
voices on the stair, a key in the door.
Here the joke renews its contract

and the pinprick dot of the television
warms into revelation again.
You look through a window
that has followed you everywhere

or it looks through you,
snaps every interior
and fixes you to the brickwork
like an image from Doisneau.

It's not that you return to the house:
the house invents your coming to it,
you wake to an armful of sun
like someone else's fiction.

The river climbs up to the garden
and the branches of the willow
have wrapped themselves carefully
around your vanished body.[7]

The summer of change arrives. The white Anglia is replaced
by a pale green Cortina, YZO 53, later to be stolen and
retrieved, a poor battered version of itself, in Dundalk. We

move from Waterford to Dublin. The house we move to is in an Edwardian street in Rathgar. I'm impressed by the pale red brick and the fact that we have the house to ourselves. If I walk down the street now it seems impossibly bourgeois, lined with fat cars. Back then it was more ordinary: many of the houses were set in flats. Some were guest houses. What was the name of the old man who left his room every afternoon at three to sit in his elderly Saab for ten minutes, turning the engine over? Music poured from open windows, throngs of people came and went. An artist lived on the other side. The mother of a famous actor lived up the road. I cut her grass once during Bob-A-Job week and was rewarded by just that, a literal bob, a single shilling. There was the Honey Man who took us with him on trips all around Meath and Kildare as he inspected his hives. I remember the farmer who led us shyly to a room above his barn where he had created a model railway world with hills and tunnels and villages. I remember Dan Donnelly's arm in the Hideout in Kilcullen . . .

The street was full of children our own age. This was a novelty. Suddenly there were knocks on the door. 'Are you coming out?' Behind our house was a field accessed by a hole in the garden wall. There we fought our wars and kept our hut. Behind the houses on the other side were the grounds of a school where we played endless football and cricket games. Here's Manolo, the Spanish exchange student who's staying with us, running contemptuous rings around us in full Real Madrid regalia. Here's his beautiful sister Carmen whom I would gladly swap for him. Here are Jack Charlton and Peter Osgood having a go at each other in the FA Cup Final barely visible through the grey interference on the set. We wander around the neighbourhood unchecked, unsupervised. We rob orchards, trespass freely, inspect the dump beside the school, collect bottles to bring to Mr Muffat's in exchange for pennies. We hang around our street, play hopscotch at the corner. And not far away is the city, town, Hector Grey's toyshop, bangers on Moore Street.

And the house itself waits patiently. In comes the coalman with coke for the kitchen boiler, hands and face black, like an emissary from a dangerous world. At the top of the house is the attic to which I repair to read, dream, broadcast radio programmes into my father's old tape recorder. At the end of the kitchen were a pantry and a scullery, concepts dimly understood, spaces from another time. I can see my bedroom at the front of the house, my clothes in their drawers, a scatter of books and comics, toys swapped and re-swapped. Up the road Charlie and his brothers share one big bedroom. The brothers are older, they listen to records and sit on the beds playing guitars, singing Simon and Garfunkel songs. Is this it? Is this where I'm from? This is Dublin: this street, this house. School is an interference, largely unwelcome. Eventually, the doorbell stops ringing. We're too old to call on each other. We go to different schools, we're an embarrassment to each other. And then we move to the house whose furniture we're smashing.

The new house is in a street of white houses built in the thirties, cars in the driveways, even the light somehow proclaiming the suburban idyll. I didn't really care. It had walls, rooms, a garden, a garage where I hung out with the lawnmower, the heating boiler and a packet of Rothmans. Teenagers don't love the houses they live in, they are not students of their own domestic architecture. I didn't love the house, but I loved *houses*. Other peoples' houses, houses I never entered but saw on my long walks around the neighbourhoods in this part of inland South Dublin. Nineteenth-century houses for the most part, houses with notions, doors set in elaborate porches. Sidelights and fanlights. The accoutrements of wealth, but it was the bricks I was interested it, the shapes, the solidity, the illusion of permanence. Maybe this was where the habit took root, or where the idea began to form that a neighbourhood, a city, was that which was wandered through incessantly.

I was escaping too, of course. Running away from myself, from the sadness of the house where my father began to get sick. From the iron hospital bed in the living room, the pain of watching him slip out of himself, steal away from us. From the sadness that settled over all of us. From this house I set out to visit my father in his city hospital and because I was angry and emotional I decided to walk it off instead of getting the usual bus, only to arrive minutes after he died, meeting the priest coming down the stairs. I cursed my walking then. Years later I found myself haunting the street where the hospital stood.

Peter Street

*I'd grown almost to love this street,*
*each time I passed looking up*
*to pin my father's face to a window, feel myself*

*held in his gaze. Today there's a building site*
*where the hospital stood and I stop and stare*
*stupidly at the empty air, looking for him.*

*I'd almost pray some ache remain*
*like a flaw in the structure, something unappeasable*
*waiting in the fabric, between floors, in some*

*obstinate, secret room. A crane moves*
*delicately in the sky, in its own language.*
*Forget all that, I think as I pass, make it*

*a marvellous house; music should roam the corridors,*
*joy patrol the floors, St Valentine's*
*stubborn heart come floating from Whitefriar Street*

*to prevail, to undo injury, to lift my father from his bed,*
*let him climb down the dull red brick, effortlessly,*
*and run off with his life in his hands.*[8]

Houses can't be held accountable for what happens in them.

They're innocent, the fruit of honest (or dishonest) labour. For years my mother lived alone in the house. I imagine the silence of that, the silence of long days in the house. And walking, as long as she was able: her long circuit of the Dodder and back up the hill past the little kiosk beside the park, past the driving test centre and into our old road. There was such loneliness in her life, especially in the last years. In the end the house itself failed to anchor her; she slipped away from it, not recognizing it, unable to remember how to lock the front door, unable to find her way home when she left the house. Her final place was a nursing home in the country not far from the city. Her room was filled with photographs from her life but by then she was beyond remembering. The corridors were lined with pieces of old-fashioned furniture: dressers stacked with dishes, cupboards and tables from a notional life. Images of some ultimate home to call the residents back to themselves, maybe. Whatever stories might have been in them stayed there. The corridors sucked what life they may once have had out of them. No one touched them or dreamed about them.

Houses are dreaming spaces. A flat, a room, a house, wherever we find ourselves, no matter how provisional or unstable, is both shelter and release, a place for daydreaming as well as for living. We carry around with us a shifting case of images from all the places we have ever lived, the steps or stairs we've sat on, the banisters we've gripped, the smell of wood or carpet, the touch of stove or knife handle . . .

> *In the dream of perfect ownership*
> *light drenches the wood, falling*
> *through windows long looked through.*
> *The wine and the oil sleep in the store*
> *and small gods have come to rest*
> *in hearth and threshold, tile and countertop,*
> *in doors, in handles smooth from long use.*
> *They inhabit radios, tumbling clothes,*
> *the silence of the winter yard, and when we're here*

*they stream through us so every breath*
*is altar and core. Robed with home we go,*
*from room to room, moving with grace,*
*lords of our little universe.*[9]

## Coda: Renga for the City

Great is the summer: when the pizzas come we are already outside.

⤸

Sun strikes the plant pots that hide the broken windowsill: the other is unhidden.

⤸

The neighbour is on the extension roof again, poking the rusty satellite dish: the world waits.

⤸

Camden Street deserted: the copper dome floats towards the mountain.

⤸

Dogs in Covid squaring off, lunging, panting: how do you explain?

⤸

Sun warms the gravel, then cools again; the red chair waits its turn.

～

Summer winter autumn spring: up at the dog's dawn again.

～

The gardens are open: round and round we go on our extended leads.

～

May: the window open, cherry blossoms on the floor.

～

Mo sits outside her front door, Butterfly weeps around her.

～

The stillest season: the frozen counterweights and jibs of cranes.

～

Ladders unclimbed, loads unlifted: hook, line, silence.

～

Someone turns on the news: the centre folds, the darkness holds.

～

Summer is here, a blatant light, a persistent rumour.

～

The dog jumps in the river: how can you not have told me it was still here?

⌣

We walk past the locked-up playground: the loudest silence yet.

⌣

A crowd gathers around the bandstand: a century ago the concert begins.

⌣

Still open, the butcher on Pembroke Street: sausages, paté, a little bread.

⌣

We walk on empty streets like a photograph of history: the city waits to begin.

⌣

We walk alive on crowded streets, tripping over people and dogs: closeness is all.

⌣

From pavements, from walls, from Georgian salons, from fanlights and doors, from treetops and canal rushes, from barges and building sites, from avenues and lanes, from cellars and mews they surge; from rooftops and gardens, from rooftop gardens, from terraces and sheds, from balconies, from footholds and towpaths, from greenhouses and barracks the populace presents itself: a reprieve, a retrieval, an interim, an interstice, a lodge for the liminal, an unresting place, you can hardly get in among them, there's scarcely a breath between them, the air is thick with bodies.

The city is a wild caress
                        great is the summer.

# Notes

*page* 10
Peter Sirr: 'The Hunt', *Bring Everything*, The Gallery Press, 2000

*pages* 11-13 *'Someone is leading our old lives'*
[1] John Montague: from 'Herbert Street Revisited', *New Collected Poems*, The Gallery Press, 2012

*pages* 15-22 *The Hurdle Ford, or the Monster's Breast*
[1] Hermann Geissel: *A Road on the Long Ridge: In Search of the Ancient Highway on the Esker Riada*, CRS Publications, 2006
[2] Colm Ó Lochlainn: 'Roadways in Ancient Ireland', John Ryan: *Féil-sgríbhinn* Eóin Mhic Néill: *Essays and Studies presented to Professor Eoin MacNeill* (1940), reprinted by Four Courts Press, 1995, p.471
[3] Barry Raftery: *Pagan Celtic Ireland: The Enigma of the Irish Iron Age*, Thames and Hudson, 1994, pp.98-111
[4] ibid. p.103
[5] ibid. p.98
[6] Colm Ó Lochlainn, p.471

*pages* 24-30 *Disremembering Dublin*
[1] *Hansard*, HC Deb, 14 December 1943, Vol.395 c.1363
[2] Yvonne Whelan: *Reinventing Modern Dublin: Streetscape, Iconography and the Politics of Identity*, UCD Press, 2003, p.200
[3] Thomas MacGreevy: 'St. Brendan's Cathedral, Loughrea, 1897-1947', *The Capuchin Annual, 1946-1947*, pp.353-373.
[4] quoted in Yvonne Whelan, p.18
[5] Thomas MacGreevy: 'Should These Monuments be Removed? The Case for Them and the Case Against', *Pictorial*, (19 November 1955), p.8

*pages* 33-41 *In the Double City: James Whitelaw's Dublin*
[1] Richard Ryan: *A Biographical Dictionary of the Worthies of Ireland from the Earliest Period to the Present Time*, Sherwood, Neely and Jones, 1822, p.629/630

*pages 47-57  The Poet and the Mapmaker*
  [1]T.K. Moylan: 'Vagabonds and Sturdy Beggars', Howard Clarke, ed., *Medieval Dublin: The Living City*, Irish Academic Press, 1990, p.195
  [2]Brian Mac Giolla Phádraig: 'Speed's Plan of Dublin: Part I', *Dublin Historical Record*, Vol.10, No.3 (September-November 1948), pp. 89-96
  [3]Alastair Reid: 'Where Truth Lies', *Inside Out: Selected Poetry and Translations*, Polygon, 2008
  [4]Colm Lennon: 'The Great Explosion of Dublin, 1597', *Dublin Historical Record*, Vol.42, No.1 (9 December 1988), pp.7-20
  [5]See the account of Speed by Ashley Baynton-Williams at http://www.mapforum.com/02/speed.html
  [6]quoted in Jacinta Prunty: *Maps and Map-making in Ireland*, Four Courts Press, 2004, p.42
  [7]See Baynton-Williams, op.cit

*pages 58-67  Directions*
  [1]Walter Benjamin: 'A Berlin Chronicle', *One-way Street and Other Writings*, Verso Books, 1979, p.298
  [2]Walter Benjamin: *Charles Baudelaire: A Lyric Poet in the Era of High Capitalism*, Verso, 1997, pp.124-25

*pages 68-90  Noises Off*
  [1]The account of the King William Statue is taken from Dillon Cosgrave, *The Irish Monthly*, Vol.41, No.479 (May 1913), pp.250-256 and Vol.41, No.480 (June 1913), pp.307-313
  [2]quoted in Peter Murray: 'Refiguring Delaney'. *Irish Arts Review*, Vol.21, No.4 (Winter 2004), p.84
  [3]Eamon Delaney: *Breaking the Mould, A Story of Art and Ireland*, New Island, 2009, p.61
  [4]ibid., p.2
  [5]A lot of the information here is taken from Micheál Ó Riain: 'Nelson's Pillar: A Controversy That Ran & Ran', *History Ireland*, Vol.6, No.4 (Winter 1998), pp.21-25
  [6]quoted in John T. Turpin: 'The Career and Achievement of John Henry Foley, Sculptor 1818-1874', *Dublin Historical Record*, Vol.32, No.2 (March 1979), pp.42-53
  [7]Much of the information here is taken from Robert Nicholson: '"Signatures of All Things I Am Here to Read": The James

Joyce Museum at Sandycove', *James Joyce Quarterly*, Vol.38, No.3/4 (Spring-Summer 2001), pp.293-298

*pages 95-102 Like Vast Sarcophagi*
[1]Much of the information on the history of trams here is taken from Michael Corcoran's talk '"Through streets broad and narrow": a history of Dublin's trams', the 10th Annual Sir John T. Gilbert Lecture (23 January 2007)
[2]Denis Johnston: 'The Dublin Trams', *Dublin Historical Record*, Vol.12, No.4 (November 1951), pp.99-113
[3]*Dáil Éireann Debates*, Vol.117 (19 July 1949)
[4]Denis Johnston, op. cit. p.101

*pages 115-125 Within and Without*
[1]Ian Cantwell: 'Anthropozoological Relationships in Late Medieval Dublin', *Dublin Historical Record*, Vol.13, No.3/4, (1953), pp.79-93
[2]T.K. Moylan: 'Vagabonds and sturdy beggars: poverty, pigs and pestilence in Medieval Dublin', Howard Clarke, ed., *Medieval Dublin: The Living City*, Irish Academic Press, 1990. Also John T. Gilbert: *Calendar of Ancient Records of Dublin*, 1907, Vol.2 pp.127, 142, 154/155

*pages 134-141 The Pleasure of Small Streets*
[1]Lance Wright and Kenneth Browne assisted by Peter Jones: *A Future for Dublin*, The Architectural Press, 1975
[2]op. cit. pp.326/327
[3]op. cit. p.329

*pages 142-147 Soul Rooms*
[1]Peter Sirr: *The Thing Is*, The Gallery Press, 2009

*pages 158-175 'The Sentiments of my Heart': John Rocque comes to Dublin*
[1]Nuala Burke: 'A Hidden Church?: The Structure of Catholic Dublin in the Mid-Eighteenth Century', *Archivium Hibernicum*, Vol.32 (1974), pp.81-92
[2]*Dublin Historical Record*, Vol.58, No.2 (Autumn 2005), pp. 129-165

*pages* 177-195 '*O commemorate me where there is water*'
  [1]from 'Lines Written on a Seat on the Grand Canal, Dublin' ('Erected to the memory of Mrs Dermot O'Brien') by Patrick Kavanagh
  [2]Alastair Reid: 'Other People's Houses', *Outside In: Selected Prose*, Polygon, 2008, p.161
  [3]ibid. pp.161-162
  [4]Antoinette Quinn: *Patrick Kavanagh: A Biography*, Gill and Macmillan, 2001, p.345
  [5]John Montague: *The Pear Is Ripe*, Liberties Press, 2007, p.77
  [6]RTÉ Radio documentary, 'The Jungle of Pembroke Road', first broadcast 6 October 1974
  [7]'Dublin and its writers', *The Irish Times* (27 July 2010)
  [8]Elizabeth Bowen: *Seven Winters: Memories of A Dublin Childhood*, Longmans, Green and Co., 1943
  [9]Antoinette Quinn, *Patrick Kavanagh: A Biography*, p.320

*pages* 196-207 *The Librarians and the Nightingales*
  [1]Alberto Manguel: *The Library At Night*, Alfred A. Knopf, 2006, p.25
  [2]Luis Cernuda: 'Library', in *Written in Water, The Prose Poems of Luis Cernuda*, translated by Stephen Kessler, City Lights Books, 2004, p.73

*pages* 208-227 *Eastward Ho!*
  [1]Anna Carnegie, Michelle Norris, Michael Byrne: *Tenure Mixing to Combat Public Housing Stigmatization: external benefits, internal challenges and contextual influences in three Dublin neighbourhoods*, Working Papers 201801, Geary Institute, UCD, 2018
  [2]For a full discussion of the Docklands regeneration see Niamh Moore: *Dublin Docklands Reinvented: The Post-Industrial Regeneration of A European City Quarter*, Four Courts Press, 2008
  [3]ibid., p.172
  [4]*DDDA Master Plan*, 2008, p.191

*pages* 239-253 *Three Houses*
  [1]André Breton, quoted in Gaston Bachelard: *The Poetics of Space*, Penguin Books, p.80
  [2]Peter Sirr: *The Rooms*, The Gallery Press, 2014

[3]Neil Powell: 'A Sense of Belonging', *PN Review* 204, (March-April 2012), p.7

[4]Ronald Blythe: *At the Yeoman's House*, Enitharmon Press, 2011, quoted in Neil Powell, op. cit. p.7

[5]Peter Sirr: *The Rooms*, The Gallery Press, 2014

[6]Peter Sirr: *The Gravity Wave*, The Gallery Press, 2019

[7]ibid., p.46

[8]Peter Sirr: *Bring Everything*, The Gallery Press, 2000

[9]Peter Sirr: *The Rooms*, The Gallery Press, 2014

# Image Attributions

page 58   'Gerry's, Long Lane' by Peter Sirr.

page 70   'Statue of King William' by Robert French (1841-1917) from The Lawrence Photograph Collection. Courtesy of the National Library of Ireland.

page 77   'Huge crowd gathered on Armistice Day at College Green Dublin, for the unveiling of a Celtic Cross in memory of the 16th Irish Division' by W. D. Hogan, 1924. Courtesy of the National Library of Ireland.

page 80   'Nelson's Pillar Destroyed' by James P. O'Dea (1910-1992) from O'Dea Photograph Collection. Courtesy of the National Library of Ireland.

page 81   'Lord Gough statue, Phoenix Park' by Robert French, from The Lawrence Photograph Collection. Courtesy of the National Library of Ireland.

page 91   Photo of Borges Station from Creative Commons. Original is a still from the movie *Moebius*, 1996, directed by Gustavo Mosquera.

page 116   'The Walls of Dublin, 1904' by Leonard Strangways.

page 134   Photograph by Peter Sirr.

page 158   Screengrab of the 1756 map.

page 166   'Noon' by William Hogarth, 1768 print. Public domain image downloaded from Wikimedia Commons.

page 208   'Samuel Beckett Bridge' by Peter Sirr.

page 210   'Docklands' by Peter Sirr.

# Acknowledgements

Poems by Peter Sirr quoted here are reprinted by permission of The Gallery Press. Lines from poems by Patrick Kavanagh reprinted by permission of the Estate of Patrick and Katherine Kavanagh.

I acknowledge all the many writers about Dublin whose work I have drawn on. Special thanks to Peter Fallon, to Maurice Earls for publishing some of these essays in the *Dublin Review of Books,* to *Graph* and to my wife Enda Wyley for enthusiastic encouragement. Two dogs and one daughter (thanks, Freya!) have contributed heavily to the wanderings which fed this book.